How to
MAKE
FRIENDS
with
WILD BIRDS

GAYLE HIGHPINE

Ҡ

Kinnikinnick Press
Portland, Oregon

KINNIKINNICK PRESS
11575 SW Pacific Hwy., Suite 151
Portland, Oregon 97223

Copyright © 2023 by Gayle Highpine
www.birdfriender.net

Library of Congress Cataloguing-in-Publication Data

Highpine, Gayle Lynne,1952-
How to Make Friends With Wild Birds
Includes Bibliography and Index
ISBN 979-8-218-03103-9
1. Birds – Behavior. 2. Wildlife - Behavior. 3. Birds – Psychology.
4. Animals – Psychology. 4. Teen and Young Adult - Birdwatching. 5.
Teen and Young Adult - Animal Behavior. 6. Teen and Young Adult -
Wildlife. 7. Teen and Young Adult - Ecology and Environment

Cover design by Damonza, from a photo by the author

Printed in the United States of America

Dedicated to my mother
who taught me how to sing to birds

CONTENTS

INTRODUCTION

CROSSING THE INVISIBLE WALL

BIRDS. THEY ARE beautiful. They are enchanting. They are the life of the skies and the music of the meadows.

Birds are all around us, in the trees, in the bushes, in the grass. We may not see them. But they see us. Birds are small and we are big, so it is easy for us to miss them. But it is hard for a bird to miss a human.

Although we can ignore them, the birds who live among us have to pay attention to *us* if they are going to survive. We call the birds part of the "environment," but we are part of *their* environment, too. Today, for many birds, the human world is a big part of their world.

To survive among us, they have to watch what we are doing. And we are odd and different from other ground creatures they see. Cows and squirrels and cats and deer are understandable and predictable. If you see enough cows, you will have a good idea what to expect from any cow you see.

But humans are all different, and they do different things. Sometimes humans do things that no bird has ever seen before. Sometimes a human may change its clothing overnight—yet it is the same human. And unpredictable changes happen in the vicinity of the humans. A field full of food may get replaced by pavement. You never know what may happen around the humans.

Some birds prefer to stay away from all of that. If we want to see those birds, we have to go to wild places, where we can watch them living their lives in their own way in their own world.

But the birds in our towns and cities and neighborhoods live with us by choice. They are the ones who are most open-minded and curious and willing to try new things. And each generation becomes even more curious and adaptable and better at figuring out new things. That is why backyard birds can quickly find a new feeder, even a type of feeder they've never seen before.

The birds among us know more about us than we may realize. A hawk, soaring above, knows the route of the letter carrier, the routine of the dog walker. The crows know the woman who feeds them, what time she gets home from work, and the car she drives. A sparrow in the backyard knows the kids who play on the swings, the gardener who tends the roses—and, of course, the human who fills the bird-feeders. (And if the feeder is empty, the birds may come up to that human to tell them about it – they may even come up to the window if they see that human in the house!)

And, just as humans love listening to the voices of birds, birds love listening to human voices. Especially high-pitched voices – women, children, or men talking in falsetto. Two women chatting on a park bench may not notice the birds around them in the trees, listening. Children playing may not notice the birds shivering with pleasure at their squeals of laughter. And the birds love to hear us sing. Music can be one of the best ways to delight the birds.

Humans are not the only birdwatchers. Birds too watch and listen to other birds. They get clues about food and danger that way, but they also seem to do it for pleasure. Sometimes, when I'm on the deck, watching the birds at the feeders, a Song Sparrow may perch near me and watch not only me but the other birds as well – the squabbling juncos, the hummingbirds chasing each other, the nuthatches coming and going at the suet feeder. We watch the birds together.

And many birds are humanwatchers. They watch us as we watch them. And they watch us as we *don't* watch them. They follow us around, flitting unnoticed from bush to bush. As the humans pass by, I look at them through the birds' eyes and ponder how they must appear to the birds.

Let's say you're in a spaceship orbiting high above an alien planet. You have been observing the planet's inhabitants for a long time. They are fascinating. They are giants – incredibly strong, able to move impossibly heavy things. They are unpredictable and do things that make no sense to any of you. But they don't seem hostile. And though they are a bit scary, they are slow and clumsy, and can't get off the ground. As long as you stay out of their reach, they might not be that dangerous.

The crew needs a volunteer to go down to the planet and try to make contact with them.

Would you volunteer?

Birds have different personalities, and some birds are explorers and adventurers. If such a bird sees a human who might understand, it may try to communicate with the human. And other birds who see a bold pioneer leading the way, and getting rewards for connecting with the human, can start getting up the nerve to do it too.

We may think that a bird doesn't like us if it flies away at our approach. We may think the robin running across the lawn isn't "friendly" because he won't come close to us. But that doesn't mean he doesn't like us. He learned from his parents to stay *just this far* from the humans. He feels safe at the proper distance.

To help birds get used to us, we need to spend time with them and among them. And it takes time and patience. How long would it take us to approach a wild tiger, even if the tiger seemed friendly? How long does it take to tell a friend our deepest secrets? It's the journey that matters, as much as the destination. As we watch the birds and get to know them, and they watch us and get to know us, the distance between us – both physical and psychic distance – slowly becomes shorter and shorter.

It never ceases to amaze me that birds can recognize us humans as fellow living creatures. We look so different. Our ways of life are so different. Yet, some of them can try to communicate with us.

Different birds will have different styles of expressing friendship. Some birds sing "whisper songs" to their human friends. Some birds follow their human friends around the yard. Some birds feed from the hand of their human friends. Some birds, especially crows, give tiny gifts – coins or keys or little plastic toys – to people who feed them.

One way we can get the attention of a bird is by imitating its call. It doesn't matter if our imitation is clumsy. We're not trying to fool the bird. (In fact, it's better if our imitation isn't perfect, so the bird doesn't take it as a rival bird.) Birds understand the notion of mimicry, because a lot of them do it themselves, and those who don't have heard other birds doing it.

Mimicking a bird's call makes us stand out from other humans. And the bird may understand that we are trying to connect. When a bird hears its call mimicked by a different kind of bird, it doesn't answer. But when a human imitates its call, the bird may reply. And we can reply back, and the bird may reply back again, and soon we are having a "conversation" back and forth.

But can we actually *communicate* with the birds? Could we understand them, even a little bit? Could they understand us?

There may seem to be an invisible wall between us and the birds. The birds, beautiful though they are, may seem alien and incomprehensible to us. That is because we are taught not to think about their feelings. Science has a rule that we can't talk about the inner life of creatures who can't talk.

But if we don't consider their feelings, it limits our understanding of the birds. And it's hard to have a friendship with someone we see as an unconscious robot with no inner life.

Birds are creatures of feeling. So are we. They experience the world by feeling, and so do we. Even when communicating about food and danger, they are really communicating feelings. And if we communicate with a bird, we are not exchanging information, but feelings.

We can never understand the birds' feelings *completely*. But we can never completely understand *another human's* feelings either. Any degree of understanding can help us start a friendship.

So a birdfriender has to break the rule against thinking about birds' feelings. Birdfrienders ask questions like—what is it like to be a bird? How does the world look through a bird's eyes? What does being a bird feel like?

When a birdfriender meets a bird, they don't ask "What is it?" but "Who are you?"

Bird emotions may not all be the same as ours, but some birds seem to share the same thrill that we feel at making a cross-species connection.

While we wait to meet an extraterrestrial intelligence, and

imagine how we might communicate with it, we can practice communicating with our fellow creatures of Earth.

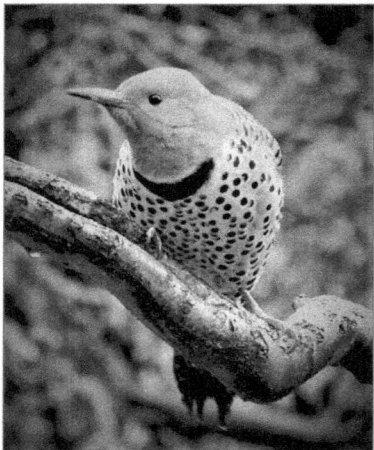

This book is about crossing the invisible wall between us and the birds. It has four parts, each part divided into chapters.

In Part One, "Birds Are Everywhere," we talk about how to make contact with the birds around us. There are five chapters in this section. In the first chapter, we talk about the birds we see every day, and how we can get them to pay attention to us, among all the humans they see every day. In the second chapter, we talk about hand-feeding birds, a joy that never wears out. In the third chapter, we talk about learning to understand the birds' communication with each other. In the fourth chapter, we talk about communicating with the birds ourselves. And the fifth chapter of Part One is devoted just to the jays, who gave me so many stories that they ended up with a chapter of their very own.

Part Two is "Bird Seasons." This section contains four chapters, one for each season. For a bird, time of year is everything. Its life changes completely depending on the season, and so does its attitude toward us. At certain times of year, the birds won't be much interested in us, even birds who are already our friends. They have more important things to do than interacting with humans. Those times of year are better for birdwatching than birdfriending.

This section is good not only for birdfrienders but for people who go to wild places where the birds don't know them – where we can enter the birds' world instead of always watching them adapt to ours.

Part Three, "What It's Like to be a Bird," is a deep dive into exploring the inner experience of birds. This section contains five chapters. One chapter is about birds' bodies. One chapter is about bird senses and how the world appears to a bird. One chapter is about instinct and how it works, for us as well as for birds. One chapter is about bird intelligence, and how it is like ours and unlike ours. One chapter is about bird emotions, and how they are like and unlike ours. (Some sections of these chapters, especially the chapters on instinct, intelligence, and emotions, might be more of interest to adults than to many young people, but this book is intended for adults and young people alike.) The more we understand what it is like to be a bird, the better we can communicate with them.

Part Four, "The Birds and Us," has only one chapter. It talks about different ways we can enjoy birds, and about different ways we can help them, and different ways they can help us. For example, birds can help our mental health. And when we make the world better for birds, we make the world better for ourselves, too.

Birds can teach us things we can't learn from books or from other people. They teach us things that can't be expressed in human language. Birds can help us to understand more deeply the experience of being a human being on this Earth.

This book is an invitation to cross the invisible wall that seems to separate us from the birds.

Part One

BIRDS ARE EVERYWHERE

Chapter One

ASPHALT ADVENTURES

BIRDS ARE EVERYWHERE. They live everywhere that we live. And a lot of places where we don't live, like the middle of the ocean and the ice sheets of Antarctica and rocky islands and remote deserts.

Birds live in forests and marshes and meadows. They also live in our cities and towns.

We have moved into the birds' neighborhoods and changed them. When we change things, some birds leave. But many birds adjust to us and stay with us.

No matter where we live, there are birds, and we can be bird-frienders. Even people who have no yards at all can make friends with birds.

Birds are everywhere.

The first step in birdfriending is to notice the birds.

In the parking lot

It's a bright June day. I'm out walking, doing errands and enjoying the sunshine. I come to the big supermarket and I decide to take a shortcut across the parking lot. Rather than dodge the cars coming in and out, and the people pushing grocery carts out to their cars, I squeeze between a row of parked cars and the neatly trimmed, waist-high hedge that separates the rows of cars.

As I walk, I notice a soft clicking sound. *TIK, TIK, TIK.* I stop and look around. The clicks come faster, in stereo, from ahead of me and behind me.

Suddenly, a bird pops out of the top of the hedge. Shiny black, not very big, he flutters up into the air – then dives down at me. Just before hitting my face, he swerves and flutters back up into the air. His yellow eyes are fixated on me, his sharp beak is aimed at my face. As I watch him, out of the corner of my eye I see another bird diving at my face from the other direction. That bird is gray, and when I turn to see it, the black one divebombs me from the other side. I turn back toward the black bird, and the gray one dives at me.

They must have fledglings in that hedge. A fledgling is a baby bird who has just left the nest, but is still being taken care of by its parents. While the babies were still in the nest, the parent birds would try to be quiet and invisible, even when electric trimmers are shaving off the top of the hedge above them. But now the clueless fledgling is out in a world full of dangers – cats, dogs, crows, hawks, humans, raccoons, coyotes, cars. In fact, a fledgling can't even fly at first, so even if it knew what was dangerous, it couldn't do much to get away.

No wonder the parents are so anxious. If any possibly dangerous creature comes near, the parent birds try to frighten it. Or make it angry. Or get it to chase them. Anything that can distract the dangerous creature so that it doesn't spot the fledgling. The clicking is not a message to me, it is an alarm to the fledgling—"*SHUT UP! HIDE! SHUT UP! HIDE!*"

Sometimes children get scared when a bird divebombs them. And a divebombing bird is certainly *trying* its very best to be scary. But birds are fragile creatures – nature made a lot of compromises to make them light enough to fly. A collision with a human could be fatal for the bird. So rarely does a divebombing bird make physical contact.

But some people don't even *notice* it when a bird is divebombing them. Even when I point it out – "Look! That bird is divebombing you!" – they don't see it. A big bird like a crow might get their attention – or an owl, who can leave bleeding gashes on a human forehead. But a little bird can have a hard time impressing someone used to watching giant rampaging monsters or exploding spaceships. The bird is risking its life to confront the human, yet to the human it might as well be invisible.

As I keep walking, two *more* blackbirds fly out of the hedge. Now four blackbirds are divebombing me. Throughout the length of hedge, clicks come fast and frantic. I go farther and still more birds fly out of the hedge and join in. Blackbirds disappear behind me as new birds take over. It's a divebombing relay!

But why nest so close to the ground at all? If I'm too close to their nesting area, whose fault is that? Plenty of perfectly good trees around. Can I see a nest or a fledgling in the hedge? I stop and peer among the leaves. I don't see anything, but the blackbirds get more upset. Alarm clicks sound fast and frantic throughout the length of hedge.

I reach the end of the hedge and I'm out on the sidewalk. Everything should be fine now. I didn't eat any baby birds. Bye-bye blackbirds. I'll go on with my errands. A couple of them follow me, doing lazy divebombs, but after a while they give up and go home.

So who are these black birds?

Some people call them grackles and some people call them starlings. But most people probably don't call them anything, because they don't even notice them.

But they aren't grackles or starlings. Nor are they the blackbirds of English songs and nursery rhymes – which we call European Blackbirds. (The European Blackbird is actually a close relative of our

American Robin, in different clothes.) These birds are Brewer's Black-birds – the parking lot bird of the west. (The parking lot bird of the east, I am told, is its larger cousin, the Common Grackle.) Brewer's Blackbirds belong to the same family as Red-winged Blackbirds, meadowlarks, bobolinks, and orioles, but they aren't as glamorous as those relatives. They don't seem to care about our admiration as they hop under parked cars or perch under grocery carts left outside.

The next day I walk to the supermarket to pick up a few grocer-ies. This time I take a different route, to avoid their hedge. But as soon as I set foot inside the lot, I hear clicking. Could the blackbirds be watching me? Surely they don't keep track of all the humans who walk by their hedge every day. But when I come out of the store, a blackbird divebombs me. And another one.

It seems it is not enough for me to stay away from their hedge. They don't want me in their parking lot at all.

A week goes by. Surely they have forgiven me by now. After all, I didn't do anything to them – all I did was walk by, so why should they be mad at me? Really? And they see hundreds of people in the parking lot every day. By now they should have forgotten about me, right?

No such luck. As soon as I set foot in their lot, I hear clicking.

I am getting tired of this nonsense. I decide to take action.

Inside the store, I buy some bread. Bread is junk food for birds, but these insect-eating birds probably wouldn't eat millet and sun-flower seeds. At least this bread is whole grain. Just this once. I start ripping up the bread. Each time a blackbird divebombs me, I throw a piece of bread at it.

At first they ignore the bread. They don't know what it is. Soon the ground is littered with fragments of bread. I walk away from the bread. When I am far enough, a blackbird lands and investigates the strange object. Pecks it. Then he starts gobbling it.

I step back, and in a moment a dozen blackbirds are on the pavement, both fledglings and adults. The fledglings are no longer hiding. The parents are no longer clicking. They are all devouring bread together. I throw bread behind me as I walk away, and they follow me like baby ducks. Hardly an hour before, they hated me.

So why do the Brewer's Blackbirds hang out in parking lots? Why do they walk under cars? Why do they nest in low bushes, when they could nest high up in the trees?

Memories of the ancestors

Traveling in the open ranchlands of eastern Oregon one summer, I finally figured them out. In the pastures among the grazing cows, the Brewer's Blackbirds make sense.

Brewer's Blackbirds can adapt to a lot of environments, but they seem most at home in grasslands. They hang around cows. Before cattle came, they followed the buffalo herds. Cows – or buffalo – scare up insects with their feet as they walk along, and drop seeds as they munch on grasses. So there is lots of food for the Brewer's Blackbirds under these huge animals.

Amid the forests of western Oregon, what resembles a herd of cows grazing in a field? A herd of cars grazing in a parking lot. Once the Brewer's Blackbirds walked under giant four-legged creatures; now they walk under giant four-wheeled creatures. Cars don't kick up insects with their hooves, but they run over insects and pick up weed seeds in their tires. So, like the hoofprints of the buffalo, the grooves of the tires are rich in food.

When a bird encounters a new situation, it tries to match that with the closest thing in its memory. A bird, like all creatures, draws on ancestral memory, or instinct. It remembers the landscapes where its ancestors lived, the foods its ancestors ate, and the dangers its ancestors faced.

Pigeons originally lived on rocky cliffs, in southern Europe and North Africa where their ancestors lived. Today the tall buildings in city centers remind them of those cliffs, the nooks and crannies of the buildings remind them of the sheltered rock shelves where their ancestors nested, and the pavement below reminds them of the rock their ancestors walked upon.

Swifts nest inside of hollow tree snags. But when people remove the hollow trees, the swifts may find another place to nest: brick chimneys, which remind them of the hollow tree trunks where their ancestors nested.

The more we know about the ancestral life of a particular bird, the better we can understand that bird. And the language of instinct can help us communicate.

The Brewer's Blackbirds' ancestors lived in places with few or no trees, so they nested in low bushes and shrubs. But that is dangerous; ground predators could find them, and there is no cover from predators from above. So they nest in colonies, so they can defend together. One for all and all for one.

I've seen teams of Brewer's Blackbirds chasing away crows in the parking lot. Crows may steal eggs or even baby birds from nests. Crows are a lot bigger than Brewer's Blackbirds, but four or five Brewer's Blackbirds gang up at once. Sometimes a crow is just innocently flying over the parking lot, and out of nowhere a bunch of Brewers Blackbirds go after it – just like they came after me, as I innocently walked by with no thought of eating baby blackbirds.

Once I saw a group of Brewer's Blackbirds chasing a Sharp-shinned Hawk. That is truly dangerous; a Sharpie could turn and grab a bird in midair with its deadly talons. But the blackbirds coordinated so that each time the hawk targeted one blackbird, another dived at the hawk from the other side. Unable to grab any of them, the Sharpie gave up and left.

Why were these blackbirds upset with me? People walk by their hedge every day. But they count on humans not noticing them. The click-alarm is meant to be a secret signal, bird to bird. It's not very loud, because it's not supposed to get my attention. It would have been a routine, casual alert. I wasn't supposed to listen to it, but I did. And the birds could see that from my body language.

But once I showed them that it could be a *good* thing to have a human pay attention to them, by giving them food, they sure changed their attitude fast.

We can start birdfriending anywhere. Birds can recognize an individual human – if they have a reason to. Some people are surprised about that, but (as we'll talk about later) birds have super-powered memories for what they see, much better than ours.

To make friends with a bird, we first have to give the bird a reason to notice us, out of all the humans it sees around it. Of course, a bird who lives with us already knows us. And once a bird knows a particular human, it can recognize that human even if they change their clothes.

Wait – the same human can change almost completely to a different color? How could that possibly make sense to a bird?

Yet birds do recognize us by our faces. That is easy to prove. In one experiment,[*] two women went to a park. They were similar in build and hair style, but one wore a yellow coat and the other an orange coat. Each sat on a different bench and put out food for the pigeons. When the pigeons arrived to eat, the woman wearing the orange coat chased the pigeons away, while the woman wearing the yellow coat let them eat. The next day, the two women switched coats and went back to the park. They sat on different benches and put out food for the pigeons. The pigeons came to the woman who had let them eat before, but they wouldn't come to the woman who had chased them away. The change of clothes didn't matter. The pigeons recognized the women by their faces. And it took only one experience for them to learn.

Of course, we don't need formal scientific experiments to prove that birds can recognize individual humans. We can find it out ourselves if we give the birds a reason to recognize us.

We can do that just by feeding the birds we see nearby. Birdfriending can begin as simply as giving them food.

Soon the Brewer's Blackbirds have eaten their fill. But I still have plenty of bread left. What to do with the rest of it? I know – the pigeons.

The athletes of the sky

The pigeons hang around way over on the far side of the parking lot, where it's mostly empty of cars. To them, parked cars aren't a cozy reminder of home, but a place danger could lurk.

I've seen people feeding the pigeons over there. Like people in cities the world over, people here feed pigeons. In some places, pigeons may offer the only chance people have for a relationship with nonhuman beings.

Humans caught pigeons and started raising them thousands of years ago, as food and as pets, and also because pigeons are very good at learning things. Pigeons can learn elaborate tricks in exchange for treats. And before the invention of phones and postal services, pigeons carried messages, including from ships at sea and from armies in wartime. People bred carrier pigeons and racing pigeons to be extra fast and strong to fly distances of hundreds of miles. People still race pigeons, and champion racing pigeons can be worth thousands of dollars.

The pigeons we see in the cities are descended from such elite athletes. And sometimes, like retired racing greyhounds, they have to let their athletic impulse come out. Every so often, a group of pigeons will burst from the top of a building in balletic flight, sweep across the sky in graceful sweeping curves and circles, then return together where they started, the whole show unnoticed by most people below.

As I walk toward the other side of the parking lot, the pigeons run away, but the moment I toss some bread, they fly right over. They know what it is and they devour it like they are starving. Unlike most birds, pigeons don't stop eating till all the food is gone. But one pigeon ignores the food. He is more interested in another pigeon eating next to him. He puffs out his chest and bows to her, cooing, but she keeps on eating like he isn't there. He gives up on her and turns to another pigeon and bows and coos to her. She ignores him too. He turns and starts bowing and cooing to another pigeon. This pigeon runs away from him. He runs after her, still bowing and cooing.

He is a single male looking for a mate. A female pigeon who already has a mate will ignore him, but a single female pigeon tells him she might be interested by running away from him and letting him chase her. In every pigeon flock, we can see at least one pigeon male doing this. They are making sure we will always have enough pigeons.

The crow-nado

I look around, and high in a tall oak tree growing behind the supermarket, I see a crow watching us.

Probably a sentry crow. Crows take turns on sentry duty, watching out while other members of the flock look for food. The oak tree is in the parking lot of the cinema next door. If there is a sentry crow, there must be a crow flock over there.

Crows are cautious birds. They have to be; the world is a dangerous place, even more than for smaller birds. They forage on the ground, out in the open where they are easy to see, and their take-off is slow. They survive by watching out for each other.

Crows pay more attention to individual humans than most birds. Any bird can recognize individual humans, if it has a reason to, just as we can recognize individual birds if we have a reason to. But crows have more reason than other birds to pay attention to individual humans: some humans kill crows. In fact, humans can kill at a distance. But if the crows took the attitude, "One human shot at us, so let's treat *all* the humans as deadly foes," it would be impossible for them to live among us. Crows need to identify the dangerous humans and stay far out of their sight. Then, as far as the rest of the humans, just keep a safe distance.

Other birds can be persuaded to come close, some even to feed from our hands. But, even if it feels friendly toward a particular human, it's hard for a wild crow to get past its caution. This may be why crows often leave small gifts to people who feed them – coins, bottle caps, plastic toys, the kinds of tokens crow friends give to each other. I think that those crows are saying, "I can't express my friendship by coming close to you physically, so let this be a sign."

I have nowhere near such a friendship with the crows. I used to think I wanted crowfriends, but when I started trying to attract crows to my backyard, the other birds threatened to go on strike. "You want *CROWS* around here??! Are you crazy?!" The robins were especially upset. "The whole reason we nest so close to human houses is that the crows don't want to come near you. What are you doing?!" The smaller birds hate crows as nest robbers. They told me I had to make a choice between the rest of them and the crows. So I made my choice.

Still, some mornings I slip over to the cinema parking lot, and I look around for a sentry crow on duty. If I see one, I hold up a big peanut. Sometimes the sentry crow will caw, a fast high-pitched *caw-cawcawcawcaw*, and one by one, crows will fly over and perch in the trees around me. And when I start throwing peanuts, they fly right down. Those crows know me.

Other times, the sentry crow will ignore me. Apparently different crow families visit this parking lot. Close up, the individual crows have distinct individual faces, but it's impossible to recognize them from a distance. So I don't know whether the crows over there now are friends or strangers. But either way, I need to bring an offering of peanuts. I go into the store and buy a big bag of unsalted peanuts in the shell, then I walk to the cinema lot.

I caw to the sentry crow and hold up a peanut. The sentry crow ignores me. So he's a stranger. Well, maybe today he will taste the first peanut of his life. I throw the peanut across the pavement. The sentry crow stares suspiciously. Slowly I walk away from the peanut, and, when I am far enough away, the sentry crow flies down toward the peanut. He looks at it from different angles. Sidles up to it. Nudges it. Taps it. Pecks at it. Cracks it open. Gobbles it down. Wow! Yum!

I throw another peanut behind me. Again the crow waits for me to move away, then he hops over and eats it. After one more, the sentry crow caws an announcement to the flock. Instantly another crow drops onto the pavement. And another. Each crow suspiciously approaches a peanut, checks it out, pecks it open, and gobbles the treats. More crows land and I drop more peanuts. A dozen crows are pecking open peanuts on the pavement.

Suddenly, a stranger appears in their midst. A gigantic monster with a huge beak. A gull. The crows look small by comparison. They don't seem to want to find out what that beak could do to them. The crows step back and watch unhappily as the gull walks over and starts gulping the peanuts whole, in the shell.

Gulp gulp gulp. But after only three peanuts, the gull stops and takes off, to the crows' evident relief. The crows go back to pecking open peanuts. But the gull still circles above us. Then it lands again. It grabs a peanut, cracks it with its beak, lets the nutmeats fall on the pavement, and swallows each piece one at a time. It picks up another peanut and does the same thing.

Observing us from above, the gull must have realized that the real yumminess was *inside* the peanuts. But the gull doesn't try to copy the crows' method of extracting the nuts, pecking the peanuts open on the pavement. The gull figured out a method that would work better with its type of beak. And it didn't use trial and error. It already had its new peanut-cracking plan in place when it landed. Wow, who knew gulls were smart?

Now I can throw peanuts to both the crows and the gull without the gull grabbing them all. I walk away, tossing peanuts behind me, and the whole group follows along. Ten crows and one gull, and me the leader of the parade!

Then, from behind me, a crow flies low right over my head and swoops ahead of me. And another and another! Another crow family arriving? More and more keep coming. Three, five, eight, thirteen, too many to count. And then they start raining down. The wind is gusting, the clouds are swirling, and dozens of crows are sailing like autumn leaves sweeping in a gale. Crows fly around me, over me, forward and back, ahead and behind, left and right, racing each other to grab the peanuts I throw ahead and behind. Gusts of wings sweep by me. A swirling vortex of crows. The vortex keeps expanding. Forty or fifty crows gliding and racing and whirling around me. The wind from all those wings seems to lift me and carry me above the ground, like a tornado sweeping across a prairie. A crow tornado! A crow-nado!

Small crow-nados happen often, but rarely a great crow-nado like the one that lifted me above the asphalt that windy morning.

Birdfriending can happen anywhere

Birds are everywhere. They bring the wild to us no matter where we live.

Some people turn up their noses at common city birds, like crows, pigeons, gulls, house sparrows. They think that only rare birds are worth looking for. They dismiss robins because they don't try to hide from us. They dismiss little brown birds who aren't colorful. And birds with colorful iridescence, like starlings and pigeons, they dismiss because there are so many of them. They think that any bird too easy to see isn't worth watching.

But the birds who are easy to see are the easiest to make friends with because they are the birds who like us. Or at least who don't mind us. We may think the robin running across the lawn isn't "friendly" because he won't come close to us. But he learned from his parents to stay *just this far* from the humans. That doesn't mean he doesn't like us. He just feels safe at the proper distance.

The birds who live among us are the most curious and the most open to new ideas. They have to be, in order to survive among us. So those birds will be the most open-minded about a new idea like becoming friends with a human.

Our neighborhoods are not just human neighborhoods. They are bird neighborhoods too. Birds have their own property lines. Each family's property is called its *territory*.

Not all kinds of birds are territorial; some kinds of birds move around and go any place they can find food. The parking lot birds are like that. But most of our backyard birds have territories.

In fact, what we think of as our neighborhood has many different overlapping bird neighborhoods. Each species has its own way of organizing its neighborhood, and the neighborhoods of different birds are superimposed. The Song Sparrows divide up their neighborhood one way, the robins another way. Their boundaries don't have to match because they don't care about the property lines of other species.

Having a territory ensures that each bird family will have enough food to support it. Since each species has its own kind of food, birds don't care if birds of *other* species come into their territories. So different kinds of birds can live together in the same yard. But they chase out other birds of the *same* kind, because birds of the same kind compete for the same foods.

Since some foods are more plentiful than others, different kinds of birds have different-sized territories. There are a lot more bugs and weed seeds for the Song Sparrows than mice for the Great Horned Owls, so a Song Sparrow territory might be half an acre, while a Great Horned Owl territory might be a square mile. So in a typical backyard, only one pair of Song Sparrows, one pair of Great Horned Owls, and so on, might show up

But people who put out birdfeeders can make their yards into such valuable real estate that it can't be claimed as any bird's private property. Such a yard becomes like a public park shared by everyone. Or maybe like a fast food place where everyone can stop by for a snack. And the more birds who are there, the safer everyone feels. And the birds connect the humans around there with that feeling of abundance and safety.

A wild area will have more different kinds of birds around, but it can be harder to make friends with them because they have more food around them, so they don't need to come near human houses to get food. City birds are used to houses as a normal part of their environment, and used to seeing humans around them. In fact, many city birds purposely nest close to humans, because crows and other predators don't want to come too close to humans. So from the time the babies hatch and open their eyes, they see humans passing close by, and see their parents acting like that is no big deal.

A natural area or birdscaped yard in the middle of a place where habitat is becoming scarce is ideal for birdfriending. I live in a tiny house with a big deck near a patch of woods. It is surrounded by shopping centers, office complexes and hotels, and a multiplex cinema across the street. The patch of woods is slated to become an office complex someday, but for the time being it, and my birdscaped yard have become a vital island of survival for the birds. Over the years I have counted about sixty bird species seen in my yard at least once, and about twenty species are regular visitors.

The best place for birdfriending is a place where we can see the same birds every day, and they can see us every day.

But people without yards can have birdfriends. Even people in apartments have fed hummingbirds, chickadees, nuthatches, finches, house sparrows, jays, and crows. I have heard of people on the twenty-fifth floor hand-feeding seagull friends.

A woman in a fourth floor apartment discovered some oatmeal full of little worms and sprinkled the wormy oatmeal on her window sill. Soon a tiny bird appeared, olive-green, with a white ring around its eye. The bird grabbed some worms and flew away. It kept coming back until the worms were gone. The bird didn't mind the human face on the other side of the window. In fact, the bird sometimes paused to study the face.

But what kind of bird was it? My friend ran through lists of Oregon birds. Nothing seemed to fit. Maybe it was a rare bird! She contacted an expert on Oregon birds and sent a photo. He replied that the bird was a female Ruby-crowned Kinglet.

Ah – no wonder she had skipped that name on the list. This bird had no colorful crown. As with many birds, the distinctive characteristic that gives the bird its name is worn only by the male. So, my friend wrote back excitedly, is this a rare bird? Not rare, the bird expert replied, but uncommon to see. Kinglets live and forage up in the canopy, almost invisible in the shadows. They rarely come down to human level, and they aren't interested in birdseed. But the tiny worms were a prize for a mother kinglet. And the trees a kinglet likes grew near the window.[1]

People in apartments or condos can set up birdfeeding stations on their balcony. Seed that is already shelled (shelled sunflower seed, shelled peanuts, hulled millet sold for human consumption) minimizes mess.[2] If seed feeders are not allowed, bird food can be placed in flowerboxes, potted plants, and hanging baskets, with no one the wiser. Suet feeders make little mess and hummingbird feeders none at all. People with no balcony can feed birds on the window sill or can hang feeders on brackets mounted on window frames. Some apartment managers may allow feeders to be hung in trees. Some might allow a community area where residents can enjoy the birds together.

But even if somewhere it's not practical or permitted to feed birds, people can put out birdbaths. Birds don't actually need our food to survive, but water is essential. On a hot dry day, fresh clean water to drink can be practically a lifesaver for the birds, and on any day, it's fun to watch them bathe in the birdbath.

---

1   Why is this the case? See the article "Why Do Birds Display?" at *www.birdfriender.net.*

2   Some people are concerned that birds will throw seeds from the feeders onto the ground, attracting rats. But that happens when the seed is a mix filled with cheap filler seed that birds don't eat – the birds throw out the seed they don't want while hunting for the seed they like. To avoid rats, don't use cheap seed mixes. Better yet, don't use mixes at all, but offer different foods in different feeders for different birds. For more information on feeding birds in urban settings, see *City Birds, Country Birds: How Anyone Can Attract Birds to Their Feeder* by Sharon Stiteler.

Ludwig the Song Sparrow, a brilliant composer

Different birds have different ways of being friends with us. Hand-feeding is just one way. One bird may sit on a branch and watch what we do. Another bird may follow us around the yard. My mother had a Spotted Towhee friend who followed her around as she gardened, and who even brought her fledglings over and introduced them. When I'm sitting and writing, sometimes I look down and see juncos and towhees hopping around my feet. Not only when I'm working out on the deck – even in the house, if the door is left open, there they'll be on the carpet, picking up seeds I've tracked in. And the chickadees come and land on the laptop monitor and watch my face as I type.

Special birdfriends can have names. Like Ludwig the Song Sparrow, who sings for me. And Daisy the Dove, who comes to sunbathe on the deck near me. And Rennie the Wren, who lands on the hammock ropes to greet me on the way to hunt bugs in the brushpiles. And Nate the Nuthatch, who signals me with a distinctive call when he arrives, so I'm holding out peanuts for him before I even see him. And Skippy the Scrub Jay, the first jay to fly to my hand for peanuts.

Daisy the Dove

And Donna the Downy Woodpecker. I met her when she got trapped inside the house and I got her out. She screeched when she saw my hand reaching toward her, but I sang to calm her down, and she finally let me pick her up. Then she wouldn't leave my cupped hands for half an hour, listening blissfully to the singing. The next day she came inside again, but let me catch her with little resistance. The next day she flew in, greeted me with eye contact and a cheep, and flew right back out. Now on the suet feeder, she makes eye contact with me and responds to my voice.

Sometimes a bird simply comes up to me and looks in my eyes. I can see a certain look in the eyes of such a bird, like an awakening or recognition. Maybe a bird can see something different in the eyes of such a human, too.

When we start paying attention to birds, the world changes a little bit. When a human and a bird make a connection, something shifts on both sides.

The first step in birdfriending is to notice the birds.

CHAPTER TWO

A BIRD IN THE HAND

I'M WALKING DOWN a tree-covered residential avenue in an unfamiliar part of town. In the canopy above, I hear a chickadee flock twittering. A familiar call sounds close to my head – the *ssis-zissit* call that the chickadees make to get my attention when they want a peanut. Without thinking, I take out the vial of shelled peanuts I carry in my pocket and hold some peanuts out in my hand. A chickadee drops to my hand and flies off with a peanut.

Then it hits me. I am in a strange part of town, and this chickadee is a stranger to me. And I am a stranger to him too.

Do I have the magic touch, to instantly tame strange chickadees?

No, more like the magic ear. Those chickadees had already been hand-tamed by someone around there. All I did was listen. Those chickadees may call to every human who walks by – but how many people pay attention to them?

The world would be a happier place if everyone everywhere could just reach out, every time they go outside, and have chickadees come to their hands.

But in each neighborhood, someone has to be the first. One kind human and one eager chickadee have to start the ball rolling. That first human may have to endure many patient hours, days, months out in the cold, as none of the chickadees wants to be the first to try it. But once one brave and adventurous chickadee finally comes to the hand, and shows that it is safe, and gets a peanut as the prize, other chickadees will follow its example. Not only that, but the other members of the chickadee flock become more open-minded toward other humans they may see holding out peanuts as well. Soon, everyone in that neighborhood could be hand-feeding chickadees.

Chickadees – like the one at the top of this chapter and the one on the cover – are very cute birds. But they are not just cute – chickadees are smart and curious, especially about humans. So are their relatives the titmice, and their cousins the tits, who live in Eurasia and Africa. Chickadees, titmice and tits make up the parid family, and everywhere, people know them as smart and friendly birds. I'm told that there are parks in snowy parts of the US where anyone can hold out food, and chickadees will land on their palm. I love to surprise someone who comes to the door by telling them to hold out their hand and putting peanuts on their palm, and then a chickadee drops onto their hand! They may never be the same again.

At first, I didn't even think about hand-feeding the birds. I just like having birds around me. I like watching them as I work on my laptop. So I took my laptop out on the deck and sat near the feeders. It felt like working in the middle of an aviary.

Gradually, the birds got used to me. They came to the feeders with me right there. The juncos started hopping close to my feet to pick up millet. Then the birds didn't come only to eat. The chickadees started landing on the laptop table next to me. Sometimes a chickadee would perch on the monitor and study my face.

So I put peanuts and sunflower seeds on the table next to the laptop. Though they could still get food from the feeders, the chickadees and the nuthatches started coming to the table for food.

Then a chickadee landed on my thigh. So I put food on my thigh. The chickadee came and took it.

So I put food in my hand and lay it across the table, palm up, as I typed with my other hand. There were sounds of fluttering around my head, as a chickadee would head toward my hand, then lose its nerve at the last second and make a U-turn for the feeders instead.

Eventually, I felt the touch of tiny bird claws on my hand. One chickadee had taken a peanut from my hand. Soon the chickadees were landing on my hand freely.

Each chickadee has its own style of hand-feeding. One flutters as it alights on the hand, the next dives in smoothly. One sits on my palm, the next will perch on the fleshy base of my thumb, another will cling to the ends of my fingertips. One grabs a seed and leaves in a hurry, another takes its time to choose. Even the feet of different birds feel different.

Now the chickadees follow me around the yard, and I carry a vial of peanuts in my pocket for them. The chickadees purposely try to get my attention. If I don't respond to its call, a chickadee may hover briefly in front of my face. Once, as I was concentrating on taking pictures of a flicker, I ignored the efforts of a chickadee to get my attention. Fed up with waiting, the chickadee landed right on the camera lens.

Often a chickadee doesn't just grab a peanut and leave, but lingers on the hand, looking at me, studying my face. Sometimes a chickadee will pick up peanut halves one at a time, and drop them, weighing and choosing them, the way jays pick and choose among peanuts in the shell to find the heaviest one. Sometimes a chickadee will drop peanuts

on the ground and peer over the edge of my palm to watch the birds on
the ground hopping over for the peanuts it is tossing. The chickadees
help me feed the birds! Feeding birds seems to be fun for them too.

The Chestnut-backed Chickadees were the first to hand-feed, then
the Black-capped Chickadees. The Red-breasted Nuthatches followed.
Like the chickadees, the nuthatches began by flying toward the hand,
then making a U-turn at the last second. But once a nuthatch had made
the breakthrough, it didn't hesitate any more. Now, when I see a Red-
breasted Nuthatch on a tree trunk, I hold my palm against the tree
trunk, and it scoots down the trunk and grabs the food.

Both Red-breasted and White-breasted Nuthatches live throughout North
America, and both come to suet feeders where we can enjoy watching
them. But Red-breasted Nuthatches can readily be persuaded to hand-
feed, while White-breasted Nuthatches can be a bit more standoffish.

This process was not quick. It took more than a year – from one
winter through the next winter – to get the chickadees and nuthatches
to hand-feed. It took a year for the Red-breasted Nuthatches, that is.
For their cousins the White-breasted Nuthatches, it took eight years!

The jay games

We hold *the* power within our hands: the power of peanuts.

I put out dried corn and millet and suet for the jays to eat whenever they want to. But peanuts are the big prize, and the *only* way they can get peanuts is directly from me. And only one at a time.

There are two kinds of jay in my region: the California Scrub Jay and the Steller's Jay. Some of my Scrub Jay friends will fly over to get peanuts from my hand, but the Stellers are more difficult to persuade. Some Stellers will let me walk up to a tree where they are perched, and they will sidle down the branch to get the peanut. But most of the Stellers won't even do that.

But all the jays play the peanut games.

The basic peanut game goes like this: I hold up a peanut and call out "Birdie!" Any jays within earshot come flying over. They land in the willow tree next to the deck. I throw the peanut onto the deck. The jays swoop down to get it.

But a more fun version of the game is "Beat the squirrel." We team up to outsmart the squirrels. As I hold up the peanut, and repeat "Birdie!" I turn and look up at the jay, look down at the squirrel, and turn back to the jay. I do this in a slow and obvious way. When the squirrel wanders toward one side of the deck, I make eye contact with the jay and pantomime throwing the peanut to the other side. The jay gets ready.

I fire the peanut. The squirrel runs toward it. But swoosh! The jay grabs the peanut from the deck, on the wing! So cool! The squirrel runs back toward where it heard the peanut land, and I throw the next peanut the other way, and another jay swoops down and beats it to the peanut. I throw another peanut. Another jay swoops for it but misses, and it takes only a second for the squirrel to grab it. Score one for the squirrel.

I could just give the squirrel a peanut. Then it would leave us alone for a few minutes. But this is more fun.

Most of the squirrels take peanuts from my hand, and many have names and funny stories. The squirrels are such characters that they could have a whole book of their own. But they will just have to wait their turn.

Each jay has its own style of getting a peanut. One jay may land and hop-hop-hop over to it. Another jay may fly right over to the peanut. Another may swoop and grab it on the wing.

Sometimes jays come up with their own peanut games. A birdfriender in Nevada reported on social media that when a Scrub Jay at a platform feeder was picking up and weighing each peanut to select the heaviest, by accident it knocked one peanut to the ground, and then jumped down, picked it up, and put it back in the feeder! Then it picked up another peanut, dropped it onto the ground, got it, and put it back again. This went on eight more times before the bird got tired of the game and retired with a prized peanut.

But at first, none of the jays would come to the deck unless I was inside the house, threw the peanut far from the door, and closed the sliding glass door after throwing the peanut. Over time, they came closer to the door. But they still insisted the door be closed. They knew the glass was a barrier. I wonder how they learned that, living out in the fir woods.

Finally, one Steller dared to grab a peanut with the door open.

That was the turning point. Now, with the door open, I could throw peanuts out one after another, bang, bang, bang. And the braver jays got peanut after peanut, while the cowardly ones didn't get anything.

The Stellers became more and more relaxed. No longer did a Steller grab a peanut in a panicked rush and fly off like its tail was on fire. They started to take their time weighing and choosing among the available peanuts. Before long, some adventurous Stellers began to come inside the door to get a peanut.

But the Stellers are still reluctant to hand-feed. Some may take food from my hand if I walk over to a branch, lay my hand there with the peanut, and stand there till the Steller sidles down the branch and grabs the peanut from my fingers. Others still prefer to chase peanuts on the deck. As with all birds, different individuals have different preferences.

Though California Scrub Jays also live here, for a few years, I had no resident Scrub Jays in my yard, only shy transients who didn't stay long. But one day a large Scrub Jay showed up and boldly landed on the back of my chair. When I turned to look at him, he flew up to a nearby low branch.

He obviously had claimed this territory. I named him Skippy Scrub Jay.

Skippy joined in the peanut games. He also would come over and get peanuts near my feet. He seemed to be showing off to the Stellers that he could get peanuts that they didn't dare to get.

I put peanuts into odd places for Skippy to retrieve – under a chair, in the hammock ropes, in a stack of firewood. Skippy seems to relish puzzles.

Though Skippy came very close to me, it took more than a year for him to take food from my hands. He let me slowly approach where he was perched, holding up a peanut in my hand, watching his eyes to see when they are fixed on the peanut, instead of on me.

Finally I am close enough that he can grab the peanut.

I started holding a peanut farther from his perch, so Skippy had to lean over to grab it. Then I held it so far he had to leave the perch to get it. I made him fly farther and farther for the peanut. Soon Skippy was swooping over to me and grabbing the peanut on the wing, like a swallow snatching a flying insect from the air. I'll bet he catches dragonflies that way. Then I walked up to him holding out the peanut, the way we used to do it. Skippy reached out – and yanked my fingertip.

Then I started raising my left wrist, and holding up the peanut in my right hand above it, and Skippy started landing on my wrist to takes the peanut.

Finally Skippy started to land on my hand to get the peanut. First he landed on my fingertips to grab it. Now he lands on the flat of my hand.

One day, another Scrub Jay flew at me out of nowhere, and tried to grab the peanut from my hand as it flew by – but missed. The jay landed, breathing hard and looking a little frightened. It watched as Skippy flew toward me and expertly grabbed the peanut on the wing. Skippy makes it look so easy.

Slenderer, shyer, this new Scrub Jay was Skippy's mate. I named her Scooby Scrub Jay.

On the next try, Scooby got the peanut. I could feel her hesitation, her tentativeness at the moment of contact. But her skills improved, and soon she was good at peanut-grabbing on the wing.

A few days later a juvie Scrub Jay showed up, apparently newly fledged from their nest. From a safe distance up in the trees, he stared at the peanut I held out to him, but wouldn't leave his perch. Finally he flew toward me -- but made a sudden U-turn before reaching my hand. He made several more starts, but each time took another U-turn. Finally, he made it to my hand.

And knocked the peanut to the ground.

He quickly flew off and disappeared. He'd finally gotten the nerve to try it, and he'd failed. I could imagine his frustration, like "I can't do it."

I named him Skyler Scrub Jay. Skyler soon mastered peanut-grabbing. But another Scrub Jay youngster still won't come near me, no matter how often it watches the others handfeed. I've named that one Scaredy Scrub Jay.

Birds are all individuals, and when we start birdfriending, we can discover their individual personalities.

The snow advantage

People who live in areas with cold snowy winters have a special advantage in hand-feeding. Chickadees and nuthatches may come to the hand much faster. Pine Siskins travel in nomadic flocks, showing up to the winter feeders in a big group, and three or four or five can come to the hand at the same time, and eat together, rather than grab-and-go like the chickadees and nuthatches. Redpolls also hand-feed in snowy winter areas. Other birds who normally might not consider hand-feeding may do it when the snow makes them a little desperate.

People in snowy areas can let the birds become used to coming to the feeders on their rounds, and then, one super-snowy day, when other food is hard to find, the flock arrives to the feeders and finds the food not in the feeders, but offered in the hands of some humans.

Some people in snowy places use the dummy technique. They create a dummy by stuffing their clothes with rags, including a head with a cap and gloved hands. They place the dummy outside and position it like a seated human, and into its gloved hand, they put bird food. The dummy sits there without moving, without changing, for days at a time. No cat or hawk stays still that long.

Eventually, the bravest member of the flock dares to approach the dummy. Closer and closer. Finally she grabs a piece of food and flies away fast. Everyone sees that she didn't die. Then the next bravest bird dares to try it. Gradually the birds decide that it is safe.

Soon, everyone in the flock is taking food from the dummy glove. Then a human puts on those clothes and gloves and sits like the dummy, holding out bird food in their hand. The birds know that a human is not a dummy, but the form has become familiar, and they have good feelings associated with it. Soon, they start coming to the real hand.

Would a woodpecker?

Downy Woodpeckers, like all woodpeckers, love suet. And Downies are tolerant birds who don't mind humans being close by as they eat, even within touching distance. Surely the Downies would hand-feed.

So I held a block of suet in my hands and offered it to them. But the Downies ignored it, eating only from the hanging suet feeder.

So I took down the suet feeder and put it next to me on the laptop table. After briefly hesitating, the Downies started coming to the table to eat the suet. But they sprayed fragments of suet all over the laptop. So I held the suet feeder up in my hand. Sure enough, before long, a Downy landed and started gobbling.

But, unlike the chickadees, nuthatches, and hummingbirds, who will fly back and forth between the feeders and the hand, the Downies, if they have a choice, will only go to the suet feeder that is hanging up, not to the feeder I'm holding. To get the Downies to hand-feed, I have to take down the hanging suet feeder, which means no suet for the other suet-eating birds like the flickers. So I rarely hand-feed the Downies.

Hairy Woodpeckers, who look like Downies on steroids, have been reported to hand-feed, but they rarely show up in my yard. In the east, some people feed Red-bellied Woodpeckers. But, like the Downies, these other woodpeckers reportedly hand-feed only when there is no other way for them to get suet.

Hummingbirds

People in the east describe the Ruby-throated Hummingbirds who live there as aggressive and fearless. I would never describe my Anna's Hummingbirds that way. Some are friendly and bold, some timid and shy, but they are all a bit cautious.

Sometimes when I am bringing out the hummingbird feeder, a hummingbird will fly over and start drinking while I am still holding it in my hands. One of my friendliest hummers, Raspberry, did that often. In fact, Raspberry was a showoff. He liked flying up in front of my face and showing off his colors.

One day, I found out about hand-held hummingbird feeders – tiny red feeders with yellow flowers like those on the regular hanging feeders. There are lots of videos online of people doing cute things with the hand-held feeders – attaching them to hats, sunglasses, etc. and then letting swarms of hummingbirds feed. How cute!

Surely, I thought, Raspberry would come to a hand-held feeder.

I bought some, cleaned and filled them. I waited till Raspberry showed up to feed, went out and held out the tiny handheld feeder next to the regular feeder. At first, Raspberry ignored me as he drank from the regular feeder. Then he flew around the hand-feeder and inspected it close-up from many angles. But he didn't feed from it.

The next time I went outside, Raspberry flew up to my face, flashing his iridescent colors, as he often did. But then he flew down to my hands. He buzzed around one hand, circling it, studying my hand carefully from one side and the other, from above and below, for about half a minute. Then he flew around to my other hand and did the same thing.

When I saw Raspberry the next morning, I came out and offered him the hand feeder again. Raspberry came straight to it and drank. Then he went to the hanging feeder, then came back to the one the one in my hand. Back and forth.

Hand-held hummingbird feeders can be an easy way to start hand-feeding birds.

The first pioneers

One bird will be the first to decide.

In 1925, a man fed a flock of Green-tailed Towhees at his home. Most of them kept a distance from him. But one bird, a juvie,

> quickly became friendly and unsuspicious, It soon learned to come to the table, at my elbow, and help itself to the litter of crumbs always kept there. Our bird was soon almost as much in the kitchen as out. It would come and go all day, eating its fill every hour or so, and often went about the kitchen on a rather complete tour of inspection which included the water pail, stove, chair backs and a dish of fresh fruit on the table. One morning, just at dawn, the "pat-pat-pat" of tiny claws on the bedroom floor announced the bird was looking for his breakfast. The door had been open. Seeing us the bird flew up and all but alighted on my head. The next morning the food box was ready and when held out to sight, the bird immediately came up on the bed via a nearby chair, hovered a moment at the box, then returned to the floor. A moment later, though, it came back to the box and ate its fill within fifteen inches of my eyes. On subsequent mornings, breakfast at dawn was the program, and it seemed not to matter to

the bird if my fingers were in the box, nor if its tail brushed my fingers…

We learned to recognize a certain squeak note as a plaint for food. It was uttered when the door was closed and no food available. A bird on the window sill looking in meant "please open the door," and in it came as soon as the door did open. But while it soon learned to accept without fright our moving about, so long as we moved slowly, we could never get between it and the door. As soon as escape seemed about to be cut off, the bird calmly flew by and out the door.[3*]

Green-tailed Towhee, a bird of the sagebrush deserts.

Only the one bird became his friend. The rest still wouldn't come near him. Birds are individuals, and they make their individual decisions.

On the other hand, birds who travel in tight-knit flocks, like Cedar Waxwings, won't leave the flock to visit a human. But in videos, I have seen a whole flock covering the arms of someone offering them fruit. That seems to happen only in areas where trees are scarce.

Getting past fear

A bird is hyper-aware of movement around it. And what part of a human moves around the most? The hands.

Any bird who has observed the humans much at all knows the power of the hands. The hands can grasp and hold things. The hands can pick up things, even things that, for a bird, are impossibly heavy.

3   J. Eugene Law, "Green-Tailed Towhee Qualifies In Intelligence Test," *The Condor*, Vol. 28 Issue 3, May-June 1926, pp 133-134 *https://sora.unm.edu/node/97139*

The hand is the scariest part of a human. The hand is also the instrument of human beneficence. The hand is scary.

If a bird is reluctant to come to the hand, we shouldn't move our hand closer to it. We should stay in one place, keeping the hand still, and let the bird choose when to approach.

To help birds get past their fear of us, we need to look at ourselves from their point of view. How dangerous are the humans? Humans are very slow, and can't leave the ground.

And the humans don't seem to be trying to catch and eat birds. But does that mean a human wouldn't eat you, given the opportunity? After all, bears and raccoons don't hunt and stalk prey, but they might take advantage of a creature who is too easy to catch.

So we need to reduce things that makes us seem dangerous. Once a bird knows us, these things are not so important, but with a bird who doesn't know us, they can matter.

If a bird hesitates to approach, we can make it more comfortable by looking at it a bit sidewise, instead of directly. Once a bird knows us, it won't care if we look at it directly, but we humans have the face of a predator. A predator has eyes in front so it can focus on the prey it is trying to catch. In fact, our faces look a bit like owls, the most deadly predator in the bird world. If we look directly at a bird, it can feel threatened. Even a bird on a power line, way up out of our reach, will likely get uncomfortable and fly away if we look at it directly.

We shouldn't make fast, sudden or jerky moves. Predators grab birds with sudden surprise moves, so a bird has an automatic reflex to fly away at a sudden movement. We don't have to be statues – we just should move slowly around them.

We should try to avoid swallowing when a bird is close. If we swallow, it means our mouth is watering, which means we are thinking about eating, and we might be thinking how delicious that bird is. (Again, that matters mainly to a bird who doesn't know us.)

When we offer food in the hand, we should be near to a bush, tree, or other perch. Birds, especially small birds, like to flit short distances from perch to perch – that saves energy and is safer.

But if a bird is hesitating to come, we shouldn't move our hand toward it. The hand should be as motionless as possible. And we shouldn't follow a bird who moves away from us. Following it is what a predator would do.

We shouldn't try to hide from the birds. We *can't* hide from them anyway, but if we *try* to hide, *try* to sneak up and watch them, we are acting like predators.

And we should not be quiet, but talk to the birds. Predators are quiet, especially when trying to sneak up on prey.[4] To make the birds feel friendly toward us, we should talk to them in high, soft and soothing sounds. Or sing to them, or whistle to them. Or mimic them. It doesn't matter if we mimic them well, they understand that mimicking is a form of communication.

If we greet them with the same sound every day, they can learn to recognize that sound. When I have peanuts for the jays, I call out "Birdie!" and they come flying across the yard, knowing what that means.

We should let them see us filling the feeders. Ideally, we should fill the feeders at the same time every day, even if the feeders don't need refilling. Shortly after sunrise is the best time – birds are hungriest then, and looking for food most actively, so they are more likely to see us filling the feeders then, and they can make a food visit part of the morning routine.

We should let the birds see us nearby while they are eating. Each day, we can move closer and closer to the feeders – even if we are behind a window – till the birds are used to us being close to them, and they associate us with food.

If a bird makes eye contact, we can communicate friendliness

---

4   This is one of the reasons why belling a cat does little, if anything, to protect birds. Much more effective are the colorful cat clown collars, sold online, which make it impossible for a cat to hide from the birds.

by slowly closing and opening our eyes – a signal of friendship and pleasure among birds.

Does hand-feeding birds put them in danger?

Some people think that if we hand-feed wild birds, then they will come to any strange human for food whenever they are hungry, and that will put them in danger. Actually, the only birds who do that are birds who were raised by humans when they were babies, and then let go. Sometimes they will actually land on strange humans and beg for food. But wild birds who were not raised by humans don't do that. They may approach a strange human and, from a safe distance, ask if the human has any food for them, but they won't fly up to a strange human, especially uninvited.

And wild songbirds, especially chickadees, are very fast. Who could ever catch a chickadee taking peanuts from the hand?

Which birds may hand-feed?

Ground-feeding birds, like juncos, towhees, and sparrows are friendly, yet they have no interest in hand-feeding. The juncos may foot-feed, if I put millet seed on my feet and sit still enough, but neither they nor the other ground-feeders will fly to my hand. I asked them why, and this was their answer: birds like chickadees and nuthatches look for their food in the trees, and flying to the outstretched hand of a human is not that different from flying to the outstretched branch of a tree. But flying up and landing on the end of a branch to get food is not so normal for a ground-feeding bird, and neither is landing on a hand.

How about if I crouched to put my hand down on the ground? Then they could just hop over to my had, right? Well, when we do something strange, it makes the birds nervous. The birds normally see us standing or sitting. A human in a crouching position would seem a bit weird to them.

I guess there's no way to hand-feed a ground-feeding bird... so I thought Then someone on social media mentioned hand-feeding a Spotted Towhee friend. How did he ever get a ground-feeder like a towhee to come to his hand? Attached to his house was a small storage shed, low enough for him to put his hand on the

The Tufted Titmouse is reputed to be just as friendly as its chickadee relatives

roof. So he laid his hand there, full of bird food. He was standing like a normal human, not crouching down, but the roof being flat like the ground, the towhee could hop over to it the way it would hop on the ground. He considered the bird's point of view and how to make it comfortable.

So how many different birds could be hand-fed? Well, in North America, the common and obvious hand-feeders are the chickadees and their relatives the titmice, the nuthatches, the jays, and the hummingbirds. Every part of North America has at least one species of chickadee, nuthatch, jay, and hummingbird. Downy Woodpeckers, another common hand-feeder, also lives in almost all of North America. Pine Siskins and Redpolls don't live everywhere (and not where I live, so I haven't talked about them because I don't have experience with them) but they commonly hand-feed in winter in cold and snowy areas.

How about other birds? Scouring videos, books and blogs, I have made a list of North American birds who have – at least once – been reported to hand-feed with somebody somewhere sometime.

Besides the common hand-feeders already mentioned, the list includes the jays' relative the Clark's Nutcracker; the Hairy

Woodpecker, Red-bellied Woodpecker, and the Yellow-bellied Sapsucker; the Rose-breasted Grosbeak, Pine Grosbeak, and Evening Grosbeak; the Spotted Towhee and Green-tailed Towhee; the Eastern and Western Bluebird; the Cedar Waxwing and Bohemian Waxwing; the American Goldfinch and Purple Finch; the Pine Warbler, Palm Warbler, Yellow-rumped Warbler, and Yellow-throated Warbler; the Scarlet Tanager; the Chipping Sparrow; the Red-winged Blackbird and Yellow-headed Blackbird; the Brown-headed Cowbird; the Boat-tailed Grackle; the White-winged Crossbill; the Ruby-crowned Kinglet; the Gray Catbird; and the Northern Mockingbird. In Europe, people hand-feed tits (European chickadees), starlings, and European Robins.

There are also reports of birds – Eastern and Western Bluebirds, American Robins, Wood Thrushes, Summer Tanagers, Red-eyed Vireos and Solitary Vireos – taking mealworms, earthworms, or caterpillars from people's hands. Most of these reports are undocumented or second-hand; Birds who are feeding babies usually don't want to take risks, because if parent birds were to die, their babies would too. But if food is abnormally scarce, and both parents and babies are faced with starvation, the parents might take desperate measures.

But bluebirds do take mealworms from people's fingers to feed their babies. The people have put up bluebird houses, and protect those houses from the bluebirds' deadly enemy the House Sparrows, so the bluebirds know those people as allies.

Owls may also take food from people's hands, even total strangers. Owls have little fear of creatures on the ground, since no ground predators hunt owls. So a scientist trying to find out how many owls live in an area will go into the woods and hold out a live mouse in her hand, andif there is an owl around watching, it will swoop down to grab the mouse right out of her hand.

Crows are another story. Though many people try to hand-feed crows, I have yet to come across a credible report of someone hand-feeding a wild adult crow. Crows can come close to their human friends, yet not too close. There are two possible reasons for this. First, crows have much slower takeoff than smaller birds, so it is riskier for a crow to come near a potential danger. Plus, some humans kill crows. It is even legal in many places to kill crows. So crows have a hard time totally trusting humans. But crows have other ways of expressing their affection for their human friends Some leave little gifts, like coins or plastic toys.

There are many ways that birds can be friends with us. Hand-feeding creates a special bond between us and the birds. But hand-feeding isn't the only way to be friends with birds. If we think it is, then we can miss the friendship of many species that will never hand-feed. Hand-feeding is not the final goal of birdfriending. It is only a step on the path. Birdfriending is a relationship. It grows and deepens as we and the birds learn to understand each other better and better. In the upcoming chapters we will talk more about understanding what it is like to be a bird. For a birdfriender, it is the journey that matters, not the destination, and the journey never ends.

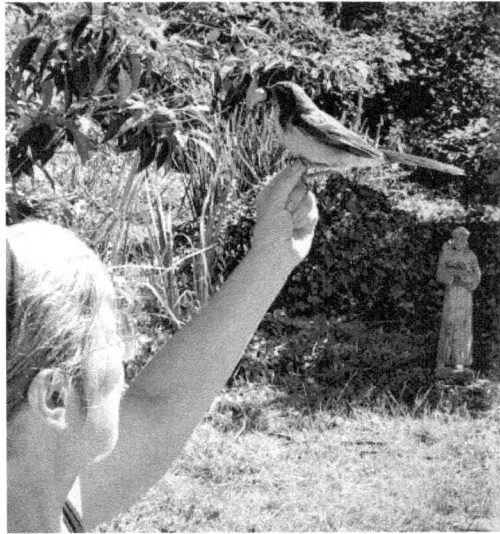

CHAPTER THREE

EAVESDROPPING ON
THEIR CONVERSATIONS

In mythology, medieval literature and occultism, the language of the birds is postulated as a mystical, perfect divine language, Adamic language, Enochian, angelic language or a mythical or magical language used by birds to communicate with the initiated. Within Sufism, the language of birds is a mystical divine language. In the Jerusalem Talmud, Solomon's proverbial wisdom was due to his being granted understanding of the language of birds by God. In Kabbalah, Renaissance magic, and alchemy, the language of the birds was considered a secret and perfect language and the key to perfect knowledge. In many folk tales (including Welsh, Russian, German, Estonian, Greek, Romany), the protagonist is granted the gift of understanding the language of the birds. The birds then inform or warn the hero about some danger or hidden treasure.

—Wikipedia, "Language of the Birds"[5]

CAN WE LEARN the language of the birds? Can the birds lead us to hidden treasures?

Maybe not to physical treasures like gold. But understanding some of the birds' communications is itself a treasure. And it helps to open the door to communication with them.

Like us, birds use their voices to communicate. Like us, they communicate with body language too. But since birds are often out of sight from each other, their communication depends most on sound.

And their most glorious sound is song.

Birdsong as communication

Birdsong is a special kind of communication. Birdsong isn't about information, like the sentences on this page. Birdsong communicates emotion. Through his song, a male songbird tries to persuade a female to marry him. And his song is a promise to keep giving her pleasure with his song even after they're married. While they build the nest, while she sits on the eggs, and whenever they get a moment's rest from raising babies, he will continue to sing, though a bit less energetically and less often.

When a female bird listens to her mate sing, her brain generates

5   Accessed April 8, 2020

the same kind of chemicals that a mammal's brain generates when it is being petted, stroked, licked, or cuddled. The shared pleasure strengthens the couple's bonds.

So it is no surprise that a female bird wants the best singer she can get. And some female songbirds sing back. Humans may not notice female songbirds who sing, but she isn't singing to the whole world, just to her special someone.

The male's song also communicates to other males of his kind. He is announcing to them that he claims a certain territory. As more birds move into the neighborhood, and things start to get crowded, they may have different ideas about where the property lines should be. They start haggling. They challenge each other and have singing contests in various disputed spots. They negotiate the boundaries by trying to outsing each other.

The competition can get fierce. The boundaries of the territories shift around. But finally the territories are settled, more or less. The best singer ends up with the best territory.

Even after territories are established, the male songbird continues to communicate with other male birds through his song. If we observe a songbird singing, we may notice that he pauses between his songs. During the pauses, we can hear the far-off song of another songbird of the same kind. And then the song of a third bird farther off in another direction. Then our songbird sings again, while the others pause.

They take turns. And even though they are rivals, the male songbird shows signs of pleasure listening to them sing. And they listen not just for pleasure. They are paying attention to each other, but why?

Song Sparrows have been studied a lot, both by scientists and by backyard birdwatchers, because they are so easy to

observe. By studying how Song Sparrows communicate with their neighbors through song,[6] researchers have found how songbirds weave a tapestry of community with their songs..

Each Song Sparrow has a repertoire of songs, which increases every year. Song Sparrows learn songs from each other, as well as developing original songs, but when a Song Sparrow borrows a musical idea from another Song Sparrow, he puts his own touches on it. A Song Sparrow's choice of songs to sing, on any given day, shows how well he is getting along with his neighbors.

Say you're a male Song Sparrow with a repertoire of fourteen songs. Two are versions of songs sung by your neighbor to the east; one is a song you learned from him, and one a song he learned from you. Three of your songs are shared with the neighbor to your south, three with the neighbor to your west, two with your neighbor to the north. And each neighbor in turn shares different songs with each of his various neighbors, creating a network of shared songs.

Every morning, you greet each of your neighbors by singing a song that you and each neighbor share. A neighbor's reply will tell you whether he is feeling friendly to you or not. Your eastern neighbor greets you with a song you both share. If you want to give him a friendly greeting back, you reply with a *different* song that you both share. If you are not feeling so friendly to him, you will reply with the *same* song that he just sang.

Answering with a *different* song that both of you share is called "unmatched countersinging," and it is a sign of friendliness toward your neighbor. Answering a song with the *same* song is called "matched countersinging," and it means you are peeved at your neighbor. Answering him with a song that you don't share at all is like giving him the cold shoulder.

By listening to who is matching and unmatching, we can tell who is getting along and who isn't. Each bird is telling the others, "Stay

---

6   For the insights on how Song Sparrow neighbors communicate by song, I am indebted to Donald Krugsma's magnum opus *The Singing Life of Birds.*

out of my territory," but at the same time, he is saying, "Hi neighbor, we respect each other's territories and we are getting along!"

Another reason Song Sparrow neighbors may communicate is to stagger their breeding schedules as not to hatch their broods at the same time. Since each couple has its own territory, which ensures enough food for their nestlings, why would it matter when the neighbors hatch their babies?

Because once their babies fledge, or graduate from the nest, the territorial boundaries will dissolve. Fledglings have no idea abut territories and they wander around anywhere. If neighbor broods hatched at the same time, their babies would fledge at the same time, and then the neighbors would be competing for the same food at the same time in the same place. Song may help the neighbors coordinate their breeding schedules.[7]

Birdsong is unique in the animal kingdom. Most animals have calls: a wolf howls, a cat meows, a cow moos. But songs are different from calls. Songs have to be learned, while calls are inherited. A duck will quack whether it has ever heard another duck or not. A dove will coo without ever hearing that sound. A rooster will crow even if it never heard another rooster. But if a songbird never hears another member of its kind sing, it will never learn to sing itself. In fact, birdsong is a lot like human language in some ways, and scientists study the songbird brain to gain insights on how the human brain learns language.

Easy-to-understand calls

All bird vocalizations other than songs are put into the category of calls.

There are many, many different kinds of calls, to communicate different things. Can we humans learn to understand their calls? We can't understand everything, but we can understand a lot.

---

7   I haven't read about neighboring Song Sparrows staggering their breeding schedules, only observed it with the Song Sparrows on my deck.

Some kinds of calls are straightforward and easy to understand. These include distress calls, alarm calls, fledgling begging calls, territorial challenges, contact calls that mates or flock members use to keep track of each other, and locator calls that they use to find each other over distance.

The *distress call* is the easiest to recognize. Practically every creature with ears knows what it means. Whether it comes from a bird, rabbit, or human, the cry of "Help, I'm in trouble!" has the same tone.

An *alarm call* is for potential danger, and is also understood by most creatures in the woods. They all listen to the birds' alarm calls, because birds, being mobile and able to see from up high, know more about approaching danger than anyone else.

What does a bird alarm call sound like? Well, let's think about another creature who makes alarm calls – a dog. When a dog barks, it's partly a warning to scare away something threatening, it's also an alarm to tell the rest of the pack that something is going on. Bird alarm calls also sound short, abrupt, and emphatic, like a dog barking at a stranger. The alarm calls vary by species – a chickadee's *"dee-dee-dee,"* a robin's *"kuk-kuk-kuk,"* a Song Sparrow's *"chip-chip-chip,"* the *"click-click-click"* of the junco snapping its beak – the birds understand each other's alarms.

Like a dog's bark, bird alarm calls can vary in tone and speed and urgency depending on what's going on. When we hear a dog barking, we can tell if it's a routine bark about someone walking by or a frantic bark about serious danger. Bird alarm calls tell each other (and us) what level of danger is around. A slow, casual alarm call can mean just to be on the lookout. A fast, emphatic alarm call can mean serious danger. When the Black-capped Chickadees give their *chicka-dee-dee* attention call as an alarm, the more *dees* they put at the end, the bigger the danger they are warning about. Birds give different levels of alarm for a cat casually strolling by and a cat who is on the hunt.

A bird listens to the alarms of other birds, no matter what kind, because a danger to one is a danger to all. And the ground animals listen to the birds too, because, being up high, the birds can see everything that's going on. Birds act as the security cameras of the woods. They let everyone know where danger is lurking, so the animals can know where to go to be safe.[8]

A deer walks by my deck. The birds say my yard is a safe place, and other animals listen to the birds.

During fledgling season, I can trace the path of a cat through the brambles by following the alarm calls of the towhees. And when the juncos are around me clicking about a cat, I feel like I am inside a Geiger counter.

I learned to find raccoons sleeping up in the trees, splayed out on a branch, arms and legs hanging down, by listening to the crows' casual alarms. Something's up there, the crows say, but not something truly dangerous like an owl. It's a day-sleeping raccoon,

One afternoon, I heard the Scrub Jays making an agitated alarm from a nearby overgrown vacant lot. I sneaked over and peered, and

8   The book *What the Robin Knows: How Birds Reveal the Secrets of the Natural World* by Jon Young explains how to find wildlife in the woods by paying attention to what the birds are saying and doing.

what did I spot? A human. He seemed to be looking for cans and bottles, but there weren't any; humans rarely went in there, as the jays well knew. I was surprised that the jays would alarm about a human; they are friendly to me and to my guests. But they knew this was a strange human, doing something unusual. That made them upset.

But the most serious danger, to a bird, is from the air. Danger on the ground is easy; just fly up too high for it to reach. You don't even have to know its exact location. But an owl or an accipiter – a bird-catching hawk like a Cooper's Hawk or a Sharp-shinned Hawk – may be lurking in the foliage, and you can't get away from it just by flying off, especially if you don't know where it is.

An owl can snatch a songbird from a branch. An accipiter can chase a songbird through the woods and catch it. A falcon can dive on a flying bird from above. No wonder fear of the winged predators is ever-present in a songbird's life.

But if a songbird spots a winged predator in the trees, how could it warn the other birds? Making a sound would give away its location.

The bird makes a high-pitched *seet* sound. Only once. That's risky enough. It's so high-pitched that the raptor can't hear it as well as a small bird can, and it is difficult to locate in the foliage.

Everyone who hears the alarm becomes silent and freezes in place. They don't fly off, because without knowing where is, you could be flying right into its claws. Even birds who didn't hear the alarm will notice the sudden silence, and they will shut up too.

Then the jays take over. They summon each other from far and wide to mob the raptor and drive it away. We might miss the songbirds' tiny *zeet* call, we can't miss the assembly call of a mob of jays or crows to call everyone together to mob a hawk or an owl.

Sometimes we may hear two birds quarreling. Chickadees who are arguing can pull out all the snarls, twitters, gargles they know. So what do birds quarrel about? In a flock, there may be arguments over rank (higher-ranked birds get first choice of food and of spots to eat). Or there could be a territorial challenge, which happens when one male bird violates another's territory. Not all territorial challenges sound like quarrels, though; the *wikka-wikka-wikka* call of the flickers is a territorial challenge.

Another call that is easy to understand is the *contact call*. Contact calls are used by mates or family members to stay in touch and keep track of each other when they can't see each other. Contact calls are soft, because they happen between birds who are close to each other. In the woods, we can hear the steady "chip... chip... chip..." or "zeet? ....zeet? ...zeet?" going back and forth in the bushes and trees. It means "here I am" and "as far as I know, everything is fine."

Chickens, ducks, quail, and other ground-dwelling species use contact calls as the babies follow their mother around. *"Cluck, cluck, cluck,"* says the mother hen. *"Peep, peep, peep,"* say the babies. The babies can hear while still inside the egg, so they know their mother's voice and will refuse to follow any other hen. Some mates, including American Goldfinches and Pine Siskins, use contact calls while in the air.

When two towhee mates are foraging together, they call to each other continually with a unique rising call that sounds like a question. If one mate suddenly goes silent, the contact call becomes louder and faster and more urgent, until it sounds truly worried. But when one mate finds a rich source of food, we can hear its tone change from "I'm here, where are you" to "Come over here quick!"

Locator calls are louder than contact calls, because they are used to find a family member other over a distance. The hooting of an owl, the piercing *kleer* of a flicker and the hoarse whisper-scream of the Red-tailed Hawk are locator calls. The hawk's call has to be loud and piercing because the mate might be a mile away.

The *begging calls* of the fledglings have a simple meaning: *"FEED ME!"* Each species of fledgling has a distinctively different begging call, because each bird parent has to be able to find its own fledglings and ignore the fledglings of other species. Yet, we can easily learn to recognize fledgling begging calls, because no matter how different they sound, they almost all have a tone of relentless nagging. (The picture at the top of this chapter is of a Red-breasted Nuthatch fledgling begging its father to feed it.)

Flock communication

We can learn to recognize and understand those calls, whose meanings are simple. But some birds have more complex vocal communication as well.

It should be no surprise that creatures who live in groups, like wolves, whales, elephants, and humans, have more complex communication than animals who live alone or in pairs. The same with birds.

Some birds belong to stable flocks. They have relationships not only with their mates, but friendships and connections with other flock members as well.

Some flock communication is easy to understand. If flock members are out of sight of each other as they forage in the bushes and trees, they may use continuous calls to keep track of each other. It's like how we humans use chitchat to feel like part of a group. "How's it going? You doing okay?"

But some flock communications are more challenging to interpret. Scientists have identified at least twenty different vocalizations used among crows, and about the same number used among chickadees.

But each vocalization may have multiple meanings depending on pitch, speed, how many times it is repeated, and the overall situation.

Chickadees are named for their "chicka-dee-dee" call. They use this call as an alarm call for danger. But the *chicka-dee-dee-dee* call is not always an alarm call. It is really a call for attention. The *chicka-dee-dee-dee-dees* ring out loud and fast when I fill the empty suet feeder on a winter morning. And *chicka-dee-dee-dee* is sometimes used as a locator call.

When scientists recorded the "chicka-dee" call and slowed it down, they found that it is much more complicated than it sounds to our slow ears. The chickadees have at least four ways of pronouncing each syllable, and different ways of combining them. Each individual chickadee has its own distinct style of "chicka-deeing" that other chickadees seem to recognize. And *chicka-dee-dee* is only one of the vocalizations chickadees have. Scientists have catalogued at least nineteen other vocalizations that chickadees make, most with lots of variations.[9] One of those chickadee vocalizations is the "gargle." (I call it "gargle" because bird scientists do, but it doesn't sound anything like the throat sounds we associate with gargling. It's more of a *chiddle-up-diplee-zikum-dingo* or something like that.)

Gargles are extremely complex, made up of many different note types, often with trills and repeated motifs. When scientists recorded the gargles and slowed them down, they found that one gargle may contain anywhere from two to thirteen syllables, and they identified up to 23 different syllables that the chickadees could combine in one gargle.

Chickadees are not born knowing their gargles. Like songs, gargles are learned. And chickadees get creative with their gargles. Individual chickadees develop their own repertoires of gargles, just as other songbirds develop repertoires of songs.

And chickadees in different places have different "dialects" in their gargles. They can tell if a bird doesn't belong to their flock by its "accent." If a bird joins a new flock, it has to adopt the "accent" of that flock to be accepted.

So what are the gargles for? What are the chickadees communicating about? One thing gargles are used for is negotiating territory and rank. Chickadees may also use gargles to gossip about each other. But humans – scientists and birdfrienders – have barely begun to interpret

9   For much of the information on chickadee communication, I am indebted to *The Black-capped Chickadee: Behavioral Ecology and Natural History* by Susan M. Smith.

chickadee communication. If we hang out with a chickadee flock, we can pick up a lot of snippets of chickadee conversation, and we know they are saying *something*. We shouldn't feel dumb if we can't understand it, because other birds who are not chickadees probably can't either. Those conversations are just meant for chickadees.

Other birds who travel together in nomadic flocks, like Cedar Waxwings, Red Crossbills, and Pine Siskins, and birds who nest together in colonies, like Brewer's Blackbirds and Cliff Swallows, may have complicated languages too. But those birds haven't been studied as much by scientists as parrots, chickadees. and crows.

The first thing to pay attention to is tone of voice. Tone of voice is a common language shared by most mammals and birds. Human babies understand tone of voice from the moment they are born. Dogs understand human tone of voice, and we understand theirs. The tone of a dog's bark can express fear, anger, uncertainty, excitement. For humans, a simple word like "what" can convey anything from curiosity to outrage – "What...?" "WHAT!" And, through tone of voice., a seemingly simple bird call can communicate many different things.

It's like being in another country where they speak a different language. We can understand a lot by listening to tone of voice and observing what is happening during a conversation. A human who spends enough time observing the same group of birds may start to understand some of what they are saying. As a crowfriender reports:

Like listening to a foreign language, in time, their sounds became more familiar to me and I was able to recognize variations in the calls... My interpretations depended upon season, context, and the individual bird. I gained insight by learning to differentiate the tenor of the call – from staccato urgency to long, drawn-out rasps.[10]

10 From *Caw of the Wild: Observations From the Secret World of Crows,* by Barb Kirpluk, p 17.

People who keep pet chickens have a great opportunity to observe what they say in different situations. Even baby chicks have a vocabulary of different peeps, tweets, and trills, expressing pleasure, discovery, distress, etc. As one chicken-keeper reported:

> I've always talked to my flocks while doing my chicken chores.... I discovered that I knew plenty of their calls – danger signals, happy calls, hellos and good nights, and even encouragement chatter. I was learning to speak chicken! ... Then one day my kids and I were visiting another flock... When we used chicken language to greet them, the response was astonishing. Their heads popped right up, as if to say, "Is there another chicken here?"... We "chatted" a bit more with them, using other intonations and sounds. Then, for a final test, I used the alarm call to alert the to danger coming from above. Every single chicken paused and became statuesque, with one eye to the sky. Just as I thought, they understood me![11]

Birds are not born knowing the intricacies of flock communication, but learn it through experience. So a bird who belongs to one flock may not entirely understand the internal language of another flock, even of the same species – never mind a different bird species.

Each flock has its own dialect and its own accent. If a parrot joins another flock, it adopts the dialect of that flock. Talking the same way makes a group feel connected, just as it does with humans. And, within the flock, each mated pair has their own special calls to find each other in the middle of the flock, and their own little love-codes, shared in the privacy of the nest. Copying each other's sounds helps the birds to bond.

And it turns out that parrots actually have names for each other[12]—

---

11   From *How to Speak Chicken,* by Melissa Caughey, p. 13.

12   Berg, et al, "Vertical transmission of learned signatures in a wild parrot"

though to us, their names (or "signature contact calls," as scientists call them) may sound like screeches and squawks. Parents give names to each offspring, mates call each other by name, and friends greet each other by name. They may even use names to talk *about* each other. There is evidence that wild parrots add an extra sound to a name when they are talking about a flock member who is dead.

If parrots have names for each other, could they have names for other things? Perhaps. After all, parrots who live with humans can learn the humans' names for different objects.

And a chicken-keeper reports:

> As I studied my flock, the meaning of one particular sound always eluded me. I simply dismissed it as another chicken greeting,....but when I paid closer attention, I realized it was in fact my chicken name! ... To me, my chicken name sounds regal. The first three sounds are low and the last one is almost an octave higher. Bup, bup, bup, baaahhhh. They use this sound when they see me, when they want something from me, and when they are snuggling in my lap.... It makes me smile every time I hear it.[13]

Private conversations

Individual birds may have private conversations – soft purrs, trills, little cheeps, and *whisper song* – intimate songs that birds sing when close to each other. Such quiet conversation happens between mates who are close together, between parents and nestlings, between friends who can't see each other in the foliage.

Conversation includes *whisper song*—intimate songs that birds sing when close to each other. Mates sing whisper songs to each other, and father birds sing whisper song to their nestlings to expose their

https://royalsocietypublishing.org/doi/full/10.1098/rspb.2011.0932

13   From *How to Speak Chicken* by Melissa Caughey, p 44-5.

brains early to the sound of the birdsongs they will need to know when they grow up. In fact, if a songbird doesn't hear his species' song while still a baby, he will never learn to sing when he grows up – much like a human baby needs to hear the sounds of talking in order to learn to talk when she's bigger.

Conversation also includes *subsong*, or baby babble. Some people might say that subsong is not about communication, it is only the babies practicing their future songs, but the parents surely share their children's pleasure as they play with sounds.

Mother birds even cheep to babies in their eggs, and they cheep back. And the babies cheep to each other while still inside the eggs![14]

Starlings, who are not territorial, use song to socialize as a flock. Starlings have wonderful singing ability, but no special song of their own. Instead, like mockingbirds, they mimic other birds, and play mix-and-match with pieces of birdsong and other sounds they like, like car alarms, to improvise long unique melodies.

Their skill at mimicking and improvising is on a par with mockingbirds, but they get much less credit than mockingbirds, for several reasons. Their voices are not as loud as mockingbird voices; not being territorial, starlings don't need to sing loudly. On the other hand, the begging call of fledgling starlings is loud and harsh, and a flock of fledgling starlings screeching together is one of the most horrible noises in all of nature, so most people associate starlings with awful screeching rather than lovely songs.

A mockingbird also gets more credit because he takes a conspicuous perch and pours out his song for the world. He wants to impress female mockingbirds and intimidate other male mockingbirds. A lone starling, on the other hand, burbles its song softly, as though singing to itself. Starlings are not territorial, they nest in colonies, and mates

---

14   Noguera, Jose C., & Alberto Velando, "Bird embryos perceive vibratory cues of predation risk from clutch mates." *Nature Ecology and Evolution*, Volume 3, pages 1225–1232 (2019)
https://www.nature.com/articles/s41559-019-0929-8

have loose, sometimes polyamorous bonds within the colony. Both female and male starlings sing, and they sing all year round, not just in mating season.

So starling song doesn't have the purpose of territory or mates, Starling song helps create camaraderie and a sense of togetherness within the flock. They repeat each other's phrases, which spread throughout the flock. We know that this creates bonding because pet starlings raised with humans, like pet parrots, readily imitate the sounds their human flocks make in order to bond with them. Groups of starlings perch together and sing together, but, unlike most songbirds, they don't take turns; they all sing at the same time, and all their lovely individual songs dissolve into cacophony. Yet another reason most people don't realize what excellent singers starlings are.

For birds who mimic and improvise, sounds seem to be a kind of plaything. Mockingbirds and starlings imitate car alarms, roosters, cats, and phones. Once I heard a wild Starling calling "Pretty bird!" in perfect imitation of some pet cockatiel it had heard.

Steller's Jays, like their eastern relatives the Bluejays, often mimic other birds. But only simple calls, not elaborate songs. (Sometimes they will whisper elaborate songs to themselves, but they seem unwilling to do it aloud.) Mimicry for the Stellers seems to be a way of creating bonds within the flock. I discovered that one year when one member of the Steller flock showed up with a brand-new melody: the song of the Red-winged Blackbird.

Red-winged Blackbirds live in wetlands and marshes. A member of the Steller flock must have visited a nearby wetlands and come back with a prize: the Red-winged Blackbird song. The Red-winged Blackbird song varies from region to region, but around here their song has three notes, the longest note being a chord with two pitches sung at the same time. (We'll talk about how they can do this in the chapter on Bird Bodies.) That sound is haunting and hypnotic, especially in he spring when a chorus of Red-winged Blackbirds are singing together in the marshes.

But most birds can't produce a chord. So the Steller couldn't really do the Red-winged Blackbird song right. Even so, the one Steller went around singing it. Soon another Steller tried it, and another and another, and soon, the whole flock was singing it. It was a hit. The Stellers started using the new song to greet each other, and even to greet me when they arrived at the deck.

But only one Steller had heard the original song. All the other Stellers had learned it from him. And his version of it wasn't a perfect copy to begin with. Other flock members began to add variations, and the song evolved, like a game of gossip. It was still lovely, but became unrecognizable. If I had heard this song and didn't know the Stellers were making it, I would have been scouring the internet in vain to identify it.

In a few years, that song disappeared. No Red-winged Blackbirds were around to keep reminding them of it. If a hit song stops getting played on the radio, how many people keep on singing it?

For the Stellers, mimicry apparently isn't just fun, but *shared* fun. Like how following a fad can make us feel connected with other followers of the fad, or using the same slang creates a bond with others who are "with it." Sharing and trading sounds seems to be one way they bond the flock together. It isn't about perfect singing, it is about the sense of belonging.

The breathy scream of the Red-tailed Hawk seems to be the Stellers' favorite. Some people say that the reason that Stellers imitate Red-Tailed Hawks is to scare other birds away from feeders. But I don't think that anyone has ever actually seen that happen. It seems absurd for so many reasons.

For one thing, the small birds show not the slightest reaction to the Stellers' Redtail imitation. They don't even react to *real* Redtail calls. In fact, they barely react when a real Redtail flies overhead.

And why would they? Red-Tailed Hawks are not a threat to them. Red-tailed Hawks are soaring hawks who hunt rodents in open fields.

On the other hand, the accipiters – the Cooper's Hawks and Sharp-shinned Hawks – *are* real threats to the songbirds.

A Cooper's Hawk and a Red-tailed Hawk belong to different hawk families and have different shapes. The long tail is a giveaway of an accipiter, or bird-catching hawk. A buteo, or soaring hawk, has bigger shoulders and a more chunky shape.

Yet, when I played a recording of the call of a Cooper's Hawk, the birds didn't react. Why? Because a Cooper's Hawk, like a tiger, a fox, or other predator, depends on stealth. If a predator is making noise, it is not hunting.

So the Stellers don't imitate hawks to get the small birds to leave the feeders. A Steller's Jay could easily just chase the small birds away. But it doesn't. Having the smaller birds around is a protection for it.

I think that the reason the Stellers imitate Red-tailed Hawks is the same reason that they imitate other birds: because it's fun. And it's shared fun, and creates bonds among flock members.

Body language

Like us, birds communicate through body language as well as sound.

Some male birds dance or bow or spread out their wings or tail feathers when courting a female. And, once they are together, mates use body language to strengthen their bonds. Mates often nibble each other's heads. To a bird, letting someone touch your head or rub your ear-holes is very intimate, a sign of deep trust.

Among practically all the songbirds, the body language of a fledgling begging a parent to feed it is the same – facing the parent and bowing below its face, mouth wide open, wings spread, lowered, and quivering.

Territorial challenges often involve body language. We may see it when neighbors who quarreled during territory negotiations, and moved far apart where they never have to see each other, run into each other at the feeders. Then we may get a brief and entertaining little show.

Each species has its own body language for this situation.[15] Some birds raise their wings, some fan out their tails. Some birds lower their wings so the tips almost touch the ground, some lift their wings and hold them out, some unfurl their wings and hold them up. Some flash their white outer tail feathers. Some birds lunge at the rival as though to peck him. Some birds even hit each other with their wings.

If neither bird gives in, the two may fly straight up into the air together, as though beating each other up, then they come down again. No one is hurt, of course. On my deck, I see this most often among the juncos. Even after they settle things and go to separate places to eat, they may go around with lowered wings or a raised tail, as though warning, "Better not mess with me, I'm a tough guy."

Feather language is a big part of birds' body language. A female bird interested in a male's singing may part the feathers on her breast, and tilt her head. A male songbird listening to another male of his kind singing will show different body language at different times of year. In the spring, when a rival sings, the feathers on top of his head may rise. a sign of intense interest and close attention. But later in

---

15   For detailed descriptions of species-specific behavior, the three-volume *A Guide to Bird Behavior* by Donald and Lillian Stokes is highly recommended.

the season, when the birds have their mates and territories secured, he may relax and show signs of pleasure in the singing of other birds – even of other kinds of birds. The tone of his own song can change, slowing down a bit and sounding more relaxed.

Birds often drop their wings when challenging each other, but they also drop their wings when taking pleasure in listening to another bird sing, like this female robin listening to her mate. The feathers on her breast are slightly parted, another sign she is feeling romantic.

Just as with us, a lot of bird body language is involuntary, not meant to communicate to someone else. Facial expressions are part of such involuntary body language. Since facial expression is such a big part of human communication, we humans are good at reading facial expressions, and that talent can help us understand the birds.

The more we understand how birds think and feel, the more we can understand their communication with each other. In upcoming chapters, we'll talk about the thoughts and feelings of birds.

CHAPTER FOUR

COMMUNICATING WITH THE BIRDS

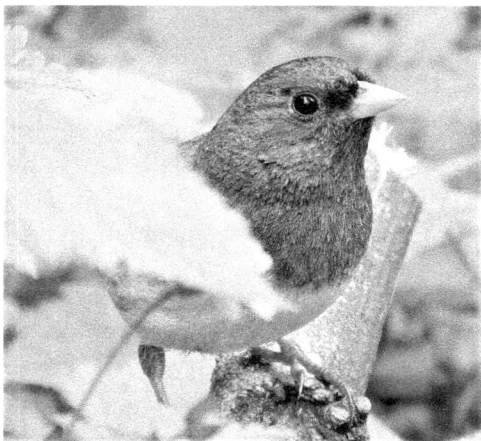

I'M WALKING AROUND the yard cutting blackberry canes. As I lean over to cut one, a junco appears in front of me, at eye level, making eye contact with me, and emitting chips of alarm.

I don't notice him at first. It's easy to miss a junco. As ground feeders and ground nesters, they are unnoticeable on purpose. But this junco is trying to get my attention. And I can guess why. I must be too close to his nest, hidden somewhere on the ground around where I am walking.

It so happens I have a camera in my hand. So I take his picture.

Then I move away, and he disappears into the brush. The picture, at the top of this chapter, shows his facial expression. A lot of people think that birds don't have facial expressions, but paying attention to birds' facial expressions helps us communicate with them – just as when we communicate with each other.

The towhee is another ground-nester. Once, when I was working in the yard, a towhee perched in front of me, facing me, and made urgent alarm calls, asking me to ask to please move away. He knew that I would cooperate, if only he could make me understand.

And more than once a Song Sparrow has come up to me, making alarm calls, and asked me to chase away a cat. Once a Song Sparrow led me some distance to a brush pile, and sure enough a cat was prowling around there. The Song Sparrow must have had a fledgling hidden in there. I chased the cat away.

Someone on social media told about a chickadee who led her to a space behind a wall where the chickadee's fledgling was trapped. She freed the fledgling.

The fact that birds can recognize us as fellow beings with whom it is possible to communicate never ceases to amaze me. And the fact that they can understand that we are on their side and will help them.

Coming in the house

When the weather is nice, I leave the door open, and birds come in and out of my house. Ground feeders like Song Sparrows and Mourning Doves walk or hop in, eating seeds I tracked in from the deck, though there's plenty of food outside. The chickadees fly in, to ask me for peanuts, and also to try to solve the mystery of where the peanuts come from. But usually a bird who flies in, instead of walking in, has come in by mistake.

And then it is confused. In the birds' world, there is no such thing as an enclosed space. And in their ancestral memory, there is no such thing as backtracking. The direction of safety is forward. The bird flies around the room, tries all the windows, and discovers that the windows are a cruel deception. It probably feels like it is in the Twilight Zone.

Different birds react to this situation in different ways. A Red-breasted Nuthatch who flies into the house usually calmly takes a perch, looks around and studies the room, then flies out straight as an arrow. I admire the Red-breasted Nuthatches and strive to handle unexpected crises the way they do.

But a jay who gets trapped in the house can panic so badly it risks hurting itself. Jays are famous for their smarts, but different birds have different kinds of smarts.

Song Sparrows and other birds who panic usually beat themselves against the windows. But when a chickadee panics, it heads not for the light of the windows, but for the darkest corners of the ceiling. Darkness seems to represent safety to a chickadee.

I used to think that, when a bird got trapped in the house, the important thing was to catch it. That is very stressful for both of us. And the bird has a traumatic experience, which it associates with me.

But finally I realized that if a bird is trapped in the house, the first thing isn't to get the bird out. The first thing is to calm the bird down. Birds can understand that we are on their side and want to help them. If we believe and feel that a bird will understand, that seems to help it come true.

Two things can calm down a panicked bird. One is darkness. If we have to pick up a bird who has been injured or stunned, we should cup our hands around it to create darkness. A bird's mind shuts down in darkness and its struggles will stop. But I can't make the room all dark, because of the windows. So I use something else – sound.

We know by instinct how to talk to someone in distress – with high, soothing, cooing sounds, like babytalk. So I sit down and talk to the bird in a high voice: "Pooooor widdo birdie! Pooooor poooor widdle birdie birdie birdieee!" " I'm in no hurry. I can keep it up all day. While I'm doing email, I coo on and on. "Pooooooooooooor liddo birdie!…"

I sing to the bird too. I'm not just trying to calm it. I want to give it pleasure. I want the bird to associate me with pleasure, with good feelings. After all, *they* give me pleasure with *their* singing, so I should repay them.

This juvie junco had been flying around bumping into windows, but she relaxed as I sang to her, and after about forty minutes, she calmly hopped out the door.

Eventually, the bird looks around and figures the way out and leaves, or else it lets me know it is ready to let me walk over, *very slowly*, to catch it. Sometimes a bird will even crouch down to allow me to pick it up.

Birds can understand our tone of voice, just as dogs and other animals do. We can convey our kind intent through our voice. If a birdfriender talks to the birds around them, it helps the birdfriend-ships develop much faster.

Singing to the birds

My mother never fed the birds. Yet they followed her around the yard, as she talked to them and sang to them.

When I was little, my mother's mother told us stories from her native Idaho, the old stories of Yaukekam the hero and his grand-mother Watak the Frog, and Skinkuts the trickster Coyote and Tsupqa the Deer and Nak'yo the Fox and Kupi the Owl and Iyamu the Buffalo and Klhaulha the Grizzly and Shinna the Beaver and other animals. I cherish those precious Ktunaxa words, that connect me to the voice of my ancestors whenever I speak those names.

My favorite stories were those of how she, herself, was friends with all the animals.

The bears and beavers would play with her, the eagle would fly down to her bare hand from the sky, the salmon would swim up to eat from her fingers – from far and wide, everybody came to visit her. I dreamed of being part of that world myself.

When I got a bit older, I realized that those stories were highly exaggerated. But they were not completely made up. My grandmother did communicate to the birds by singing to them. And not just to the birds. She sang to the plants in the garden; she said it made them happy and made them grow better. She sang prayers of thanks to the wild medicine plants she gathered. She talked to insects and spiders as though they were people. And she passed these things to my mother as well. And my mother passed them to me. (And, as I grew up, I discovered that such ways are common to most Indigenous peoples.)

My mother taught me to sing to plants in the garden. It doesn't matter that plants don't have ears – they can feel our songs. And I saw that that was true, because even though my mother never fed the birds, her bird friends followed her around as she worked in the garden and talked and sang to them.

When a bird calls, she said to call back to it. Not to try to fool it, of course, but to get its attention. Even though a bird may seem to ignore a human's reply to its call (after all, it isn't calling the human, but other birds of its kind) the bird does notice and remember that human.

And sometimes when I answer a bird's call, the bird does reply back to me. Then we can have a conversation. I repeat a *chickadee's dee-dee-dee* attention call, for example, with the same cadence, same number of *dees*, same notes, same rhythm, and the chickadee responds reproducing the same cadence, and we do that over and over. When a Steller's Jay imitates a Red-tailed Hawk, I answer with an imitation of its imitation, and we may do that back and forth. When a flicker makes its *kleer* call, which is meant to locate another flicker, I answer it, and occasionally the flicker will turn its attention to me and start answering me even though I'm not a flicker.[16]

Sometimes a flicker will answer me back when I reply to its kleer call, but even if it doesn't, over time that flicker becomes friendlier and more approachable. I also reply when a Steller's Jay imitates the Red-tailed Hawk. Often the Steller will answer back and we go back and forth. Once I heard a Redtail imitation that sounded a bit thinner than usual, and I answered, and we called back and forth for a while. Then the bird emerged from the foliage, and it turned out it wasn't a Steller. I had been talking to a starling!

A bird may not realize at first that we are trying to communicate with it. But at the very least, it seems to make the birds friendlier.

My mother taught me to talk to the birds. When she was outside, she talked to them constantly, and sometimes sang to them. And she taught me how to sing and whistle to the birds. She taught me how to watch their reactions, so I could tailor my singing or whistling to what they liked.

Later, I started playing the flute for them. And then I started playing recordings of entire orchestras for them. That blew their minds.

Communication through music is a deeper kind of communication than a message about danger or food. Shared pleasure creates bonds. To bond with a dog or cat, we pet it. When a dog or cat is petted, it brings back the feeling of being a baby licked by its mother. That makes pleasure chemicals that create bonding. For birds, music and sound generate such pleasure chemicals. Birds bond through the pleasure of sound.

We and the birds both love music. And we love each other's music. Humans love to listen to birdsong, and birds love listening to

---

16 See the Youtube video "Conversation with a flicker."

human music, at least at the right time of year (as we will talk about in the section on Bird Seasons) and the right kind.

But why do we both love music? Music serves a practical purpose for birds, to attract mates and establish territories. So some people say that, for birds, singing is only business.

But music serves no obvious practical purpose for us. Why did we develop a music instinct?

Some people say that we did for the same reason as birds – to attract mates. They point out that romantic love is the most common subject of popular songs, and that rock stars get lots of girlfriends.

But musical performers who show off for audiences are a recent development in human history. And of all the people who sing or play music, very few are stars who perform on stage. And most people don't pick mates based on musical ability.

Yet we have a strong instinct to sing together, play together in groups, chant together, dance together. Why is it fun to sing together around a campfire, move in synchrony to the same music?

Because human music was originally communal and ceremonial. It still is in Indigenous cultures. The original human purpose of music was to create group unity. This may be why human music[17] is founded upon something absent from birdsong: meter. *ONE-two, ONE-two,* or *ONE-two-three, ONE-two-three,* or *ONE-two-three-four, ONE-two-three-four.* We are born with the instinct for meter: *WOULD you LIKE them IN a BOX, WOULD you LIKE them WITH a FOX.* Meter synchronizes us. Meter lets us dance together, chant together.

This is different from bird music. Not only does bird music *not* have a regular meter, but we humans like to accentuate the meter of music with drums, tambourines and other rhythm instruments. Our first musical instruments were percussion instruments such as drums and rattles. And percussive instruments like that are just what birds *don't* like.

---

17   With a few exceptions, such as monastic chant, shakuhachi and duduk music, etc.

All the birds seem to dislike percussion and any kind of sudden loudness. One day a pair of friendly Mourning Doves came in the house, attracted by the music I was playing. Then the music ended with a burst of applause, and the doves took off in panic, crashed into the windows this way and that, finally making it out. I never saw that pair again. Now I am careful that the music I play for them contains no surprises like that.

But human music is a marriage of meter and melody. After drums and rattles, the next human instruments were flutes. The Native American flute has become popular in recent years for relaxation and meditation, but its original purpose was courtship; a young man on the Plains would softly play his flute melodies to catch the ear of a young woman he was interested in. The idea of using flute melodies to court a mate very likely was inspired by birds. In fact, the notion of melody itself may have been brought to us by birds in the first place. The birds may have introduced us to the whole idea of singing.

So it's no wonder that the birds seem to "recognize" melody, and appreciate it when we play it for them.

Other animals, including cows and elephants, seem to respond to music as well. Slow, soothing classical music appears to make them calm and happy. Considering that a high soothing tone of voice seems to be a universal language understood by every creature with ears, it seems no surprise that music with that quality would please many animals even more.

Soothing, relaxing music can help a bird who is panicked or under stress. But different species have different preferences, and some song-birds get excited by lively melodies. We can let their reactions guide us to the music they like.[18]

---

18 The website *www.birdfriender.net* contains links to music that has proven popular with my birds, including both music for a bird under stress and music for happy birds.

Birds listening to us

Top row: Birds often face the source of music as they listen to it.
Bottom row: Birds cock their heads to hear music from different angles.

The first sign that a bird is listening to sounds we are offering is that it turns its face toward us. We turn our faces toward something to watch it, but a bird does the opposite – if it faces something, it is *not* watching it. Birds' eyes are on the sides of their heads. The visual field of a bird's two eyes overlaps only a little bit in front of its face, so that it can focus and aim its beak at close-up things like seeds and bugs. To look at something farther away, a bird will turn one side of its head toward it and watch it with one eye. When a bird faces us directly, that means we aren't a threat. We're not even worth watching. The bird's mind is on something else.

But why does a bird face us directly when listening to music? It's actually trying to face the source of the music, to hear the music with both ears. It may cock its head, or flick its head, or move its head in little jerks, to hear the music from different angles.

We humans get "goosebumps" from hearing beautiful music, and so do birds. When a bird has "goosebumps," its feathers fluff up.[19] A

19   Birds fluff their feathers to keep warm too, but fluffing for cold and fluffing up for pleasure look different. A cold bird will fluff up evenly all over, and stay fluffed up, avoiding movement, so as not to lose the precious pocket of warm air. A bird who sits fluffed up without moving when the weather is not cold is a sick bird.

bird taking pleasure in anything it hears or sees may briefly fluff up, but when a bird is inspired by music, its feathers may rise till they almost stand out straight from its body. It may slowly move its feathers up and down, or hold them out for a long time. The bird may expand until it "explodes."

A bird listening to human music may show the same signs of pleasure that a female bird shows when she listens to a male sing. She may part the feathers in the middle of her breast. She may raise the feathers around her ear holes. A bird listening to music may start preening. Birds preen more when they are happy. So good feather condition is the sign of a happy bird.

Top row: Birds get "goosebumps" and puff up when they are enjoying music.
Middle row: Birds listening to music may part their breast feathers.
Bottom row: Birds often preen when listening to music.

So what kind of music do birds like? Exactly what one would expect them to like – flutes, violins, oboes, and other high-pitched instruments, and high-pitched singing voices. (I don't think birds even recognize low-pitched notes as music.) Birds who sing fast, agile, complicated melodies like fast, agile, complicated melodies, while other birds prefer slower music with long, sweeping notes.

It turns out that music inspired by birds is popular among the birds. Beethoven's Pastorale symphony, especially the passages inspired by birdcalls, is a hit. Vivaldi's lively flute and violin concertos, which evoke bird-filled meadows in springtime, are favorites of the Song Sparrows, while Ralph Vaughan Williams' "The Lark Ascending" is the hit of the Steller's Jays.

Songbirds aren't the only birds who love music. Flickers, Mourning Doves, and Anna's Hummingbirds are music lovers too. The hummingbirds like the sound of whistling. They don't care if it has a melody, but they like fast notes. Mourning Doves swoon over the voices of human sopranos and altos, especially harmonizing. Surprisingly, the flickers have similar tastes to the Mourning Doves. In fact, birds of these two species, who are not related and normally don't associate, may even listen to music together. Once I took a photo-

graph of what appeared to be a pair of Mourning Doves intimately listening to music together in a tree. When I blew up the picture, to my astonishment I found it wasn't a pair of Mourning Doves, but a Mourning Dove and a flicker.

Bird facial expressions

For us humans, facial expression is a huge part of our communication, so our facial muscles make our expressions obvious. Our mouths smile or frown. Our eyebrows accentuate our expressions. Birds' beaks can't smile or frown, and they have no eyebrows. Their expressions are are in their eyes. A bird's facial expression may be subtle, but fortunately we humans have an instinct to perceive facial expressions, even subtle ones. When we get a "feeling" from looking at a bird's face, we should pay attention to that feeling.

One exercise to help us read birds' expressions and personalities is to do an image search, typing in the name of a bird species plus the word "face." Then study the pictures that come up. All are of the same species, but we can see they are different individuals, with distinct faces and different personalities.

This White-crowned Sparrow has an expression of relaxed alertness until I start talking to it, then its eye shows pleasure. A camera with a zoom lens can help us see these subtleties.

And we can see a bird's state of mind in a photo as well. A photo taken in a wild place may show a bird in a state of alertness – watching the photographer with one wide round eye, feathers pressed tight against its body, legs poised for flight. A photo taken in a backyard may show a bird with relaxed posture, an affectionate smile in its eyes, its toes barely showing under fluffed feathers.

Since mates see each other's faces up close, birds have a well-developed eye-language of love. Mates blink slowly or half-close their eyes when they are together, showing relaxed pleasure, affection and trust. We too can use the slow blink to communicate affection to birds.

Two eye expressions we can use to communicate with the birds are the eye-smile and the slow-blink. The eye-smile is similar for us and the birds. In the slow blink, we meet a bird's eyes, close our eyes slowly, and slowly open them again. The bird may do the same thing back, sharing a smile with us.

The Mourning Dove and flicker demonstrate the slow blink; the crow is covering its eye with its translucent inner eyelid.

But a bird has some eye-language that we don't. Besides its regular eyelid, a bird has a translucent inner eyelid that protects its eye from dust and wind while it is flying. When a bird is intensely interested in something, its inner eyelid may flick. A male songbird listening to a rival singing and a female songbird on the nest listening to her mate singing both flick their inner eyelids.

These are just some of the subtle fine points in bird facial expressions. But the first thing to know is that if a bird *appears* to be looking at us, it is indeed looking at us, and if we study the bird's facial expression and body language, we can perceive the bird's attitude toward us.

Body language

Birds can use body language to communicate with us. They can signal us when they need food. The hummingbirds may fly in front of my face if their feeders are empty; the Stellers perch in the willow and stare at me until I throw them peanuts; the chickadees hover in front of the glass door to tell me they are hungry.

Birds can read our body language too. They can learn how to figure out what a human is up to from our body language.

Once, in the supermarket, I saw a Brewer's Blackbird inside the store. He was in the produce section, flying from one vegetable display to the next, taking bits of this food and that. He had hit the food jackpot! He ignored the shoppers who reached for vegetables inches from him. I pointed him out to a store employee. The employee pointed to a net on a long pole leaning against a wall. "That's for catching birds," he said. "And the bird knows it. When I don't have the net, that bird lets me get close to him," he sighed, "but as soon as I reach toward the net, before I even touch it, he flies to the other end of the store. When I put it down, he comes back." The blackbird had learned what the net was for and what it meant when the man reached for the net.

Birds are especially sensitive to body language that can suggest that someone may be after them. When a feral cat is around, a bird may send either a casual alarm or a red alert – it can tell by the cat's body language whether the cat is just strolling by or is on the hunt. A bird can tell when a human is after it, too.

Once a crow was damaging a man's house.[20] Who knows why. The crow did it in plain sight of the man as the man did yard work. The man tried to scare the crow away, but the crow ignored him. So the man decided to shoot the crow. He went into his house to get his gun. When he came out the crow was gone. He went back to working in his yard. The crow came back and started attacking the house again. The man went back in the house again to get his gun. Again the crow was gone. The man went back to working, and the crow came back. This time, as soon as the man turned toward the house, the crow flew away. The crow seemed to have figured out that when the man was headed for the house, he was going for his gun.

---

20   Described in *Animals In Translation*, by Temple Grandin (p 245)

The man gave up on the idea of shooting the crow and went back to work. But when he headed to the house for a cup of coffee, the crow didn't fly away. The crow knew the difference between a man striding into the house with murder on his mind and a man strolling into the house for a coffee break.

One day I was working on my laptop on the deck. I had a pile of peanuts next to me for the jays. A friend dropped over, and, as we chatted, my Scrub Jay friend Skippy kept coming to the pile of peanuts. As jays do, he picked up peanut after peanut, testing its weight, before finally making a choice and flying off with it. Fascinated, my friend wanted to take a video of that – would he come back and do it again? Of course he will, I said, he's been doing it all morning. My friend took out his phone and aimed it at the pile of peanuts so he could catch Skippy's arrival.

Skippy returned to the curly willow tree next to the deck and poised to fly down to the peanuts. My friend aimed the phone and waited. But Skippy stayed in the tree. We watched him and talked about how long he was taking. Skippy acted oddly nervous and finally flew away without ever coming for the peanuts. I realized why. He didn't mind a stranger being there, but the fact that we were talking about him and paying attention to him must have seemed weird to him, so he left.

Seeing and feeling

Some people communicate with birds and other animals by mentally sending images to them. Some people say that, if we quiet our minds, we can receive images from the birds, too. Of course, that isn't scientific, so some people would say that it can't be true. But, true or not, we can understand the birds better if we can picture how the world looks to them and consider what we can communicate that would make sense to them. (That helps with understanding our fellow humans as well.)

So we need to think about what we can communicate that makes sense in their world.

For example, the jays always want the biggest, heaviest peanuts. So when Skippy arrives, wanting a peanut, I go out with a clear cannister full of peanuts and pick up one dinky peanut after another, hold it up for him to see, then drop it back into the cannister, before finally choosing a prize big peanut for him. He understands the reason I am making him wait – I am choosing the biggest peanut for him. Birds can understand the idea of doing things to make someone else happy; we know that because mates do things that give each other pleasure. And birds understand the idea of "liking" and "disliking" someone; individual birds can like or dislike each other. So birds can like individual humans, and they can understand that we like them, too.

Compare the expression and body language, and the overall feeling, of this junco to the concerned junco at the top of the chapter.

I believe that birds may understand that they are making *us* happy when they come to visit us. And I believe that that makes them feel happy too. And that, when they feel that, they may come visit us for more than just the food.

I believe that birds can feel it when they are welcomed – just as if we could feel if we were welcomed or not in a foreign country where we didn't speak the language. I believe that a bird can understand our kind intentions if we expect it to understand. Birds understand the language of feeling.

What can birds communicate to us? We can't learn that from books. Only the birds themselves can give us those treasures.

Communication with the birds is more invitation than information. Birds are emotional creatures who communicate in a language of feeling. Even messages about food and danger are really about feelings. We understand the birds through sensing their feelings. That can make us better communicators with humans, too.

Communicating with the birds means sharing a sense of life, on our journey together on planet Earth.

CHAPTER FIVE

A COUPLE OF JAYS LATER

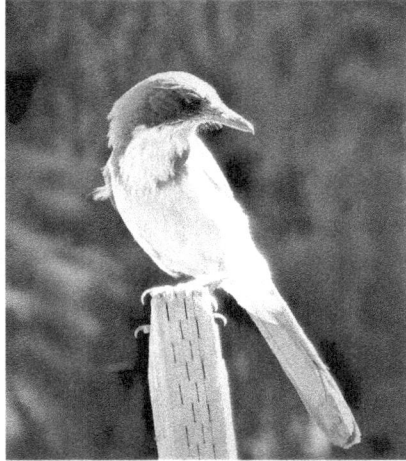

THE SCRUB JAY alarm was the first bird alarm I learned. "Listen! He's saying *Cat! Cat!*" my mother would say, as she pointed out how the Scrub Jay was following a cat we couldn't see, staying safely out of its reach about six feet off the ground. *Shriek! Shriek!* He's warning all the other birds, she told me.

The Scrub Jays have been a part of my world since childhood. But I had little knowledge of Oregon's other jay, the Steller's Jays. Only when hiking in the woods did I see those elusive blue shadows.

The full name of our Scrub Jays is California Scrub Jay, because there are other Scrub Jay species, like Florida Scrub Jays and Mexican Scrub Jays, and, as their name implies, they come to Oregon from the south. The Steller's Jays, the provincial bird of British Columbia and common in Washington, come to Oregon from the north. Oregon, where I live, is where the two jays meet.

But, even in Oregon, Scrub Jays and Steller's Jays are rarely seen together, because they prefer different habitats. Scrub Jays like open habitats with scattered oak trees. In fact, they don't even need actual trees. They got the name "scrub" jays because they were first recorded in "scrublands," dry areas with sparse shrubs and stunted vegetation. Steller's Jays, on the other hand, like dark conifer forests.

So the Stellers and Scrubs probably hardly ever met each other.

Until I came along, bearing peanuts.

To one side of where I live is a stand of Douglas firs, and to the other side, an open field with scattered small trees. So I live between Steller's Jay habitat and Scrub Jay habitat. And both jays come to visit me. And I am constantly struck with how different these cousins are.

East of the Rocky Mountains live the beautiful Bluejays,[21] and they seem different still. I know them only through videos. Though they are close relatives of the Stellers, the Bluejays seem smaller, lighter, quicker, more agile. I've seen videos of them catching peanuts tossed in the air. I can't imagine a Steller doing that. The Bluejays seem daring, curious, and funny. Surely people must love those jewel-like birds.

Yet apparently a lot of people who live with Bluejays don't like them. People describe them as "loud," "brazen," "rude," "aggressive" "bullies." They say the Bluejays threaten smaller birds. They say that the Bluejays attack the feeders in noisy groups and drive small birds

---

21 I write their name "Bluejay" because both Scrub Jays and Steller's Jays are also *blue jays*, and in fact, most people around here call both Scrub Jays and Steller's Jays "blue jays." To learn about birdfriending Bluejays, check out the Youtube channel LesleytheBirdNerd (the best birdfriending channel on Youtube, in my opinion).

away. Some people put up feeders designed to let only small birds eat and keep Bluejays out.

The Stellers are very different from these descriptions of their sibling species the Bluejays. The Stellers are downright courteous, both to one another and to other birds. They come to the feeders one at a time and don't harass other birds. They are rather timid and skittish. And they don't make noise except when there is a reason.

Bluejays live east of the Rocky Mountains

At least, *my* Stellers are like that. To my surprise, sometimes I see Steller's Jays described with words like those used for Bluejays – words like *cocky, impudent, raucous, brazen, boisterous, blustery, plunderers, pigs, bullies.* I've seen descriptions of Steller behavior that astonish me. My Stellers are so shy it's hard to persuade them to come close, but Stellers in national parks are reported to grab food off picnic tables, even to grab sandwiches right out of people's hands. Well, there's no downside to stealing food from humans in a national park – the humans only laugh and tell the story on social media. It makes sense that the boldest ones would thrive in national parks, but still, it's amazing how much the Steller flocks vary. Each Steller flock has its own personality, its own culture and rules and customs.

Steller's Jays belong to flocks, and they ask other flock members for advice. Sometimes they may disagree with each other's opinions, but one Steller doesn't go it alone and ignore what the rest of the flock thinks. Steller's Jays make group decisions. When it came to birdfriending the Steller's Jays, I had to convince the whole group.

The Scrub Jays, on the other hand, don't belong to flocks.[22] And that makes a big difference in how we approach birdfriending them. Scrub Jays definitely observe and learn from each other, but each Scrub Jay figures things out for itself. Each Scrub Jay has its own attitude toward humans. Each Scrub Jay makes its own decisions.

Both Scrub Jays and Steller's Jays play a big part in other chapters of this book, but they gave me so much more material that they finally just had to have a chapter of their own.

Scrub Jays have been studied a lot by scientists who do experiments testing their intelligence. (Scrub Jays are rated among the most intelligent animals in the world, as we will talk about later in the book.) But those studies are done in laboratories with tame Scrub Jays raised in captivity. Few scientists study the behavior of California Scrub Jays in the wild (although the communal behavior of *Florida* Scrub Jays has been studied quite a bit).

And it seems that few scientists study the social life of Steller's Jays. This is surprising. Steller flock behavior is so fascinating and so easy to observe.

But any of us can be a bird scientist. A scientist is a person who adds to humanity's knowledge about the world. Although a *professional* bird scientist, or ornithologist, needs special training, anyone, even a kid, can add to humanity's knowledge about birds.

We can practice bird science while we are birdfriending. Every day I see birds doing things that have probably never been recorded by science. Any of us can make discoveries about the birds, just by going outside.

---

22 When I say just "Scrub Jay," I mean California Scrub Jay, the kind we have in Oregon. The Florida Scrub Jay has a very different way of life, living and breeding in communal colonies.

"Making discoveries" doesn't have to mean observing something that no one has ever seen before. When we pool our experiences and compare them, we can discover what is unusual and what is common. For example, when choosing among several peanuts, my jays will pick up each one, seeming to weigh it, drop it, pick up another, take their time choosing. Is that unusual? Is it only my jays who have this cute and funny practice? No, turns out it is common to see jays doing that. By sharing our observations, we can find out what is common and what is unusual in what we see, and we also add to humanity's total knowledge about birds. And if we do that, we are bird scientists.

I share my experiences with my jays in hopes that other people will observe their local jays and compare their observations with what I write here. Just about everyone in the world has jays of some kind living around them, or the jays' close relatives the magpies, or their big cousins the crows and ravens. Every kind of jay has its own way of life, and each flock has its own culture, and each individual has its own personality, so the jays provide us some of the best opportunities to make new discoveries.

Bird science and birdfriending are both about making discoveries. They are both about observing the birds and trying to understand them. And combining birdfriending and bird science together makes them both even more fun.

The Steller flock

From deep within the dark Douglas firs the sudden yell of a Steller's Jay explodes – *KA KA KA*! Another Steller voice joins in, and another and another.

Stellers are flying in from all directions, headed to one spot in the trees. yelling together. I look out, as I always do when I hear this sound. Because I know what is happening. They are mobbing a raptor – a Cooper's Hawk, or maybe an owl. Maybe if I'm really lucky, I'll see the raptor get flushed.

It's all going on in dense foliage, and I rarely see anything, except the Stellers popping in and out of the foliage, like popcorn. But occasionally I get lucky. Once a large Cooper's Hawk flew out straight toward me. She passed just a few feet over my head and I saw her face close up. Her expression looked strained and haggard, and she was panting; her stress was obvious. And one of her tail feathers was hanging broken. Clearly, being mobbed by jays was no game for her.

Most birds, seeing a Cooper's Hawk hiding in the trees, wouldn't dare confront it. A Cooper's Hawk can snatch a bird right off a branch. It can grab a small bird out of the air. So most birds, seeing a Cooper's Hawk, will give a quick alarm and freeze, hoping the hawk won't spot them in the foliage. Why and how do the Steller's Jays, among all the birds, go right up to the raptor and try to drive it away?

The Stellers have even more to fear from the raptors than small birds do. They are big enough to make a good meal, they are slower at getaway, and, being big, they are harder to hide. That may be why, wherever Stellers live, they make their home among evergreen trees, which never lose their leaves and leave them exposed and visible. In the shadowy fir forest, a Steller's Jay can be almost invisible, its dark pointy head blending in with the pointy fir branches.

The Stellers can mob dangerous raptors because they don't do it alone. They wait until a group has arrived before going after the raptor. They keep moving constantly so the raptor can't focus on any single one to try to catch it.

The key to Steller survival is the flock.

Steller's Jays belong to family flocks. Except, the Steller flock isn't what we usually call a flock. Normally we call any group of birds that is together a "flock," whether they are together only for the moment or for years. But the whole Steller family flock never seems to be together all at once.

Yet it is a connected group. It contains several mated pairs, maybe four or five, plus unmated youngsters. The family flock shares one big territory, which seems to be roughly a square mile or so. Within the flock territory, all members are free to go where they want. They spread out in their shared territory and each family makes its own living. But they stay in touch with each other, and, at a moment's notice, all the Stellers can join together for the common defense.

The Steller flock members are quite individual, especially seen close up.

Not many birds have family flocks. Cedar Waxwings, Brewer's Blackbirds, and some swallows do. Among birds that do have family flocks, each species arranges things differently. Florida Scrub Jays build communal nests and help each other. Pinyon Jays travel around in flocks together, and nest close together, one nest per tree; within the flock territory, only mated pairs are allowed, and unmated youngsters are kicked out. Crow family flocks are set up like wolf packs; each flock has one mated pair, plus their unmarried children from previous years, who may stay around for years to help their parents raise the new babies.

The Steller family flock is like the Pinyon Jay flock in that it contains multiple mated pairs. It is like the crow flock in that it contains unmated youngsters from previous years. An adult Steller doesn't just teach its own kids, but may help teach any youngster in the flock.

But I don't know if the unmated youngsters help the new babies, the way crows and Florida Scrub Jays do, since I can't observe their nests.

But I have come to know much about the relationships and the etiquette rules within the Steller flock. I learn about them through the games I play with them – especially the peanut game.

Like most animals who live in groups – flocks, herds, packs, colonies – the Stellers have social ranks. The highest ranking individual eats first, then the next highest, and so on. This system may seem unfair to us humans, but creates harmony in the group by preventing fights over food.

But when the youngsters first fledge, they don't know the rules of etiquette. They quarrel over the peanuts and screech at each other. They squawk at the adults instead of bowing to them. They want the adults to keep feeding them, even after they have started to learn how to feed themselves. As they wean, the young Stellers begin to learn the rules. The youngsters may quarrel with each other, but they defer to the adults. As the youngsters grow up, they find their places in the flock hierarchy, and abide by it. The flock is well-regulated.

The Scrub Jays

The Scrub Jays come from a different environment from the Stellers. The Stellers live in the woods, but the Scrubs come from open habitat, where hiding is not an option. So Scrub Jays don't even try to hide. A Scrub Jay's survival depends on being observant and aware.

The silhouette of a Scrub Jay, watching the world from an exposed perch with a wide view, is a familiar sight in cities and towns in western Oregon. They are common and conspicuous birds around here.

Unlike the Stellers (and unlike Florida Scrub Jays) California Scrub Jays don't belong to flocks. They pair up, and stay together, if not for life, then for years at a time. Each pair has its own territory. The pair establishes a territory together and defends it together, keeping other Scrub Jays out. Most songbirds don't bother defending territories in the winter, but Scrub Jays do, perhaps because they have cached food for the winter throughout their territory.

Scrub Jay parents will let their kids stay on the territory for the winter, but come spring, the youngsters will be expected to leave. Then the unmated youngster may wander around, or may join with a flock of unmated youngsters until he or she is ready to settle down with a mate in their own territory.

Scrub Jay youngsters seem to catch on to things more quickly than Steller youngsters. Just days after Skippy started flying to grab a peanut from my hand, Skippy's fledglings caught on to the idea. Not that they *mastered* it, but suddenly, all at once, they were making the attempt. When a Scrub Jay parent teaches its youngster, the youngsters learn fast, often catching on the first time.

Scrub Jay youngsters may have to learn their parents' lessons faster because they have a shorter time with their parents, less than one year. The Steller youngsters spend years with their parents, and with other adults as well, so they can take their time to learn, and that allows them to be more cautious.

Peanuts bring them together

So did the Scrubs and Stellers ever cross paths before I came along and brought them together with my peanuts?

Maybe not, I thought. When I first moved here, I saw Scrubs and Stellers run into each other on the deck. They quarreled. Usually, the Scrubs would run the Stellers off.

Stellers and Scrubs just don't get along. So I thought. At first.

But it turned out that I was wrong. Over the years, I witnessed their relationship change and evolve.

When I first moved here, the ruling Scrub Jay was Valentina Velociraptor. I gave her that name because she reminded me of the velociraptors in the kitchen in the movie *Jurassic Park*.

Like a lot of Scrub Jays, she had a sneaky, cunning air, like she was trying to get away with something. Her mate was like that too. I called him Vincent Velociraptor. But he was much shyer than Valentina, so I didn't see him much.

Though Valentina was an enthusiastic player of the peanut game, I'm not sure I could call Valentina a friend. She acted more like an opponent. She couldn't simply take a peanut. She had to outsmart me to get it. I would throw a peanut onto the deck for her, and, no matter how far away the peanut was from me, she would watch me, waiting for me to turn my head before she would snatch the peanut. As though it was no fun to get a peanut unless she was tricking someone.

The Steller's Jays were more timid. But they weren't afraid only of me, they were afraid of Valentina.

At first, the Stellers would not come to the deck, so I spread food on the ground off the deck for them – shelled sunflower seeds and peanut fragments, small but delicious bits that would be swallowed in a gulp, so that they would stay and eat, rather than flying off with a whole peanut.

So a Steller lands in the willow tree, sees the food, and yells. Soon two or three other Stellers arrive. They study and discuss the situation. The ground is a scary place, they agree. But on the other hand (or on the other wing) there are no hiding places for predators around my deck – no bushes for cats to hide behind, no canopy above for Cooper's Hawks to lurk in ambush. But then again, they agree, it is uncomfortably close to the unpredictable humans.

Finally one Steller is picked to be the one to find out if it is safe. He cautiously flies down, grabs a sunflower seed, and flies off with it. The others see that nothing bad has happened, and indeed the brave one has gotten a yummy reward. One by one, the Stellers fly down to eat the bits of food scattered on the ground.

The only way a large, conspicuous bird like a Steller's Jay can be safe eating on the ground is to be part of a group of eyes looking out. If one bird is startled, it flies off instantly, and all the birds fly off in a flash, no questions asked.

So the Stellers are nervous while eating together on the ground. I'm hoping they are starting to feel like my house is a safe place, but they are obviously on hair trigger, and I try not to make even the smallest move that could startle them.

Suddenly there's an explosion of loud alarm shrieks – *"DANGER! DANGER! DANGER!"* as a big shadow appears out of nowhere and plunges at the Stellers. All the Stellers explode into panicked flight.

It's Valentina. She didn't do this to eat the Stellers' food. There's plenty of food for her on the deck. She just seems to think that it's fun to scare the Steller's Jays.

And why are the Stellers such wimps? They are bigger than the Scrub Jays. And there's three or four of them, versus one Scrub Jay.

But as I came to know the Stellers better, they helped me to understand. They're already nervous, exposed on the ground, and then that big shadow descending from above, the piercing shrieks of alarm, the flapping of panicked wings all around?

Yes, the Stellers are bigger. But that's not an advantage. A bigger bird is more vulnerable. It's a better meal for a predator, it's more conspicuous, and it has slower takeoff. The Stellers felt exposed and vulnerable. They were nervous.

But over time, I saw the Stellers' relationship with the Scrubs change. It changed as their relationship with me changed. As the Stellers came closer and closer to me, they started to stand their ground with Valentina as well. It became harder for her to scare the Stellers into flight, and even when she did, they would come right back.

Then Valentina vanished. I saw her mate Vincent alone once or twice, then he was gone too. And for a few years, I had no Scrub Jay regulars – only transients, unmated youngsters scouting for territories. But they were easily frightened by the newly emboldened Stellers, and didn't stay around.

Then Skippy moved in.

Skippy Scrub Jay is so different from Valentina Velociraptor. While Valentina seemed cunning and sneaky, Skippy is dignified and straight-forward. Seeing Skippy and Scooby together so much has made me realize how seldom I saw Valentina and Vincent together. I had figured that must be normal for Scrub Jay mates. But bird marriages, like human marriages, vary. Some pairs act like co-workers in a business relationship, others spend every possible moment together.

Skippy and his shyer mate Scooby

And Skippy has a completely different relationship with the Stellers. He abides by the Steller flock rules. I have never seen a quarrel between him and the Stellers. He treats the Stellers with respect, and they treat him like one of them. If there is any doubt whose turn it is to get the next peanut, they communicate through body language until there is an agreement.

Deception

One noticeable difference between the Steller's Jays and Scrub Jays is that the Steller's Jays mimic other birds, while the Scrub Jays don't. And the Steller's Jays are tremendous music lovers, while the Scrub Jays have a mild fondness for music. There may be a connection there. Steller's Jays seem to use their mimicry to bond the flock like fads, as they pass new calls back and forth. They also find other ways to use mimicry for fun.

One day I heard the *wikka-wikka* call of a flicker. Flickers make this call back and forth as they chase each other and play hide and seek through the trees. I used to think this was courtship; it looks so flirtatious. But it turns out to be the way male flickers argue about territory. Near me, another flicker answered with his *wikka-wikka* challenge. I looked and found him – but he wasn't a flicker. It was a Steller's Jay making a perfect imitation of a flicker *wikka-wikka* call.

Then the real flicker appeared and looked around. The Steller made the *wikka-wikka* at him, and he jumped up, flew at the jay and drove it away. Then another male appeared, and the two flickers resumed *wikka-wikka*-ing and chasing each other. But there were still three *wikka-wikka*s moving through the trees. Once again the Steller tricked the flickers to come to him. Both flickers drove the Steller away, but the Steller didn't go far. He flew into a nearby tree and started *wikka*-ing again, and got the flickers to chase him again. It was a game.

Jays may also deceive with their alarm calls.

One day, I notice a couple of crows in the parking lot across the street. I've been needing crow portraits for this book, so, armed with peanuts and a camera, I head down toward the parking lot.

As I walk down the driveway. I see Skippy in the trees, following me and eyeing the tub of peanuts in my hand. I toss him a peanut and continue across the street.

I throw peanuts to the crows, they caw and summon the flock, and soon fifteen crows surround me. They are cautious about approaching me as I throw peanuts toward them and try to coax them close enough to get good shots of their faces.

Suddenly, from a nearby tree comes the piercing alarm of a Scrub Jay. *"SHRIEK! SHRIEK! SHRIEK!"*

I look around. Nothing but a big empty parking lot. Nowhere for any predator to hide. But the Scrub Jay's alarms get faster, urgent, frantic.

"SHRIEKSHRIEKSHRIEKSHRIEK!" the Scrub Jay screams. *"EMERGENCY! EMERGENCY!"*

He's facing me. Me? Seriously? He sees me as a danger? And he cares so much about the safety of crows? Are you kidding?

I raise my camera and get a shot of the jay in mid-shriek. Through the zoom lens, I recognize Skippy. He has followed me across the street.

Skippy?! I thought you were my friend! You taught your mate and kids to take peanuts from my hand! And now you bad-mouth me to other birds like that?

But the crows start nervously backing away from me, like, "Ummm…." And as the crows back off, Skippy swoops down and snatches the very biggest peanut from the pavement. Before the crows have a chance to react, he's back for the second biggest one.

In that instant crows catch on to the joke. They all quickly hop over and grab the rest of the peanuts, even though a moment ago they were afraid to get that close to me.

One Scrub Jay versus fifteen crow giants – he has to use some cleverness.

But wait, he gets plenty of peanuts at home, and probably has a zillion stashed. He's not starving. He's just having fun. It seems as though any Scrub Jay, even one who is normally polite and well-behaved, thinks that food just tastes better when you can outsmart someone to get it.

Anyway, the crows didn't seem to hold it against me at all. After all, crows are capable of the same tricks. They get it.

Nest robbers

Like their cousins the crows, Scrub Jays have a reputation as nest robbers. Nest-robbing means eating another bird's eggs, nestlings, or fledglings.

But I think that their nest-robbing may be exaggerated. I base that on the way that other birds act around them. Crows are hated by the other birds, but they don't seem to care what other birds think of them. The Scrub Jays, on the other hand, live as part of the greater bird community. They are feeder birds, like the rest. When there is an individual nest robber among the Scrub Jays, the birds, including other Scrub Jays, treat him as an individual criminal. If Scrub Jays were all nest robbers, they would *all* be treated as outlaws by the other birds.

I once knew a nest-robbing Scrub Jay. He got a Downy Woodpecker nestling somehow. Maybe that was the only incident, but once may have been enough. Whenever he showed up, he was scolded by other birds. And he was also shunned by the other Scrub Jays. Scrub Jays are not social birds, so one would think that shunning would not matter to him. And birds' body language is subtle, so I wondered if I was imagining it. But he became more and more unkempt, neglecting his preening and feather care, which is the sign of an unhappy bird. And after a while, I didn't see him anymore.

I witnessed one other incident of outlaw behavior by a Scrub Jay. One summer morning I heard a big ruckus from the bushtits. Bushtits are tiny birds, but they can be loud. A flock of bushtits was mobbing a Scrub Jay. It appeared that the Scrub Jay had tried to grab a bushtit fledgling, and that he was unsuccessful, but the bushtits weren't letting him off the hook. They were announcing to the world that this bird was a criminal. This was a young transient, not one of my residents, and I never saw that jay again.

I believe that nest robbers are rare exceptions among the Scrub Jays and that nest-robbing is not socially acceptable among them. Other birds, including bushtits, normally seem to be perfectly fine with the Scrub Jays. When they single out one Scrub Jay, there is a reason.

Individual and flock friends

Skippy chose to be my friend. He made a definite decision at a definite moment.

But with flocking birds, like the Juncos and the Stellers, friendships don't usually happen one at a time. Some Juncos come closer to me than others, but they don't seem to be trying to establish individual connections with me. The Stellers changed their attitudes toward me gradually, with a lot of dithering back and forth in the group. Making friends with them meant making friends with the flock. It meant getting flock consensus.

Sometimes a particular individual bird – a Song Sparrow, a hummingbird, a towhee, a chickadee, a nuthatch – may single itself out, and we develop a relationship with *that bird*. Such birds, like Ludwig and Scooby, often get names.

With other birds, each interaction with one member is like a thread that connects me with the flock, and slowly those threads weave a network of connection, drawing the whole flock closer, until I feel the flock enveloping me. It is like being initiated into the flock.

Every species, and every individual bird, has its own personality. Our back yards can be wonderlands for finding new friends.

Part Two

BIRD SEASONS

IN THIS BOOK, I capitalize Bird Spring, Bird Summer, Bird Fall, and Bird Winter to distinguish them from the spring, summer, fall, and winter on our human calendars. The dates of the Bird Seasons don't necessarily match our calendars, but vary depending on latitude and climate and the type of bird. In fact, in tropical latitudes, where the temperature doesn't vary much through the year, Bird Seasons may happen any time of year. Bird Seasons are defined by the birds' breeding cycles, not by our calendars.

It is important for a birdfriender to understand the Bird Seasons, because a bird's attitude toward everything – including us – depends on what Bird Season it is in.

The Bird Season it is in determines everything in a bird's life: the routine of its day, how and where it looks for food, the kinds of foods it looks for, and how much food it has to find. How far it travels during the day. Where it sleeps at night. The Bird Season affects a bird's attitude toward new things. What it listens to. What it pays attention to. How interested it is in new things. How much it is willing to take risks. How it acts with other birds. How it acts with its mate. (Or if it even has a mate – many birds get divorced when breeding season is over.)

In order to know what a bird is doing and thinking, we have to know what Bird Season it is in. But in order to know what Bird Season a bird is in, we have to watch what it is doing. And different birds can be in different Bird Seasons at the same time.

A bird's year is divided into two halves: breeding season and non-breeding season. Bird Spring and Bird Summer are breeding season, and Bird Fall and Bird Winter are non-breeding season.

Bird Spring and Bird Summer come at different times in different places. And even in the same place, different birds start Bird Spring and Bird Summer at different times. That way, different kinds of birds who eat the same food can share the same territory; they need the most food while feeding babies, and if each is feeding babies at a different time, they won't compete.

Bird Spring is really two Bird Seasons. In Early Bird Spring, birds establish their territories and find mates, or rekindle the romance if they keep the same mates year after year. Early Bird Spring is the easiest season for humans to recognize, because we hear all the birdsong. In Late Bird Spring, the birds build their nests, lay their eggs, hatch their eggs, and feed their nestlings.

In cold and snowy regions, Bird Spring may not begin until April or May. But where I live, the winters are mild, and the earliest Bird Spring, Song Sparrow Spring, begins as early as February or even late January.

Bird Summer begins when the young birds fledge, or leave the nest. During Bird Summer, the parent birds care for their fledglings, teach them how to survive, and try to keep them from getting killed. They are just as busy as they were when the babies were tiny and in the nest – or even more busy, because the babies are scattered all over the place trying to get themselves in trouble. Where I live, Bird Summer begins in May or June for most birds.

It should be no surprise that, during Bird Spring and Bird Summer, making friends with the humans is the last thing on a busy bird's mind. Bird Spring and Bird Summer are a great time for watching birds, but not for making friends with them. Our job during Bird Spring and Bird Summer is to be easy for the birds to ignore as they take care of business.

Bird Fall begins when the youngsters can find food themselves and no longer need their parents to feed them. The weaning of the youngsters marks the end of breeding season. Where I live, Bird Fall begins in August.

During Bird Fall, birds prepare for winter. Fortunately, fall is harvest time, when food is most abundant. Newly weaned youngsters can hone their food-finding skills while food is still easy to find. Birds preparing to migrate store up energy for the journey. Birds who cache food to eat during the winter can find plenty to store.

Then in Bird Winter, survival becomes tougher. Our human calendars say that winter begins on the winter solstice, around December 21, but I doubt that there is any place where Bird Winter begins that late. Bird Winter begins in early November, around the Day of the Dead. In colder places, it may start even earlier.

During breeding season, a bird has to be cautious, because if it makes a mistake and ends up caught by a predator, its whole family may starve.

But in Bird Winter, a bird can afford to be braver. There are no babies who will starve if it dies. And food is harder to find. So a bird can take more chances and risks in Bird Winter. It is more open to trying new things and discovering new things – including the possibility of becoming friends with the humans who live around it.

So Bird Winter is the best time to begin trying to make friends with the birds. Therefore, Bird Winter is where we will start the birdfriender's year.

CHAPTER SIX

BIRD WINTER: SEASON OF SURVIVAL

WHERE I LIVE, it hardly ever snows. A few flurries now and then that hardly ever stick. A little frost on the ground some winter mornings. A hard freeze occasionally that freezes the birdbath. But hardly ever any snow worthy of the name.

As kids, we longed for snow. We envied the kids we see in pictures making a snowman together and having snowball fights and sledding down the snowy hills. Not to mention how beautiful the snow is to look at! But winters in western Oregon are mostly just rain.

But every few years, we get some real snow. Enough to cover the whole world with sparkling whiteness. And then the kids get a snow holiday! Just two inches of snow closes the schools, and, while the grownups gripe about traffic snarls, the kids get a free day to celebrate and play in the snow.

No wonder, when kids are sitting in a classroom, and a lonely snowflake falls from the sky, some kid yells out "Snow!" and all the kids rush to the window. No wonder that when the snow stays on the ground for more than a day or two, it is such a festival for the kids.

But it is a catastrophe for the birds.

The birds who could have left for the south but didn't. And the birds who left some frozen northland to spend the winter here. They were here because they had trusted that it wouldn't snow.

Cold isn't the problem; feathers are great insulation. The big problem is food. Or, rather, the lack of food.

When it's cold, birds have to eat more, to keep their bodies warm. But when it snows, food is hard to find. Insects are hiding under tree bark or dead leaves. Seeds are locked in frozen dirt, instead of standing up high waving in the wind. And if the water freezes, there is nothing to drink.

No wonder some of our birds, like the Rufous Hummingbird and the Black-headed Grosbeak, leave for sunny Mexico during the winter. But most of our birds stay. Migration is hard and dangerous, and they may have a better chance of survival by staying home. As long as it doesn't snow.

The snowy disaster hardly ever happens. But when a freak snowfall happens and lasts for more than a few days, that is one of the few times that people who feed birds may actually save their lives. I live in that kind of place.

Migratory birds

Where I live, winters are chilly, but it barely frosts, and snow is rare. So only a few of our birds leave for warmer climes. And only a few birds consider this a winter destination, like the Golden-crowned Sparrow, who comes to Oregon all the way from Alaska, and the Fox Sparrow, who just travels from the mountains down to the valley, a trip of only a few hours.

Winter visitors: Golden-crowned Sparrow and Fox Sparrow

And then there are the robins. Robins are here all year round, but there are a lot more of them in the winter. Robins arrive in flocks from Canada, a hundred or more in a flock. Each flock chooses one particular tree to be its winter roost. In the morning, the flock breaks up into smaller flocks and each group goes off to a different place to forage. The migrants look for where the local robins are foraging, and join them, since the residents probably know the best places to eat. In the evening, the small flocks return to headquarters and roost together as one big flock again, their red breasts making a bare-branched maple look like a Christmas tree covered with red ornaments.

But as winter nears its end, the resident robins start hinting that they want the visitors out. It's getting close to time to establish breeding territories, and they don't need extra robins around. The migratory robins don't argue. They leave and go back home to their breeding grounds in Canada.

The Fox Sparrows disappear back to their mountains by Ground-hog Day, while Golden-crowned Sparrows wait until May to leave for their breeding grounds in Alaska.

These are the migrants I know of around here. Where I live, most of the birds stay home all winter.

Birds who stay home

Every place has some birds in the wintertime. Warm places may have more birds in the winter than any other time, because not only do their regular birds stay home, but many refugees from the wintry places join them.

But even snowy places have some birds who stay at home all year. Every part of North America, except the polar regions, has chickadees, nuthatches, and some kind of corvid – crows, ravens, magpies, or jays. And many snowy places have birds like cardinals. And nomadic flocks, like pine siskins and crossbills, traverse the snowy landscapes, showing up unexpectedly in big groups. But how do these birds survive the snowy winter, while other birds have to leave?

Each species has its own secrets. Crossbills have unique beaks designed to extract the seeds of pine and fir cones. Tiny kinglets hunt tiny insects with their tiny beaks among the evergreen needles. Cardinals and robins eat berries hanging on bushes.

And some birds make sure in advance there will be food for them in Bird Winter, by caching food during Bird Fall. To cache (pro-nounced "cash") means to store something in a safe hidden place until later. Chickadees and nuthatches cache seeds in spaces in the bark of trees. Jays and other corvids usually cache food in the ground.

When winter comes, the bird remembers where its caches are. Not one or two or ten or twenty caches. Thousands! And not just approximate locations. If the bird was even an inch off, it wouldn't find the food. The bird goes straight to the exact location of seeds it hid many months before, with no poking around or searching. Even though the location may be covered with snow or dead leaves.

Winter flocks

Most songbirds break up their territories during Bird Winter. Of course the birds who fly south have to give up their territories when they leave. But even most birds who stay home give up their territories during Bird Winter.

The whole point of having a territory is to ensure there is enough food for the babies, and birds aren't raising babies in the winter. Defending a territory is work, and simply surviving is hard enough. When the birds aren't breeding, most consolidate the territories and let everyone just move around freely.

When the territorial boundaries break up, a species has two choices. Individual birds can go it alone and wander around in search of food by themselves. Song Sparrows, towhees, wrens, and woodpeckers are some of my bird neighbors who go it alone in the winter.

The other choice is to get together and travel around as a flock, making regular circuits around its flock territory, and defending their flock boundaries against other flocks of the same kinds.

Flocking has advantages. More eyes looking out for danger. More eyes looking for food. More knowledge of the best place to forage. More chance to watch what other birds do, and see what happens when they do it.

Some flocks are made up of only one kind of bird, like bushtit flocks. Bushtits, who live only in the west, are tiny round birds that look a bit like gray chickadees with long tails. They sound like tinkly little jingle bells as they move through the canopy. When a flock of bushtits lands on the suet feeder, packed together with their tails sticking out, they remind me of a pincushion.

But birds of different kinds can flock together if they are near the same size and can forage in the same places. There are two main flocking communities where I live – the tree foragers, like the chickadees and nuthatches, and the ground feeders, like the juncos and sparrows.

When the junco flock stops to eat, they are often joined by Song Sparrows, Golden-crowned Sparrows, Fox Sparrows and towhees. But these birds don't seem to travel around together as a flock.

Bushtit flock descends on suet feeder

The chickadee flock, on the other hand, can contain many species traveling together. Where I live, the chickadee flock contains three species: two kinds of chickadees (Black-caps and Chestnuts) plus Red-breasted Nuthatches. But other observers have reported White-breasted Nuthatches, Golden-Crowned Kinglets, Red-eyed Vireos, Brown Creepers, Tufted Titmice, Downy Woodpeckers, and different kinds of warblers flocking with chickadees.

These different birds can forage for insects in the same tree because they look for their food in different ways. Chickadees hop along tree branches as they search. Nuthatches look for food on the trunk, often head downward. Kinglets may hover under the tips of twigs. Titmice may hang upside down from heavier limbs. Woodpeckers pound holes with their strong bills to get insects hiding deep under the bark, while the Brown Creepers scuttle up and down tree trunks extracting insects from nooks and crannies with their pointy beaks.

Although the flock may contain various kinds of birds, the chickadees are the leaders,[23] and the other birds follow them and pay attention to their communications. The chickadees are the best at spotting danger and giving warnings. The chickadees decide where to go and where to forage, and where to roost each evening.

Many of the other birds who mix with the chickadee flock also belong to their own flocks with their own boundaries. The chickadee flock might share half of its territory with one nuthatch flock and half with another. As the chickadee flock crosses into different nuthatch flock territories, the nuthatches of one flock drop out and those of the other flock join up.

Flocking birds learn from each other's discoveries. An example is what happened in Britain in the early twentieth century. Milk used to be delivered to homes in glass bottles left on people's doorsteps. The milk was not homogenized, so cream separated and went to the top of the bottle. The bottles were covered with aluminum caps. Blue Tits and Great Tits, relatives of the chickadee, learned how to pierce the caps with their beaks and drink the cream from the top of the bottle. By the 1950s, Blue Tits and Great Tits all over Britain had learned to pierce the caps and steal the cream. [24]

They were not the only birds to do this. Some European Robins and European Blackbirds did it too. But only a few of them. The Tits, as flocking birds, learned from each other and spread their knowledge. European Robins and Blackbirds, however, stay in their own territories and chase off others of their kind. So they don't get a chance to teach or learn from others.

---

23   For much of the information about chickadee flock behavior, I am indebted to *The Black-capped Chickadee: Behavioral Ecology and Natural History* by Susan Smith.

24   "The Opening of Milk Bottles by Birds," h*ttps://britishbirds.co.uk/wp-content/uploads/article_files/V42/V42_N11/V42_N11_P347_357_A059.pdf*

Within a flock there are ranks, and it is often the lowest ranked birds who make the new discoveries. Higher-ranked birds get the first choice of food and of places to feed, lower-ranked birds get last choice. It may not seem fair to us humans, but the ranking system keeps the flock from fighting over food.

When the flock is hunting insects in a tree, the safest place is the middle of the tree, and the most dangerous place is the outer branches, where a bird is more exposed to predators. The low-ranking birds eat in the risky places. When the flock comes across a new source of food, they may send the low-ranking bird to try it out first and see if it is safe. So a "bold" bird who is the first to approach humans or try something new and risky is probably a low-ranking bird in the flock.

Flocks bring together a lot of different personalities, and some individuals like each other and some don't. Normally, that's no problem. While they are foraging, birds in a flock spread out and scatter around, so birds who like each other can stay closer together and birds who don't like each other can avoid each other. Simple.

But when they all come to the birdfeeders, they find themselves all eating close together. Even birds who don't flock, like the towhees, run into each other at the birdfeeders. And then their attitudes toward each other come out. Some birds like to be near each other, but others seem to get on each other's nerves, and when they meet there can be drama. The juncos, especially. Often two juncos on the deck explode into a fluttering fight in the air. But we have to be quick to see it, it can all be over in two seconds.

Though most songbird pairs break up for the winter, mated pairs of chickadees, nuthatches, and bushtits stay together all winter and join their winter flocks as couples. Mates stay close to each other within the flock. Meantime, within the flock, widowed birds find new mates, unmarried youngsters hook up, and some birds even trade mates.

So, unlike most songbirds, whose males find territories first and look for mates afterward, the chickadees and nuthatches are already paired in advance of spring. Come spring, a couple will establish a territory together, which may not be too hard because they know their neighbors pretty well, having spent the winter together.

The chickadee flock

Chickadees are the supreme winter survivors. Native peoples who live in places of severe winters revere the Black-capped Chickadees, because these tiny birds not only survive, they act cheerful and optimistic in the harshest winter. Black-capped Chickadees live throughout the northlands, all year round, anywhere there are trees – even deep in the interior of Alaska,. And so does another chickadee, the Boreal Chickadee. How do they do it?

One of their secrets is caching food under tree bark. No matter how deep the snow gets, the trunks of the trees and the underside of the branches will be snow-free. There are insects hibernating under the bark, too.

But another survival secret is that chickadees also eat meat. Like the other great feathered winter survivor, the raven, the cute little chickadee feeds on the remains of deer, elk, and other animals that have either starved to death or been killed by predators like wolves and mountain lions. While the big predators are eating, the tiny chickadee darts in and out, snatching beakfuls of meat, or better yet, fat. Chickadees are too small for the large predators to care about, and too fast for the predators to catch even if they did care.

This might explain why chickadees are so bold about

During Bird Winter, chickadees come to the hand for food many times a day.

approaching us and taking food from us – their ancestral memory associates large animals with food. It could also explain their fondness for suet, which is rendered animal fat.

But a problem with this hypothesis is that birds of the chickadee family live in all different climates, even the tropics, and everywhere they live, they are reputed to be as friendly, smart, and bold as the Black-capped Chickadee.

And another problem with this hypothesis is that chickadees don't merely *tolerate* us being close to them, the way they might tolerate wolves sharing a deer carcass. Chickadees actually *like* us.

And the chickadees *try* to communicate with us. It's their idea. In the winter, walking around the yard, I will often hear a *ssis-zissit* call near my ear. So I always carry a vial of peanuts in my pocket for the chickadees. If I don't have the peanuts with me, they will follow me to the house and wait while I get peanuts for them.

But once Bird Spring arrives, I won't see my chickadees again for months.

The winter hummingbirds

Birds appreciate human feeders, most of all in the winter, but (barring freak snowstorms) they can survive without us feeding them. Birds have survived without our help long before we humans came along.

With one exception. There is one bird whose survival depends on us, at least during the winter.

That is the Anna's Hummingbird.

Hummingbirds originate in South America, and nearly all of the 362 recognized hummingbird species live in the tropics. Only about a dozen species venture as far north as the United States, but most of them are seen in the southern parts. A few species live in the northern states and even Canada, but they are there only during the summer. They all leave for Mexico or farther south before winter hits. (See Chapter Nine for more on migratory hummingbirds.)

Anna's Hummingbirds live along the Pacific coast, but not long ago they lived no farther north than southern California. The only hummingbird regularly found farther north along most of the Pacfic coast was the copper-colored Rufous Hummingbird. But in the mid-twentieth century people started feeding hummingbirds, and also planting more plants that hummingbirds like, and the Annas started to spread northward, till they reached the Pacific Northwest. Unlike other hummingbirds who migrated south in the winter. the Annas didn't have the custom of flying south because they had always lived in a warm place. And they didn't need to fly south, because of the hummingbird feeders provided by the humans. Year by year the Annas spread farther and farther north, until by now they have reached Sitka, Alaska.[25]

People who feed Anna's Hummingbirds in the winter have to figure out ways to keep the feeders from freezing – covering them in Christmas lights, or taking them inside at night and putting them back out right at dawn when the hummingbirds need them the most. In their northern range, Anna's Hummingbirds live only where there are people to feed them, so besides being the only winter humming-birds, they are surely the most urban of all hummingbirds.

The Annas seem to know they need us, so they are friendly and curious about humans. Like other hummingbirds, Annas will fly up to the people who fill the feeders to let them know when the feeders are empty. But they also fly up to people out of interest and curios-ity. Often a new Anna will fly over to my face and investigate me minutely, hovering in front of each eye, the nose, the mouth. It's a little unnerving to see that sharp needle beak pointed at my eyeball.

---

25 See "Winter range expansion of a hummingbird is associated with urbanization and supplementary feeding," https://royalsocietypublishing.org/doi/10.1098/rspb.2017.0256; "Hummingbirds March North, Fueled by Sugar Water," https://www.sierraclub.org/sierra/hummingbirds-march-north-fueled-sugar-water; "Meet Alaska's Winter Hummingbird," https://ianajohnson.com/meet-alaskas-winter-hummingbird/

And sometimes Raspberry will display for me the way he does for a female hummer, blazing his iridescent red head feathers in my face.

Meanwhile, the Rufous Hummingbirds seem to be getting rarer and rarer. No one is positive about why, but it may be because so much of their winter habitat in Mexico is being turned into cattle pasture. So the Rufouses, who fly south expecting to find winter food supplies, may be starving to death during the winter, while, back home, the Anna's Hummingbirds who depend for their winter survival on human love are thriving.

The arrival of Bird Winter

Whether we live in a place with cold winters or warm winters or in-between, Bird Winter is the best time of year to begin feeding the birds.

But don't wait for December 21, winter solstice, which our calendars call the "first day of winter," to start. That's way too late. Bird Winter begins in November, and the feeders should be out before that to give the birds time to discover them.

Winter sets the cycle of birdfriending in motion.

But as Bird Winter turns to Bird Spring, life will change dramatically in the bird world. For the birdfriender, too.

CHAPTER SEVEN

BIRD SPRING: SEASON OF SONG

WE KNOW WHEN Bird Spring is here. It is announced by birdsong.

Where I live, the earliest songs of Bird Spring start well before it begins to look like spring. The Song Sparrows don't stop singing completely even in the winter, but before the leafless trees begin to bud and the spring flowers break the soil, the Song Sparrows start filling the air with the sounds of Bird Spring.

Over weeks and months, more voices join the chorus.

By the time the flowers are blooming, the meadows are buzzing with bumblebees, the cherry blossom petals are swirling in the wind like pink blizzards, the bird symphony reaches its peak and sounds like a celebration.

The two seasons of Bird Spring

Bird Spring is actually two seasons: Early Bird Spring and Late Bird Spring.

In Early Bird Spring, a bird establishes a territory and finds a mate. That is when all the displays and the most intense singing happens. In Late Bird Spring, the birds build nests, lay eggs, incubate the eggs, and feed and care for the nestlings.

Bird Spring doesn't start at the same time for all birds or in all places. Some birds are already starting Late Bird Spring while other birds are in Early Bird Spring.

Bird Spring is the best time of year for birdwatching and for birdlistening.

A cowbird and a catbird displaying

Singing isn't the only way a male bird woos his mate. If we are lucky, we can see birds display. A starling fans out his wings, a catbird fans out his tail. The cowbird spreads his wings and bows to the female while gurgling a bubbly song. A hummingbird does an acrobatic display. A Red-naped Sapsucker drums on a hollow log. A flicker pounds on the chimney, terrifying the dogs inside the house.

We might see a pair courting. A pair of swallows bow to each other. A pair of Downy Woodpeckers dance with each other. A pair of Cedar Waxwings pass berries back and forth. A pair of Steller's Jays chase each other through the trees.

At the same time, other birds may already be in Late Bird Spring. We can watch those birds gathering materials for their nests: sparrows picking up pieces of dried grasses, swallows taking beakfuls of mud, crows getting twigs, wrens taking animal fur. Later still, we may see those same birds flying with caterpillars in their beaks and disappearing into the foliage, and then we can hear the excited chorus of the baby birds.

Bird Spring is the best time for bird*watching*. But the worst time for bird*friending*.

The birdfeeders look deserted. The winter flocks have disappeared. The few birds who show up are mostly singles. A chickadee once in a while. A pair of bushtits on the suet feeder now and then. Why are the birds gone from the feeders?

One reason is that the birds are on their territories. A bird has to stay on his territory he is claiming, because if he leaves, someone else could claim that territory. And, unless his territory is right next to the birdfeeders, to get to them he would probably have to cross another bird's territory, and could get in trouble with the owner of that territory.

Besides, the feeders mainly offer seeds, and in Bird Spring, most songbirds want insects, not seeds. Insects have a lot more protein, which birds need to lay eggs and which baby birds need to grow. The parents feed themselves on insects as they gather insects for their babies. So the seeds in the birdfeeders don't attract the birds much in Bird Spring.

So during Bird Spring, we can put bird*friending* on hold. Bird Spring is the season for bird*watching*. We can watch the birds living their lives in their own ways in their own world, in our own backyards.

Staking out a territory

Most songbirds gave up their territories and split up with their mates when breeding season ended last year. So when Bird Spring comes, the first order of business for a male songbird is to claim a territory and find a mate. With most songbird species, though not all, it happens in that order. For both establishing a territory and finding a mate, singing is the key.

A territory ensures that there will be enough food for the family. A good territory is the most important thing that a male songbird has to offer to a female. So he claims a territory, or tries to. He decides where he wants the boundaries of his territory to be, and announces it to the world by singing. He moves from perch to perch along the edge of the boundary, and in each spot, he loudly sings the best song he possibly can.

While the males have their singing contests, the females are flying from territory to territory, shopping around, checking out the territories, and the singers.

Ultimately, the best singers win. But some birds end up without territories – like losers in a game of musical chairs. Those birds don't get to breed, at least not that year. They are left to sneak around the different birds' territories.

A youngster in his first year may not even try to claim a territory. He has to skulk around other birds' territories, sneaking around looking for food. As long as he doesn't sing, the older birds pretend not to notice him. He makes a soft warble that says, "Don't mind me, I'm just a youngster, I'm not trying to claim a territory here."

But although he isn't singing, he is listening. Listening to everyone's songs. Listening and learning. He practices under his breath, experimenting and developing his own style.

But how can he really learn to sing unless he can sing out loud once in a while? One day, he dares to practice singing out loud. That arouses the instant rage of the territory's owner, who immediately drives him out.

The unmated youngsters may be the only birds at the feeders in

Bird Spring. The feeders won't be part of anyone's territory. It is too valuable a piece of real estate for any one pair to claim. At least, usually. But one year, in my yard, a Black-headed Grosbeak actually did that. He flew from feeder to feeder – even the feeders he didn't use, like the hummingbird feeder – and sang his very loud song. There were two other male Black-Headed Grosbeaks in adjacent territories, and if he caught them daring to come to the feeders, he drove them away. I have never seen any bird do this before or since.

Once a female bird chooses a mate, she is supposed to stay in her own territory. (Although sometimes a female bird may quickly sneak into the next door neighbor's territory and cheat on her husband.)

Finding that special someone

A bird wants somebody to love. A bird wants to fall in love and get married.

Most other animals in the world don't fall in love with their mates. Few animals other than birds form one-to-one partnerships. We humans do it for the same reason that birds do: because human children need two parents to raise them.

Most baby birds are born helpless and completely dependent on their parents to feed them. Unlike most creatures in the world, they need two committed parents. So the parents' falling in love helps the species survive.

A widowed songbird might manage to raise a brood, as a single parent, but the work will be much harder, and success much less certain. And young male songbirds need their fathers. They need to hear him singing when they are still in the nest; if not, then when they grow up, they won't be able to sing well enough to secure territories and mates for themselves. So their generations would end there.

Most larger birds, like eagles, geese, parrots, mate for life. Not many songbirds mate for life, but some – like chickadees, bushtits, nuthatches, cardinals, crows and jays – stay with their mates for years. The mates go through the winter together.

But most of the small songbirds split up with their mates at the end of breeding season. Still, songbird mates may occasionally become so attached to each other that they do stay together through the winter. (I have seen this with Song Sparrows, who normally break up.) But most songbirds look for new mates in the spring.

We might think that a couple must not have strong feelings for each other if they don't even intend to stay together after the kids are raised. But for birds, whether the relationship lasts for a season or a lifetime, the fire burns fiercely. Even if the love lasts only till the children are on their own, the continuation of the species depends on couples falling in love,

For a bird, the most important thing in life is finding that special someone.

The Song of Love

Most songbirds use songs to attract a mate. Even those who also use color or displays.

Songbirds are not the only ones to use sound to advertise for mates. Doves coo, roosters crow, bitterns boom. And frogs croak, crickets chirp, cicadas buzz, all to call females.

But songbirds are different from all other creatures in the symphony of nature, even other birds.

When a frog croaks, he croaks the same thing over and over and over again. When a cricket chirps, he chirps the same thing over and over and over again. When a rooster crows, he always crows the same crow. When a dove coos, he coos the same coo again and again. Hour after hour, day after day, as long as it takes. The ten-thousandth coo the same as the first.

For these creatures, their mating calls are ancestral knowledge. They don't have to learn them. Even if a male dove never hears another dove in his life, he will start cooing when he gets old enough. A rooster doesn't have to hear another rooster to know how to crow. A frog is born knowing how to croak.

But songbirds have to *learn* their songs, like humans have to learn how to talk. If a songbird never hears another member of its species sing, it might make some sounds when it grows up, but it won't sing real songs. If a human baby never heard another human talk, it might babble, but it would never learn how to talk. In fact, scientists have found parallels in the way we learn language and songbirds learn song, and they are studying the way a songbird brain learns song to learn more about human language learning.

And of all creatures on Earth, only songbirds and humans can be creative with their voices. Only songbirds and humans create new songs. Only songbirds and humans practice their songs and work to get better and better. Only songbirds and humans borrow ideas from others and work them into new original forms. (In fact, some songbirds, like mockingbirds, catbirds, and starlings, may even borrow sounds like car alarms and meowing cats.)

The joy of creating music is yet one more thing shared by songbirds and humans.

Not all songbirds sing. Crows are technically songbirds, but they don't sing at all. Other songbirds sing only a simple song, one practical for an ID. What the males offer depends on what the females want.

And apparently, female songbirds want singing. A female Song Sparrow apparently doesn't give a whit for pretty colors. She wants the best singer she can get.

So, what kind of singing does she like? Louder? Faster? Longer?

It turns out that almost all female songbirds prefer variety. And songs that are more complicated and difficult. And original – not exact copies of another male's song. She appreciates creativity. A Song Sparrow can copy another bird's song, but he has to put his own original twist on it. The variations may sound almost the same to our ears.

Birds can hear fine details in the songs that we usually don't notice. But with practice, we can learn to hear these details too.

Songbirds, male and female, have a special area in the brain for learning song and appreciating song. Testosterone flows in the male songbird in Bird Spring and impels him to sing. A female songbird injected with testosterone will sing too. Female songbirds do sing sometimes, but more often a female songbird prefers to sit back and listen. But her musical brain makes her a sophisticated listener.

It takes years for a bird to become a top singer, just like it takes years for a human to become a great pianist or gymnast. And just the fact that a bird has *survived* long enough to become a master singer makes him a good catch. Creativity and the ability to survive may go together.

Birdsong is advertising. And the whole point of advertising is to be noticed, to get attention, to tell everybody who you are and where you are and why you are so great.

And she enjoys the singing. One of the things he is advertising is the pleasure he will be able to give her with his songs. If she didn't enjoy the singing, he would stop singing once she has chosen him, because there is no longer a practical reason for singing.

But he will continue to sing. He will continue to sing for her as she incubates the eggs, and she will close her eyes and puff her feathers in pleasure.

And she will not not be the only one listening. All the Song Sparrows in the neighborhood will keep track of each other by listening to each other's songs.

Late Bird Spring: Eggs and babies

Once a bird pair is mated and has a territory, it is time for their Late Bird Spring to begin. We can watch them gathering materials for their nests. Pieces of grass, twigs, moss. Mud. Soft animal fur. Lichens. Hummingbirds use spiderwebs.

Each kind of bird has its own kind of nest. No one teaches them what kind of nest to build, or how to build it, or where to build it. They inherit that knowledge as ancestral memory. The only thing they have to decide is *where* to build it. If they can't agree, the female's opinion will prevail. After all, she's going to be spending the most time there.

Bushtit nest woven into the branches of a fir tree. On the back side, it looks like a hanging sock.

Among some birds, both mates build the nest together, while among others, the male gathers the material and brings it to the female, and she builds the nest. Among other birds, the male may build the nest first and then bring the female over to see it. Among some birds, like some wrens, the male builds multiple nests throughout his territory and then the female gets to choose one, though she may rebuild it in a way she likes better.

The robins are building a bowl shaped cup nest out of grass and small sticks stuck together with mud, on a tree branch. The Song Sparrows are weaving a cup nest out of long pieces of grass, placed in low bushes close to the ground.

A pair of crows is building a nest of sticks high in an oak tree. The Barn Swallow pair is making a nest out of mud, glued to the side of a barn. The bushtits are weaving a suspended nest in the fir needles. The House Sparrows are making a nest in a potted plant on the front porch. In a bramble bush, the Mourning Doves are making a sloppy pile of little sticks that hardly seems to qualify as a nest.

The juncos are nesting right on the ground, behind a tuft of grass under a boulder. Nesting on the ground might seem dangerous; a predator could get to a ground nest more easily than to a nest in a tree. But the predator has to find the nest in the first place. A nest in a tree is easier to find than a nest on the ground. A nest in a tree has to be somewhere in a tree; a nest on the ground could be *anywhere*. The ground is full of places where a junco nest *could* be.

The killdeer mother lays her eggs out on the ground, in the open, but they are placed among rocks and dead leaves that are the same color as her eggs, making the eggs invisible.

And a whole bunch of birds – cavity-nesters like woodpeckers, wrens, chickadees, nuthatches, bluebirds, and even some owls – are looking for dead trees with holes to nest in. Woodpeckers make the nest holes in trees for all kinds of cavity-nesters to use. But if humans clear away the dead trees, then a lot of these birds have no place to nest and can't raise families. Fortunately for some, humans may provide birdhouses to take the place of the dead trees.

The work of an experienced nestbuilder can be intricately crafted. A hummingbird rehabber describes a nest brought to her:

I gazed in wonder at the skill and craftsmanship involved in sculpting this elegant work of art.... It would take a human hundreds of hours of patient practice to create a structure equally beautiful and functional. Like snowflakes, each hummingbird nest is unique.... Looking at hummingbirds' astonishing creations opens the door to a magical and other-worldly realm.[26]

Finally the nest is built. Then the female bird lays eggs, one egg per day. The egg contains all the food and water a baby bird needs. The yolk is the food and the egg-white holds the water. As the baby absorbs the food, it will grow and grow until it fills up the whole egg and has to come out.

If the eggs get too cold, the babies inside will die. If the eggs are warmed, the babies inside will grow. But if the eggs are neither warm nor cold, the babies inside won't grow, but they won't die either. Most birds want the babies to hatch at the same time, so they don't begin incubating (keeping the eggs warm so the babies will grow) until the whole clutch of eggs are laid. But some birds do the opposite, and start incubating as the eggs are laid so that the babies *won't* all hatch at the same time.

When the baby songbirds hatch, they are tiny and blind and naked, and can quickly die of cold if they are not constantly kept warm. So at all times, one of the parents has to sit on them to keep them warm. This is called brooding them.

Some songbird parents take turns sitting on the nest — one does incubation and brooding while the other searches for food. Among other songbirds, the female stays on the nest, while the male finds food for her and the babies.

26 From *Fastest Things on Wings: Rescuing Hummingbirds in Hollywood,* by Terry Masear (p. 8)

Each baby needs to be fed at least every twenty minutes. The baby birds need insects, worms, spiders. And those critters are mostly hiding. He has to search them out. He has to bring food for one baby every five minutes. Or enough food for four babies every twenty minutes. Not to mention finding food for mom and himself. All day, from sunrise to sunset.

And once in a while, maybe in those moments when everyone's belly is filled, he can take a break and sing a little too. Is there any reason for him to sing anymore? He has his territory, he has his mate. Yet, he still sings, when he gets a break from his duties. He sings to please her, because she likes it – why else would she have searched for the best singer she could find as her mate? And he sings to stay in touch with his neighbors.

And the tiny babies need to hear his song. A human baby needs to hear humans talking, while still a baby – otherwise, it won't learn to talk when it grows up. And a male songbird needs to hear his father's song while still in the nest if he is to sing when he grows up.

But when babies are hatched and hungry, there isn't much spare time for dad to spend singing. There is work to do. Soon the babies will be feathered out and leave the nest. But the work doesn't stop. In fact, life will get even more complicated in Bird Summer.

CHAPTER EIGHT

BIRD SUMMER: SEASON OF GRADUATING

BIRD SUMMER ANNOUNCES itself to our ears with a new kind of music.

The warbling birdsong of Bird Spring is gradually replaced by a sonic tapestry of breathy buzzes and hissing trills and burbling squeals and squeaky hums and gurgly whistles and croaky squawks and hoarse quacks, layering over each other.

This is the sound of fledglings yelling to their parents, *"FEED ME!"*

As we move from Bird Spring into Bird Summer (which begins around early May where I live) the world fills up with fledglings. A fledgling is a baby bird who has fledged, or graduated from the nest. A fledgling still depends on its parents to feed it, protect it, and teach it about the world. Once it can take care of itself, it is no longer a fledgling, but a *juvenile*, or "juvie."

But while it is still a fledgling, wherever it may wander, it calls out to its parents. Just as every songbird has its own song, so every kind of fledgling has its own distinctive begging call, so that its parents can find it in the crowd of buzzy, raspy, croaky, trilly, gurgly *"FEED ME!"* calls all around.

For songbird parents, Bird Summer may be even more work than Bird Spring.

During Bird Spring, they laid the eggs, incubated them, and hatched them. Then they started the frantic period of feeding the babies. But without feathers to cover them, the baby birds quickly would die of cold. Mom has to stay in the nest to keep them warm until they feather out. Or the parents take turns. The babies have to be all together in the nest to be covered all at once.

In just a week or two, a baby bird grows from a naked blind morsel the size of a human thumbnail to a fully feathered creature almost as big as its parents. Once covered with feathers, the baby doesn't need mom to keep it warm. And its eyes are open and it can move around, so it no longer *has* to stay in the nest. Whether it is in the nest or out somewhere else, mom and dad could feed it. So should the baby leave the nest, or should it stay?

Surely mom and dad would want the babies to stay in the nest. It is easier to feed them all in one place. Mom and dad know where they are. If they were out of the nest, mom and dad would have to look for them and travel around to feed each one separately. And a baby bird can easily get lost.

And the outside world is full of dangers. Cats and dogs and hawks and raccoons and cars and human children. A fledgling bird is an easy lunch for all kinds of critters.

Surely the baby should stay in the nest as long as it can, flapping and strengthening its wings and growing up, Then it will be able to fly almost immediately when it leaves the nest, and could better escape dangers.

And some parent birds do take that option, letting the youngsters stay in the nest till they get so big they can't fit any more and push each other out.

Yet most songbird parents encourage the babies to leave the nest as soon as possible. Even if they can't fly yet.

Why? What's the hurry?

The nest isn't a safe place either. The longer the nest is active, the more likely it is to be discovered.

The voices of the growing babies are getting louder by the day. Every time mom or dad arrives at the nest with food, bursts of *"FEED ME! ME! ME! ME!"* calls explode from the foliage. All four throats together make extra volume. The choruses are so loud they are even obvious to us, yards away.

And each day that passes increases the chance that a crow or squirrel or bird of prey will observe the parent birds going in and out of their hiding place.

The nest is an all-or-nothing gamble. Maybe nothing will happen to it and everyone will be fine. But if a predator discovers a nest full of eggs or babies, *all* of them get eaten. The entire brood is gone.

But if the babies are spread out, hiding in different places, something might happen to one baby, but then the parents have lost only one. They would still have the other babies in different places. There is a better chance that some of their babies will make it.

The fledging of the fledglings

Not only do they still have to find food for three or four hungry babies, but now the babies are all in different locations, and the parents have to keep track of each one, and fly around to them.

Back in the nest, mom or dad would arrive with food about every five minutes. Now, in four different places, each baby has to wait a lot longer for a parent to show up. A hungry baby bird could get restless and impatient. It might flex its growing muscles. And when dad finally shows up with food, he might find the baby gone.

Fortunately, fledgling birds make a lot of noise when they are hungry. The parents listen for its voice.

But maybe they can't find its voice. Maybe the baby is nowhere to be found. Maybe it is dead.

A fledgling is clueless about danger. And the big world is full of dangers. Hawks. Raccoons. Coyotes. Owls. Crows. Weasels. Skunks. Snakes. Foxes. And, of course, cats. It could be picked up by a dog who treats it as a feathered tennis ball. Or carried off by a human child who uses it as a toy. Or it could fall into a puddle and drown. Or fall into a hole and starve to death in darkness. Or get hit by a car.

Its parents try to protect it. If dad sees a dangerous creature approaching, he makes an alarm call. *"SHUT UP! SHUT UP!!"* And the fledgling shuts up.

But it shuts up only for as long as it hears the alarm. As soon the alarm stops, the fledgling starts yelling *"FEED ME! FEED ME!"* again. So dad has to make the alarm call continuously, as long as the danger is present. It doesn't matter that he is betraying his own location by making noise. It is more important that his fledgling not be discovered.

But while he is trying to protect that fledgling, its siblings, scattered around in other locations, are getting hungrier and hungrier, and yelling *"FEED ME!"* and nobody is telling them to shut up. So maybe *that* fledgling doesn't get eaten by that cat, but its little brother may not be so lucky.

The bird-catching hawks

For an adult bird, a ground predator, like a fox or a cat, is a relatively easy problem. The bird just has to know it's there.

But a bird-catching hawk – an accipiter, like a Cooper's Hawk or a Sharp-shinned Hawk – is a different problem. There is no safe perch, no place to be out of its reach. A winged predator can snatch you from a perch high or low. It can grab you as you fly through the air.

The Cooper's Hawk has hungry babies too. Fortunately for the Cooper's Hawk, just when it needs lots of food for its babies, there are lots of songbird fledglings available to catch. According to one calculation,[27] on average, each baby Cooper, from the time it hatches until it is weaned, consumes 66 songbirds. So a brood of four baby Coopers would eat about 264 songbirds, mostly fledglings. And the parents have to feed themselves too. That may mean that it could take

---

27 *What the Robin Knows: How Birds Reveal the Secrets of the Natural World*, by Jon Young, p. 46.

nearly four hundred songbirds to support one family of Cooper's Hawks during the breeding season.

But, once they have fledged, about fifty percent of accipiters starve to death in their first year of life. Catching birds is not easy. It takes skill to hide, skill to know the right moment to go for the prey, skill to maneuver at top speed through the trees, skills to grab something moving through the air with your talons. Many juvie raptors don't live long enough to develop the hunting skills they need to survive.

The population of songbirds and accipiters stays in balance, and life goes on.

Fun at the feeders

During breeding season, the birds don't usually have much interest in us. Breeding season – Bird Spring and Bird Summer – is time for birdwatching, not birdfriending.

But for people who feed birds, Bird Summer can be the greatest time for backyard birdwatching, because we don't have to go looking for them, the birds come to us.

Not to *us*, exactly – they come back to the feeders, which had looked so lonesome in Bird Spring.

If the birds had discovered the feeders back during Bird Winter, they found out then that it is safe to be around the humans. Bird Winter is the time for taking risks and making new discoveries. Bird Summer is not the time to take risks with something new. Especially since there is plenty of other food around in Bird Summer.

In Bird Summer, we can offer to make the job of the parent birds easier. They are frantically trying to feed their kids while at the same time keeping them from getting killed. Out in the big world, the food is spread out, and not always easy to find, and the parents have to leave the kids alone and unguarded to go find it.

Not only is food easy to get at the birdfeeders, the parents can bring their fledgling to the food and feed it right there. And if the food is in a place where hawks and other predators can't hide, then it is actually safer than the big wide world.

Not to mention the birdbath, always full of fresh clean water to drink. Water may be in short supply on hot sunny days.

Since the fledglings know nothing about territorial boundaries, territories are becoming irrelevant in Bird Summer. So the feeders can be hopping with birds in Bird Summer.

Bird Summer can give us the best birdfeeder show of the year, as the parent birds teach the fledglings how to eat on their own.

If you are a fledgling just out of the nest, you have no idea how to look for food. You don't even really know what food looks like. Food is something carried in your parents' bills or regurgitated from their gullets. You never got a good look at it. You don't know how they got it in the first place. You don't know how to search for food on the ground or on a tree trunk or hiding on the underside of a leaf. You don't even know how to pick up food.

The only way you know to get food is to beg your parents for it. So you open your beak wide and shove it into dad's face, shivering and quivering your wings, squawking *"FEED ME!"* Dad picks up piece after piece of food and puts it in your mouth. Once in a while, he grabs a bite for himself.

After a few days, dad starts to do things a little differently. He eats a piece of food himself before giving a piece to you. Then he eats another piece himself. Then another piece for you. Feed, eat, feed, eat. He makes you wait. You quiver and buzz and impatiently nag, "*HEY! I'm HUNGRY!!!!*"

But he makes you wait longer and longer between feedings. Now he eats two pieces of food before giving one piece to you. Then three pieces for himself, then finally just one piece for you. He eats some more, one, two, three pieces, seeming to ignore your wailing complaints.

Impatiently, you look around. Right there is another bird who looks like your parents. Maybe *he* will feed you! You hop over to that bird and stick your open beak in his face and quiver your wings and buzz at him. But he ignores you. How about that bird over there? You hop over to try your luck with that one, but he only quivers and buzzes and begs back at you, "Why don't *you* feed *me*?" He's a fledgling too. So you hop back over to dad to resume nagging him. Dad, all this time, has been calmly eating as though everything were fine.

With hungry intensity, you watch what he is doing. In the nest, you never got to observe how adult birds feed themselves. Now you see what food looks like and how to pick it up. And you are getting hungrier and hungrier as dad makes you wait longer and longer. Finally, you can't wait any longer. You pick up a piece of food and swallow it. You've done it!

You still have a lot to learn. How to find food. Where to search for it. How to recognize different kinds of food. And what to do with it when you find it. Not all food can just be gulped down whole. Many seeds need to have the hull removed, and there are different techniques for different seeds – from grass seeds to hard-shelled sunflower seeds. Some seeds need the fluff removed. Some insects can be swallowed whole, while other insects need their heads or wings or legs removed before they can be eaten.

Some bird parents don't bring their fledglings to the feeders. Like other dove and pigeon parents, Mourning Doves feed their babies "pigeon milk." The parents eat and digest the food, then the baby dove puts its beak down the parent's throat and drinks the liquefied food using its beak like a soda straw. Gulls and other seabirds feed their babies that way too.

A young hummingbird just out of the nest is fed by its mom for the first few weeks, but mom doesn't teach it to find food; the fledgling hummer has to figure that out on its own. It knows by instinct that its food is associated with eye-catching colors, so it goes around investigating everything colorful. They copy other birds; they try the suet feeder and other birdfeeders where they see other birds eating. They investigate everything brightly colored, especially red things. Once I saw a hummingbird fledgling poking at the red spot on the back of a Downy Woodpecker's head.

The big imposter

Predators are not the only threat to a songbird brood.

A strange (suspicious?) looking Song Sparrow

One May day, I heard a loud "*FEED ME!*" call from a rhododendron bush. I saw a Song Sparrow go into the bush with food. I sneaked over and looked through the leaves. A nest! With a baby Song Sparrow in it! It was a little odd-looking for a Song Sparrow... kind of ugly, actually, but... maybe that's how Song Sparrows look at that age? I snapped its picture as it stared at me from the nest.

I should have been suspicious about the fact that the baby's begging call was so loud that it led me straight to the nest. The voices of four baby Song Sparrows put together shouldn't not be as loud as this one guy.

And I should have been suspicious that there weren't other babies in the nest. Why was he the only one there?

Two days later the youngster fledged. But he didn't act like a normal Song Sparrow baby. He didn't hide in the bushes. He chased his parents around. Whenever they landed, he was right behind them, demanding food with his nagging calls and his great big open mouth. His "*FEED ME*" calls were not the little buzzy trills of a Song Sparrow fledgling. His calls were loud and harsh.

And when he planted himself in front of one of his parents, opening his big mouth in her face, I could see he was much bigger than the parent bird. What gives?

Then I knew. He wasn't a Song Sparrow. He was a cowbird.

And I realized what had happened. A month or so before, a female cowbird had been sneaking around, looking for unguarded nests with eggs in them. When she found this Song Sparrow nest, she laid an egg of her own and left.

She let the Song Sparrows hatch her baby. A cowbird doesn't raise her own babies. She lets other birds do it. (In Europe, the cuckoo does the same thing.) And she chooses birds smaller than cowbirds. So when the cowbird baby hatches, it will be the biggest mouth in the nest.

This Song Sparrow probably won't make the same mistake again

To a bird, the open mouth of a baby is a powerful instinctual cue, a signal passed down through ancestral memory. And the bigger the mouth, the more powerful the cue. The biggest mouth gets the most food. So most of the food the Song Sparrow parents brought went into the big mouth of the cowbird. The cowbird baby grew while the other babies starved to death. He got all the food that normally would have gone to four Song Sparrow babies. So, by the time I saw the cowbird in the nest, he was the only baby there.

The Song Sparrows appeared frazzled and frantic as they tried to keep up with the cowbird's loud nagging and endless pursuit. They seemed to realize that something was wrong. They probably realized that when the cowbird was still in the nest. Yet they didn't stop feeding the cowbird baby.

It's bad enough when a brood is eaten by a predator. At least that story is over and done with, and the pair can start a new nest if enough time is left. But when the brood is destroyed by a cowbird, the cowbird adds insult to injury by making its foster parents work their tails off to feed and care for it.

The Song Sparrows who made the nest in the rhododendron bush must have been first-year birds. Only inexperienced birds would make a nest so easy to find. But they learn from experience. They learn how to hide their nests better. And they learn about cowbirds. Next time these Song Sparrows find a cowbird egg in the nest, they will push it out. If they can't, they might build new nest right on top of the old one. If the cowbird returns and destroys the nest in revenge, as cowbirds sometimes do, the pair might learn that the best thing to do when you find a cowbird egg is just to abandon the nest and build a new nest somewhere else. Better to take the loss of their eggs than to be stuck with a cowbird.

And one day, I heard an intense, agitated Song Sparrow alarm call outside my door. I looked out and saw a Song Sparrow confronting a female cowbird, yelling with a ferocity I have never seen in a Song Sparrow. "*YOU! YOU! YOU!*" the Song Sparrow shouted. "You're the one! You did it! I saw you!" The cowbird just sat there, like, "Yeah, whatever," as the Song Sparrow kept getting in her face, "*YOU! YOU! YOU!*" Obviously this Song Sparrow had caught the female cowbird in the act. He had identified the culprit and was letting the whole world know who it was.

And apparently, everyone does get wise to the cowbird trick. Some summers there are five cowbird fledglings on my deck, each with junco or Song Sparrow foster parents. But the female cowbird may have laid eggs in forty different nests. The vast majority of birds who had found cowbird eggs in their nests were not fooled. And the following summer, I see no cowbird youngsters at all. It seemed that everyone has learned.

But in a few years, new generations come up that don't know about the cowbirds. Then the cowbirds will again find victims they can fool.

So the cycle goes on.

Birdfriending is generational

Once upon a time, where I live, the flickers were extremely shy. If I wanted to watch a flicker, I had to hide. I set up the suet feeder so that I could hide and watch it if a flicker showed up. But if the flicker caught the slightest glimpse of me, off it flashed.

Then, one July day, I heard the loud nasal *"DEER!"* call of a flicker – the call that flickers use to locate each other.[28] Mates use it to find each other, and parents and fledglings do that too. I followed the sound to a dead tree. There was a nest hole high up in the tree, and sticking out of the hole, not twelve feet from me, was a flicker head, loudly calling *"DEER!"*

Wow, a flicker so close! She was the only one in the nest hole. I could see the flicker was a female. I answered, *"DEER!"* Of course, my

---

28   Some people render it *"KLEER!"* or *"KYAH!"* or *"KING!"* or in other ways. Judging from recordings, the flicker call sounds a bit different in different places.

clumsy flicker imitation sounds nothing like a real flicker. But that didn't matter. She answered me, "*DEER!*" I answered "*DEER!*" again. We went on and on, back and forth, watching each other as we called.

I worried that any second, one of her parents would come and say, "Don't associate with those humans! Bad! Danger!" And that would be the end of my incipient flicker friendship. But no parent showed up.

She must have been the last one in the nest. The parents must have stopped bringing food to the nest. Sometimes birds do that to make the last baby leave. So no one came around to warn her not to be friends with me.

I named her Flora the Flicker. The next day I visited her again, and we conversed for over an hour. No one was feeding her, and she must have been extremely hungry, and I couldn't do anything about that. But I also sensed that she was lonely and frustrated. She seemed glad for the company. Maybe she was glad to have a friend who would listen as she poured out her frustration.

But the third day, the hole was empty. Flora had gone. Good luck, Flora. Could she find her parents? If not, would she be able to find food on her own?

But the next day, she was on the suet feeder on my deck. And she didn't mind me being near her as she gorged herself.

And she didn't come just to eat. Sometimes she would come just to visit and sit near me, like some of my Song Sparrow, Steller's Jay, and Mourning Dove friends.

Through summer, and fall, and winter, Flora came to eat suet every day, and sometimes just to sit near me. But then when Bird Spring came, Flora quit showing up. I wondered if I would see her ever again.

Flora the Flicker feeds her fledgling on the suet feeder.

Then when Bird Summer arrived, she was back. And she had three fledglings of her own. She led them straight to the suet feeder, and stuffed suet into their mouths, day after day. And she taught them that it was no problem that I was right there. She taught them I was a friend.

And suddenly I had not one but four friendly flickers visiting me. And when those friendly flicker fledglings grew up, they brought their own fledglings to the suet feeder. And now, although Flora is no longer with us, I have lots of friendly flickers visiting. They are very tolerant of humans around. And some, like Flora, hang out just for company.

And when I hear the flickers calling *"DEER!"* I always answer. Usually they ignore me – after all, they are calling for someone else, not me. Sometimes they reply anyway, and we call back and forth. But whether they reply or not, I sense that the flickers feel more friendly toward me when they hear me try to speak Flicker.

Flora the friendly flicker fledgling was a fluke, because she made friends with me all by herself. (Her parents would undoubtedly have been against it.) But she showed me how a friendly parent can raise children who are even more friendly.

Another summer, I discovered a Mourning Dove pair nesting

in the blackberry bushes. I went near the nest every day – no closer than twelve feet – and sang to them. The two youngsters turned out friendly indeed. My friend Daisy the Dove was one of them, and now she comes to the deck almost every day, not only to eat, but just to sit with me, and hear me sing to her.

Daisy the Dove, as a nestling with her mother (can you spot her mother?) and a year later as an adult.

Birdfriending is generational. Birdfriendships develop year by year. Every generation becomes a little friendlier than the last.

The birds who began to be our friends at the feeders during the Bird Winter, bring their fledglings to the birdfeeders in Bird Summer.

In Bird Summer, we want the parent birds to ignore us. They are glad to ignore us, because they don't want to think about us in breeding season anyway. So Bird Summer is not the time to try to get the birds' attention. Bird Summer is the time we should make ourselves easy to ignore.

If a fledgling sees its parents fly away from the humans, it learns that the humans are a threat. But if the fledglings see their parents ignoring us, they learn to accept us as part of the scenery. And if they see their parents acting friendly to us, they learn we are friends.

Our birdfriends may bring their fledglings to meet us. My mother had a towhee friend who did that. My chickadees and jays may bring their fledglings to me, and even show them how to hand-feed. But we should let that be their own idea.

We shouldn't approach too close so that the birds fly away. If the young bird sees that, it learns to associate humans with fear. But otherwise, it just observes other birds keeping a cautious distance from the humans, and learns that humans are okay as long as you stay just that far.

When Bird Winter comes, that young adult bird will be even more open-minded than its parents to being friends with the humans, and come much closer than its parents would have suggested. And its own youngsters will in turn come even closer. Each generation of fledglings sees its parents more relaxed around the humans – especially *these* humans who live in *this* house. All because of what it learned in Bird Summer.

And sometimes we can cheat a little. I once lived in a house where a House Sparrow pair were nesting in the eaves outside my bedroom window. I spread millet seed outside my window for them, but if the sparrows saw me so close, they would fly away. I had to use a mirror to watch them.

When their babies fledged, the parents brought them to eat the millet seed outside the window. I would sneak over and stand in front of one side of the window where the babies could see me very close, while the parents, off to the side, were blocked by the wall from seeing me. The babies didn't realize that the parents couldn't see me. All they knew was that their parents seemed fine with my being only a few feet away. So when they grew up, they didn't mind me being close.

Birdfriending is generational. The relationship between birds and their humans develops over generations. Older birds pass on what they know to younger ones. Like knowledge of the migration routes, so does knowledge of the human world, and its opportunities and dangers, flow through the generations.

Bird Summer is a key stage in birdfriending. During Bird Summer, we have first contact with the younger generation, and can make a first impression on their impressionable little minds. And first impressions are lasting.

CHAPTER NINE

BIRD FALL: SEASON OF PREPARING

THE BIRD SEASONS announce themselves to our ears. Bird Spring by birdsong. Bird Summer by fledgling *"FEED ME"* calls. Bird Fall by... bird silence.

The trees seem strangely empty of birds. This is because Bird Fall is the time of molting – the time that birds replace old feathers with new ones. Birds who are going to migrate need good feathers for flying. Birds who are going to stay home in the winter need good feathers to keep them warm. Juvie songbirds who had camouflage coloring when they were fledglings are getting adult plumage now.

During molting season, birds are missing a lot of their feathers, and they hide, because they can't fly as well and would have a harder time escaping danger.

So the feeders look deserted. No more parents at the feeders stuffing food into the fledglings' mouths. Bird Fall means breeding season is over. Courting, nesting, incubating, feeding nestlings and fledglings – all done. The parents can take a break now. In fact, with the kids on their own, most songbird couples will split up.

The youngsters can feed themselves now, and they are on their own, learning how to find food. Fortunately for them, food is easy to find in Bird Fall, and this is another reason the feeders look deserted: the birds don't need them. All kinds of grasses are going to seed. Nuts and acorns and berries are ripening. Delicious insects are under every leaf and in every bark crevice. Human gardeners get their biggest harvest in the fall, and birds do too.

Where I live, Bird Fall begins in August. For the humans, August is summertime, when the livin' is easy. For the birds, the living is easy then, too. At least it is for some birds.

Migratory birds

Yet, above us, rivers of birds are flowing through the sky. But it's an invisible river, because most migrating birds are too small for us to see up there. Only the big ones like the geese and cranes give us an idea of what is happening high above us.

Like truck drivers crossing the country, migrating birds need rest stops where they can fuel up along the way. So people lucky enough to live on migration routes may see more different kinds of birds than anyone, including outstandingly beautiful birds, like the warblers.

People who feed birds on migration may actually help those birds to survive, especially when the migratory birds lose an area they used to depend on. When a tall-grass meadow is turned into an apartment complex, the migratory birds who used to stop there may discover that one of their refueling stations is gone. A bird on migration has little time or energy to search around for new food sources. And if it can't refuel along the way, it will die.

A bird on migration can remember the location of one birdfeeder in the backyard of one house on one street in one town that it visited one time, a year ago. Some birds even show up at a particular feeder around the very same date every year.

A migratory bird also needs to know where it is headed. A good place for spending the winter should have plenty of food and water and be safe from danger.

But if a bird has never migrated before, how can it know where to go? Already exhausted from its superhuman journey, a bird has little energy to fly aimlessly around a strange place looking for food.

Like caching birds, migratory birds need a superpowered memory. Specifically, the ability to remember what it sees. And birds have that. They are much better at remembering what they see than humans.

A bird feels restless as it prepares for the long flight:

> He can feel it: a stirring in his bones and feathers. It's time. Today is the day he will once again cast himself into the air, spiral upward into the clouds, and bank into the wind, working his newly molted flight feathers for real. After weeks of flight testing, he feels ready. Day after day, he has spent the non-feeding hours carefully smoothing the barbs on each feather vane to seamless perfection. Now there are no gaps for the wind to pass through and slow him down. He has packed all the fuel he can… His inner GPS is set for north, The whole flock is rippling with anticipation, chattering, waiting for one of them to make the first move. [29]

The first time a migratory bird makes the trip, it follows other birds. Next year, it can remember the whole migration route, all the landmarks, all the stopover points, and the destination. It can remember the location of one birdfeeder behind one house on one street in

---

29 Phillip Hoose, *Moonbird*

one town that it visited once a year ago. It may even show up at that feeder on the very same date each year.

Migratory birds have far longer memories than resident birds. Longer than resident birds of closely related species. Longer than resident birds of the *same* species. When scientists compared the memories of migratory and resident warblers, the resident warblers could remember where food was hidden up to two weeks later, but the migratory warblers could remember it *an entire year* later.[30] Other scientists studied Dark-eyed Juncos and White-crowned Sparrows, and found similar memory differences among migratory and resident groups *of the same species*.[31]

Migratory birds depend on familiar landmarks, and they trust things they have seen before. They distrust new things. If something looks different than it did last year, a migratory bird tends to avoid it. Scientists put farm equipment in a field and observed the reactions of different birds. The resident birds were curious and investigated. But the migratory birds stayed away from anything that wasn't there last year.

To a resident bird, who sees the same scene every day, any new thing stands out. And it has plenty of time to study the new thing. For a resident bird, changes usually happen gradually, not suddenly. A new apartment building goes up; the resident bird witnesses every step for months, and has plenty of time to adjust to it. But when the migratory bird shows up, after a long absence, it sees a shocking change.

Yet a migratory bird may be less curious about new things than a resident bird. A bird on migration is constantly bombarded with newness, passing over a lake one day and a mountain the next. The world can completely change from one morning to the next. A bird

---

30   Claudia Mettke-Hofmann and Eberhard Gwinner, "Long-term memory for a life on the move." *https://www.pnas.org/content/100/10/5863*

31   "The relationship between migratory behaviour, memory and the hippocampus: an intraspecific comparison," *https://www.ncbi.nlm.nih.gov/pmc/articles/PMC1635458/*

on migration has to be able to resist its curiosity. If you'll be in a place for only a day or two, there's nothing to gain by exploring. Wandering away from the flock is at best a waste of precious energy, and at worst dangerous. So a migratory bird who is less curious will survive better. And its children will inherit less curiosity.

So how does a migrating bird find feeders in the first place? Passing through for a day or two, hundreds of feet in the air on a migration route a hundred miles wide, over thousands of human roofs?

It watches the resident birds. On a stopover, it observe the locals and find out what they know. So if we want migratory birds to discover our feeders, we need to have resident birds feeding there already.

A migratory bird might take longer to discover bird feeders, but once it does, it is loyal to places it knows. And also to humans it knows. When a migratory bird forms an attachment, it may last a lifetime.

The heroic hummingbirds

Migratory birds make hard and dangerous journeys. Some birds like terns and knots fly from the Arctic to almost the Antarctic, and back, a journey almost like flying around the world. But the Ruby-Throated Hummingbird may make the most courageous journey of all.

A Ruby-throated Hummingbird takes off from the Gulf Coast and makes a nonstop trip to Yucatan, Mexico, over 900 miles of ocean. It flies continuously, day and night, for nearly 24 hours. Unlike the marathon-flying seabirds, a hummingbird can't stop and eat along the way. There's no food for a hummingbird in the ocean, and it would drown if it gets near the water.

The hummingbird can't rest for even a moment, because there is no place to rest on the ocean. And it has to fly at top speed, beating its wings at a blurring speed of over 50 strokes *per second*. because its tiny body can hold only enough fuel to last 24 hours, and if it doesn't make it to its destination before running out of fuel, it will drop into the ocean. So a headwind that slows it down can be fatal.

No one knows how many Ruby-throats meet that fate. But in 2017, three hurricanes, Harvey, Irma, and Jose, hit the Gulf of Mexico back to back during the height of Ruby-throat migration season. The next spring, as reported throughout social media, people who were expecting the spring return of the Ruby-throats to their feeders saw much fewer hummingbirds than usual, and some people reported they had no hummingbirds at all. Apparently many Ruby-throats had been caught in the hurricanes.

For most migratory birds, there is lots of food in Bird Fall, just when they need it most. But hummingbirds need flowers to fuel up, and flowers can be scarce in the fall.

So a Ruby-throat who finds a precious patch of flowers may claim it for himself and guard it. Hummers may try to chase each other away and battle over the flowers, pretending to stab each other with their beaks. For the Ruby-throats, the battle is a fight for their lives. People who feed Ruby-throats are amazed by the tiny birds' ferocity. Why are they so greedy and unwilling to share? There is plenty of food for everyone.

But the Ruby-throats' ancestral memory is of flowers. A single flower has only a bit of nectar, and once someone gets it, that flower is done. And so they do battle over the feeders.

People often stereotype hummingbirds as being aggressive, because they notice the fierce ones, amazed that such tiny jewels can be so ferocious. But a hummingbird rehabilitator who has cared for hundreds of hummingbirds says,

> To label all hummingbirds as mean and combative misses one of the most fundamental truths every rehabber comes to recognize: hummingbird dispositions are as varied and diverse as those of any domestic pet. Some are tough as nails, others

fragile; some show high intelligence and learn everything immediately, others take more time; some rush in and boldly take charge of every social situation, while others are fearful and shrink away from confrontation. And finally, some display childlike dependence, while others are fiercely self-reliant and can't wait to get away from their caretakers....

The youngest fledglings usually like one another a great deal, poke each other gently in the chest with their bills when sitting side by side on their perches, and snuggle close together when sleeping at night. But even at this tender age, a few antisocial firebrands refuse to coexist with other birds and prefer to throttle their cage mates ruthlessly. Such offenders can usually be cured of their aggressive tendencies by being paired with either an entirely nonconfrontational introvert who lets them assert their egomaniacal need for dominance or a self-possessed and more experienced veteran who won't put up with it.[32]

But (although some people on social media testify differently) in my experience the Anna's Hummingbirds are not combative like the Ruby-throats. They rarely fight or try to keep each other from feeding. Two Annas who meet at the feeder may share it peacefully, or may break out into a game of tag. In fact, I have seen hummingbirds perch next to each other at the same feeding port and take turns feeding.

And people describe the Ruby-throats as bold and fearless around humans. But my Annas are cautious around humans. An Anna may watch and study a human for days before approaching.

Of course, hummingbirds, like every other bird, have individual personalities, but there are overall species personalities too. I think that the difference between Ruby-throats and Annas has to do with

---

32 From *Fastest Things on Wings: Rescuing Hummingbirds in Hollywood*, by Terry Masear (p, 155, 149)

the fact Ruby-throats have to be bad-ass to go on such an epic migration. And they have to be aggressive to get enough food to fuel that migration. Annas don't have to migrate, so they aren't so desperate.

But still, flowers disappear in Bird Fall. And Anna's Hummingbirds spread to the Pacific Northwest only in the twentieth century when people started feeding hummingbirds and planted plants they like. The Annas here expect humans to feed them in Bird Fall and Bird Winter, when flowers are scarce. So here, too, Bird Fall is a season of hummingbirds.

The games of Bird Fall

The jays and I play peanut games year round, but Bird Fall is the best. This is because Bird Fall is caching season. In Bird Fall, they are storing food for the winter. They always want more peanuts so they can bury them in the ground. The more, the better.

In Bird Fall, the jays would play peanut games with me all day if I was willing. While working on the laptop on my deck, I can throw peanuts to jays.

Bird Fall is the time to introduce myself to the next generation of jays. Bird Summer is when other birds bring their fledglings to the feeders to feed them there, but the jays don't bring their youngsters to the deck until Bird Fall, after the youngsters know how to feed themselves and don't need anyone to put food into their mouths. When young birds can feed themselves, they are no longer called "fledglings," but "juveniles," or "juvies."

The Steller juvies are klutzes and can be comically clumsy in their landings.

They tend to have a rather raggedy look, in contrast to the sleek adults, because they are not yet good at preening themselves.

We start with the basic game: I throw a peanut onto the deck. The adult jays swoop down to grab it. The juvies sit in the willow tree and watch.

A juvie Steller's Jay vainly begs its parent for food. Molted feathers hang from its tail. Unlike the adult, the juvie doesn't know it should pull them out

Then sometimes a juvie arrives alone to the curly willow. I throw a peanut onto the deck, but instead of flying down, the juvie stays on the willow branch and yells "Ack ack ack!"

An adult Steller shows up right away. It sees the peanut, grabs it, and flies away, leaving the juvie peanut-less.

Why did the juvie call out? That caused it to lose the peanut.

But apparently the lesson was more important to the juvie than the peanut. The young Steller was asking the adults to come and show it what to do.

Sometimes when I call out 'Birdie!' and throw the peanut, a juvie flies straight to the willow tree, and aims its body to go for the peanut on the deck. And then an adult Steller arrives. The juvie sits back while the adult gets the peanut. All adults in the Steller flock seem to outrank all juvies.

And sometimes, when an older bird shows up, a juvie may start begging like a fledgling, quivering its wings and squawking. But the adult will refuse to feed it. Instead, (just as all the songbird parents do with their fledglings) the adult will demonstrate to the juvie what to do and expect the juvie to apply the lessons for itself.

With most songbirds, when a fledgling can feed itself and has basic survival skills, the parents are done teaching it. But there are exceptions. Crow youngsters spend several years with their parents before eventually going off on their own. They help take care of the next generation of youngsters, experience which probably will be valuable when they raise their own families.

I don't know if Steller's Jays do this or not. But from my observation of Steller's Jays, I think that some youngsters stay and some go, and its on a case-by-case basis.

Steller parents, like crow parents, demonstrate advanced food-gathering techniques and food-finding skills to the juvies who stay with the flock. And not just their own parents. If a juvie calls out for help, three or four adult jays may show up at once. All the adults seem to watch the juvies, parents don't watch just their own kids.

The Steller juvies are just beginning to learn about the world. I want the young Stellers to see the elders getting peanuts from me. I want them to learn that playing peanut games with the humans is a normal thing to do. And this happens in Bird Fall.

Time for concerts

Birds love music. They love the music of other birds. They love our human music, if we play the right kind of music for them.

But only during Bird Fall and Bird Winter, the non-breeding season. During breeding season, Bird Spring and Bird Summer, a bird closes its ears to all but its own kind. In Bird Spring, it is listening for songs of its own kind, and in Bird Summer, for fledgling calls of its own kind.

But after breeding season is over, the birds can finally listen to other birds. Songbirds can take time to enjoy each other singing, regardless of species.

Unfortunately, in Bird Fall, no one seems to have a lot of drive to sing. Everyone seems to want to listen to someone else do it. During the spring, the male birds were full of testosterone (masculine hormone). Testosterone creates the desire to sing. Not just the desire, but a drive to sing, a need to sing. Female songbirds have the equipment to sing, but with less testosterone, they sing much less than males. Female birds given testosterone will start singing, and in Bird Fall, perhaps the hormone balances change for some female birds.

But when breeding season is over, the male bird's testosterone goes down, and he doesn't feel the same strong need to sing. He may still sing, sometimes, but not with his former urgency. Now, if he sings, it's casual, leisurely, like some female songbirds sing. If he bothers to sing at all. But he wants to listen. We can see from their body language that, in Bird Fall and Bird Winter, the birds enjoy anyone's singing – not just that of their own species. Everyone seems to want someone else to sing. This time of year, birds seem to appreciate a good performance.

The Song Sparrows are the stars of Bird Fall, at least where I live. When a great Song Sparrow musician like Ludwig gives a concert, other Song Sparrows, and other birds too, assemble to listen. He will take a perch and unleash a bubbling flood of song. Not discrete phrases with pauses in between, like the Song Sparrow songs of Bird Spring, but a continuous warble, a bit like a House Finch, yet made up of Song Sparrow phrases. Not loud – *he's* not trying to drive away rivals or attract a mate – but not soft whisper song either. He's singing just to sing.

But singing takes a lot of energy. Each bird, it seems, would just as soon listen while someone else makes the effort, so he or she can just relax.

That's why Bird Fall and Bird Winter are the time of year to introduce the birds to human music.

The key to birdfriending is spending lots of time among the birds. I spend as much time as possible on the deck around the birdfeeders.

I don't have a television, because the birds are so much better entertainment. I work on the laptop outside, as weather permits, and I usually play music as I write, but the birds appear to utterly ignore my music until Bird Fall comes.

The Song Sparrows are not only great performers, but great music lovers

The Song Sparrows are the biggest music fans. They show up from all over, and don't listen from hidden places like many other birds. They take the best seats they can find, close to the music, arranging themselves like an audience at a concert. They cock their heads, dreamily close their eyes at the slow notes, jerk their heads this way and that at the lively fast notes. They preen, fluff up and puff up and blow themselves up like balloons.

One sunny winter day, I played a Vivaldi flute concerto that sent a lot of Song Sparrows into paroxysms. A few hours later, as I sat on the deck working on my laptop, I became aware of a faint, far-off warbling. It was soft, like bird baby babble, a cascade of warbles, trills, burbles, gurgles, and quotes, bubbling out without pauses or definite beginnings and endings.

The song was so soft that I thought it was far away, so I didn't expect to spot the singer. But I looked, and there was Ludwig, perched in the bamboo, just yards from me, at eye level, watching me.

When we made eye contact, he started singing a little faster, but no louder.

The magic music was quiet, like the private burbling of mates as they cuddle, like the murmurs parent birds make to their babies, like the soft babbling of babies making their first efforts to sing. Those sounds have to be soft, because the birds don't want to give away their location to predators. Whisper song is only for the family. A sound of intimacy.

His beak hardly moved, his throat hardly quivered. The song he wove was as quiet as baby subsong, but it showed his years of practice and sophistication.

Ludwig kept eye contact with me as he sang. He knew he was performing for an audience. After all, songbirds usually are. And it doesn't always have to be the same audience. After about forty minutes, Ludwig flew to the willow tree, where I got a picture of him. That photo is on the back cover of this book. To me, he looks proud of himself.

Song Sparrows are not the only birds who whisper song. I once heard a robin singing whisper song. By pure luck I was walking under a tree as that lovely soft burble come from a nearby branch. Mockingbirds, catbirds, and Bluejays are reported to sing whisper songs. Starlings often sing whisper songs in large groups, but that just sounds to us like a burbling chaos.

Steller's Jays love music with long sweeping notes.

The Steller's Jays are not considered singers, just mimickers. But every once in a while, in Bird Fall, a Steller's Jay will take a perch facing me, and, very softly, start to sing. Really sing. A waterfall of liquid notes, clicks, trills, whirrs, whines, and quotes from the songs of other songbirds. A performance worthy of a mockingbird, but so soft that it could hardly be heard more than ten feet away.

If the Steller can sing like that in whisper song, why doesn't it sing aloud? To me, it seems as though the Steller is quietly confessing its secret dreams. "I could have been one of the great songbirds, but I am too embarrassed to try..."

Of course birds don't think that way. But still, the whisper song seems meant to be intimate. And when offered to me, maybe it is intended to reciprocate for my musical offerings. After all, what better gift could a bird offer but his song?

Part Three

WHAT IT'S LIKE TO BE A BIRD

CHAPTER TEN

MADE OF AIR: BIRD BODIES

WHEN I WAS a little kid, like four years old, I decided to see if I could fly.

After all, if birds could do it, why couldn't I?

I didn't have wings, but I had a beach towel. I stretched it out like a pair of eagle wings, and flapped hard up and down. But I didn't even get an inch off the floor.

Maybe I needed a little altitude to get started? I climbed up to the top of the sofa, stood up like an eagle on the edge of a cliff, spread my terrycloth wings, waved them hard, and took off. And soared up to the ceiling!

Actually, no. I crashed down onto the floor. Luckily, the carpet was soft.

I wasn't completely surprised. A towel wasn't quite like a bird's wings. But I still had to try.

I didn't know then that people had been trying to fly for a long long time. Long before airplanes were invented, people tried to figure out ways to fly with their own power, like a bird.

Surely this flying machine will work?

But even if we could make wings that worked like bird wings, we still couldn't fly like birds. We are much too heavy.

It's not just us. It's all mammals.[33] A hamster and a sparrow are about the same size, but even if we could put sparrow wings on a hamster, the hamster couldn't fly, it would be too heavy. And if we held a hamster in one hand and a sparrow in the other, the hamster would feel substantial, but we would barely feel the sparrow except for its claws.

---

33 How about bats, you ask? Bats have a different flying technique that is good for catching insects in the air but doesn't allow them to travel long distances or do other things birds can do.

Birds are light. A little bird can land on a tiny plant stem that couldn't support our little finger, and it hardly bends.

And birds made a lot of compromises to become light enough to fly.

One thing they gave up is teeth. We could scarcely live without teeth, and neither could dogs or cats or horses.

But for birds, teeth would be too heavy. Birds' beaks are made from the same light material as our fingernails, called keratin, and a beak made of keratin can crack the outer hull of a seed. But that's not enough. Food has to be crushed before it can be digested. And birds eat hard foods like seeds and grains, which we need to cook or grind before we can eat them. But birds just swallow them. So how does a bird chew its food without teeth?

We chew our food first, but a bird chews its food *after* swallowing it. A bird chews its food inside its body. How? With rocks! Birds swallow tiny rocks. Birds swallow rocks?! The tiny rocks go into an organ called a gizzard. The strong muscles in the gizzard move around the tiny rocks to grind up the food before the food continues on to the stomach.

To stay light, birds don't get pregnant. A mother bird couldn't fly with babies growing inside her body. Instead, she lays eggs, and puts all the nutrients to feed the growing baby into the egg.

A bird's body not only has to be light, but streamlined. Anything causing wind resistance had to go. Legs have to be small enough to tuck against the body in flight. No external ears, just holes in the head. No external genitals, just an all-purpose hole called a cloaca (clo-AY-ca) for mating, laying eggs, and peeing/pooping.

In order to be lighter, birds shrank their internal organs, or even got rid of them when possible. For example, no bladder. Liquid is too heavy to carry around. Instead of making liquid urine, a bird concentrates its pee into a thick white stuff called uric acid, which it mixes with its poop to excrete together. The mixture is called guano. If we ever look at bird guano, most of it is white – that is the concentrated pee. Pee is super acidic; we know how a little pee can cause painful diaper rash. The concentrated pee in bird guano is so acidic that, over time, it can eat through paint and rust metal.

And a bird's lungs are proportionately half the size of our lungs. Yet a bird needs lots more oxygen than we do. A migrating bird may fly very high where the air is very thin. Plus they have to keep their own bodies warm in the freezing air. So they need a lot of oxygen.

So how does a bird manage to get enough oxygen with smaller lungs?

A bird breathes into its bones! A bird's bones are hollow. The hollow bones help to make a bird very light. In fact, a hummingbird's feathers weigh more than its bones. A bird has little air sacs throughout its body, like balloons, most of them inside the bones. This helps the bird get enough oxygen to fly.

Lungs like ours would not work for a bird. We breathe in, out, in, out. That means that oxygen is coming in only half the time. But, to fly, a bird needs oxygen nonstop. So when the bird breathes in, some of the air gets stored in the air sacs, and then when the bird breathes out, the oxygen from the air sacs gets pulled into its body. (Bagpipes use the same principle.) So, whether breathing in or out, a bird gets a continuous flow of oxygen into its body.

Hollow bones also enable a bird to sing nonstop without stopping to take a breath. Some birds can even sing while flying!

But a bird's hollow bones, and its small, delicate internal organs, make it very fragile. The air sacs can easily be clogged or damaged by air pollution. Many a pet bird has died from fumes from a self-cleaning oven or non-stick coating on pans. Coal miners used to bring a canary in a cage down into the underground mines with them, and if the canary suddenly died, the miners knew that there were poison gases in the mine, and they would leave the mine before the poison gas got them too. We use the phrase "canary in a coal mine" to mean someone who is the first to be affected by a problem, but who may not be the last.

On the edge of starvation

The life of a bird[34] is very expensive. Birds need a lot of energy to survive. A bird has to maintain a high body temperature – around 105 T or 40 C – and if it loses its body heat it will die. And wing-flapping burns energy like an Olympic runner.

A small songbird eats half its weight every day. What is half your weight? What if you had to eat that much food every day? A little bird who *doesn't* eat that much will starve. The birds with the most expensive lifestyle, the hummingbirds, consume up to eight times their own weight every day!

We mammals can store extra energy in the form of fat. A bear can store so much fat that it can go the whole winter without eating. But a bird can't save up energy for times when there is no food, because the heavier it gets, the harder it would be to fly, and if it can't fly, it's doomed.

So birds always live on the edge of starvation.

A bird eats only what it needs right now. A tiny bird picks up tiny seeds with its tiny beak for a few minutes, stops eating, flies off. It may look as though that bird doesn't eat much. But it burns off that energy quickly and has to eat again. Eat and burn, eat and burn.

When the small birds act hungry, especially in the winter, they are not kidding.

But a bird has a big problem every day: night. It can't look for food in the dark, so night means long hours without food. To prepare for night, a bird has to choose a spot sheltered from the wind. And then, from its last reserves of energy, the bird generates a pocket of heat, and fluffs up its feathers to hold the pocket of air next to its body. This helps the bird stay warm till morning.

But maybe one night, disaster strikes. A raccoon climbs the tree. In panic, the songbird jumps off its perch. But, unable to fly in the dark, it tumbles to the ground. In its blind effort to escape, it collides

---

34 A flying bird, at least. This doesn't necessarily apply to ostriches or turkeys.

with a tree. It flutters up the trunk, gropes its way to the lowest branch, and sits panting.

The songbird has escaped the raccoon. But it may be doomed anyway. It lost the pocket of air that was keeping it warm, and it has no more energy reserves to generate a new pocket of warm air. If it's not too cold and morning is not too far, and it can find food at the crack of dawn, the bird might make it. Maybe.

Larger birds eat less in proportion to their size than small birds. And they can eat more at one time. A Cooper's Hawk may eat "only" about one-eighth of its weight every day. So a larger bird won't be as desperately hungry as a chickadee.

Smaller birds use more energy, because smaller bodies lose heat faster, and it takes much more energy for a smaller bird to fly.

Wouldn't it be glorious to fly like a bird?

People often say "I wish I could fly like a bird." Wouldn't that be wonderful?

But before we ask our fairy godmother to grant us that wish, we first should figure out *what kind* of bird.

The birds we see soaring up in the sky, the eagles and hawks, the seagulls, the swifts, the ravens, make us yearn for the joy of flying.

If we want to fly for fun, we shouldn't be a songbird. Songbirds fly only when they have to, and keep flying to a minimum.

That's because that there two styles of flying: flapping and gliding.

The eagles and ravens and gulls glide through the air with out-stretched wings. They can stay up all day, because flying is little work for them. A gliding bird surfs on air currents, hardly moving its wings, except to steer. Some birds, like swifts, even sleep in the air.

But small birds have small wings, and small wings don't glide. Small wings flap. And every flap costs precious energy. So small birds can't afford to fly around for fun. A songbird saves energy by not flying unless it really has to. And when it does have to fly, it flies no farther than it has to. When a small bird has to cross the yard, it doesn't do it in one long flight, but in short hops from tree to tree or bush to bush. The chickadees further save energy by alternating flaps with short glides, *flap-flap-glide*, *flap-flap-glide*. It sinks with each glide. so its flight looks like a series of dips and rises.

And when a chickadee comes to a hand for food, it likes to travel no more than just one *flap-flap-glide* from the perch. And when a songbird has to escape from another creature, it flies only high enough to be well out of the animal's reach.

Taking off can be hard work if you are a large bird with big wings, like this swan.

So why don't small birds have long wings?

Long wings have one huge disadvantage: slow takeoff. A swan has a hard time getting up out of the water. An eagle has to flap pretty hard to lift off. A vulture can't even get in the air by itself – it has to wait for a rising column of warm air to carry it to the sky. An albatross has to run like a plane on a runway to get lift-off.

But a swan or an eagle rarely has to worry about predators, so slow takeoff is not a big problem for it.

Some small birds do have long wings: the swallows and swifts. These birds catch insects in the air, And for them, danger comes from the air. Falcons catch birds in flight. The swallow's long pointed wings make it maneuverable, so it can pursue flying insects and escape a falcon.

But for other songbirds, danger is a cat or a fox or a hawk or a mink, which might be lurking anywhere, waiting to pounce. So they need fast takeoff.

Nevertheless, on migration, birds flap, because they need to get to their destination as soon as possible. And when a big bird, like a goose, flaps, it is working even harder than a small bird.

So geese have a way to reduce the work of flying. Migrating geese usually fly in diagonal lines, sometimes connected into a V. This is because each bird flies in the wake in the air created by the bird in front of it, like a wake created in the water by a fast boat. Riding the wake, a goose need a lot less energy to travel. The front goose has to work hardest, but when it gets too tired, it drops to the back to fly in someone else's wake for a while. The geese take turns being front goose.

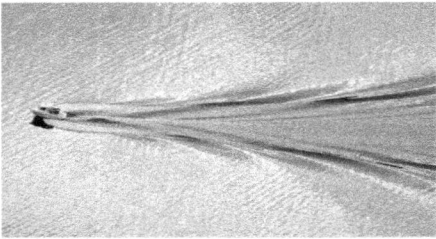

Taking off can be hard work if you are a large bird with big wings, like this swan.

Starlings use the air currents from each other's wings when they fly in huge synchronized shapeshifting flocks called murmurations. They ride on the air currents created by the pointed wings of their neighbors, and they may even communicate with each other in some way through these air currents.

Birds must have a sense that air is *something*, that the world is made of air, in part, and that the air is what connects things together. Trees, houses, they are all connected through air. A bird has to be aware of what the air is doing – what direction the wind is coming from, how fast it is blowing.

The air sacs in a bird's body may help it to monitor changes in air pressure, which would tell it something about the weather coming.

Birds have more air inside their bodies than any other kind of creature. Birds are not only creatures of the air, birds are *made* of air.[35] (At least in part.)

A murmuration of starlings. The birds turn in unity,
communicating through the air with their wings.

---

35   Credit to Sy Montgomery for the phrase "birds are made of air," which is a chapter title in her lovely book *Birdology: Adventures with a Pack of Hens, a Peck of Pigeons, Cantankerous Crows, Fierce Falcons, Hip Hop Parrots, Baby Hummingbirds, and one Murderously Big Living Dinosaur.*.

The birds' secret

Though birds are delicate, they have a superpower: feathers. For keeping warm, feathers work much better than fur. Fur is thick and heavy and would get in the way of flying. Feathers are light and streamlined, yet they hold in heat better than fur.

Plus, feathers are adjustable. When it's cold, a bird puffs out its feathers and traps a pocket of warm air around its body. The feathers form an airtight surface that holds the air pocket. As the temperature goes up or down, the bird can instantly adjust how much warm air is trapped by its feathers. It's like a magic coat that could change between a light sweater and a heavy overcoat at the speed of thought.

When it's cold, a bird needs to be constantly aware of the wind direction. A bird has to face into the wind, otherwise the wind may ruffle its feathers and cause the loss of its precious heat pockets. Observing their chickens do this, farmers used to fashion weathervanes in the traditional shape of a rooster and place them on top of their barns to show the direction the wind was blowing.

The superpower of songbirds

Songbirds are birds who sing. Or who could sing even if they don't.

"Songbird"[36] means a member of the passerine order, the "sparrow-shaped" birds. There are 23 bird orders, such as the ostrich order, the penguin order, the hummingbird order. Ducks, geese, and swans belong to the order of "goose-shaped" birds. Parrots, cockatoos, and budgerigars belong to the order of "parrot-shaped" birds. Herons, egrets, and pelicans belong to the order of "pelican-shaped" birds. Peacocks, pheasants, and turkeys belong to the order of "chicken-shaped" birds. And so on.

All our common backyard birds are songbirds except the woodpeckers, the doves, and the hummingbirds. Songbirds, or passerines, are defined by two characteristics. One is their feet. Each bird order

---

36 Rhymes with "canine" and "feline."

has its own kind of foot, designed for its way of life. Ducks have webbed feet, for the water. Eagles have talons to grab prey. Sandpiper feet are designed to run on sand. Woodpeckers have two toes in front and two in the back, designed to hang vertically on tree trunks.

Songbird feet have three toes in the front and one in the back, designed for grabbing and holding a perch. A songbird's feet lock when it crouches, so it won't fall off its perch even when it is sleeping. Even a windstorm can't blow a songbird out of the tree. So songbirds are also known as "perching birds." As ducks were designed for a life on the water and quail for a life in the grass, passerine birds are designed for life in the trees.

The other defining characteristic of songbirds is that they all have the vocal equipment and the special brain areas for creating and appreciating song, whether they use it or not.

Birdsong is often too fast and complex for us to hear. The only way we know the details is by recording the songs and slowing them down. How can songbirds produce such fast and subtle music? The secret is their voiceboxes.

Like all creatures that breathe, we have a windpipe that connects our noses to our lungs. At the top, where we breathe in, the windpipe is one tube, and farther down, the windpipe branches into two tubes, one for each lung.

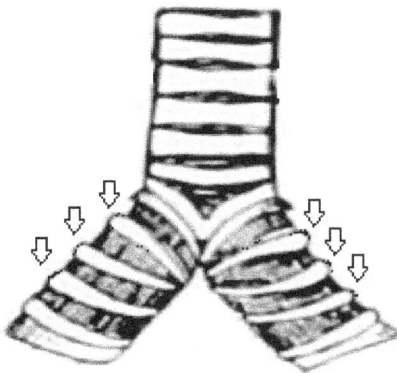

Bird syrinx

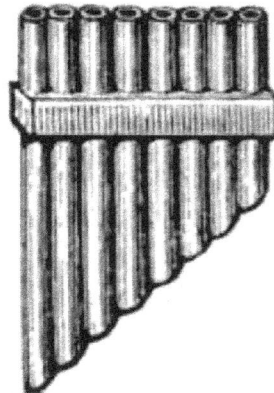

Panpipe

Our vocal cord is near the top of this tube. We call this our voicebox, or larynx.

Birds' vocal cords are located in a different place. They are in the branched part of the windpipe. Two vocal cords, one for each branch. Each vocal cord has a slightly different quality in its notes.

Together, this double voicebox is called a syrinx *(suh-RINKS)*, from a Greek word meaning panpipe – a musical instrument consisting of multiple small pipes that each produces a different pitch.

A human singer sings a melody by changing the notes coming from their voicebox. A panpipe player plays a melody by switching back and forth between one pipe and another. A bird can do both of those things – at the same time! A bird can switch back and forth between the two sides of the syrinx, each side singing a different note.

And each voicebox can change notes and effects much more quickly than a human singer can. We humans have a muscle-like ring of tissue around our voiceboxes that changes the notes we sing, and the way our voices sound. A bird has not one but three rings of muscle around each of its voiceboxes –totalling six control rings.

Not all "songbirds" even sing, but they still have those song brain areas. And some songbirds, like crows, have repurposed their song brains to communicate in other complex ways.

More bird superpowers

Some birds have special superpowers of their very own. The most superpowered birds of all are without doubt the hummingbirds.

Hummingbirds live at super-speed. Their hearts beat at 60 times a second. They can flap their wings up to 200 times per second, They can fly forward and backward, up, down, and sideways. They can hover in one spot, and move with perfect accuracy from blossom to blossom.

Woodpeckers are another superpowered bird. In most ways, woodpeckers are as delicate and fragile as other birds. Yet in one way, woodpeckers are the strongest and toughest creatures on Earth.

A woodpecker smashes its head into hard wood, with a force that would destroy a human's brain, break our neck and pop our eyeballs from their sockets. And the woodpecker doesn't smash once, but over and over and over – up to 16 times *per second*, twice as fast as a submachine gun! Just one second of that would turn the brain of any other creature to jelly. How does the woodpecker do it?

The woodpecker's skull is lined with sponges – thick spongy bone – that protect the brain from jolts, like styrofoam protects an object in a package, but way stronger than styrofoam. The woodpecker also has thick neck muscles that spread out the force of the blows so it doesn't break its neck. And a third inner eyelid that prevents its eyeballs from popping out. And it has slit-like nostrils covered with fine, wiry feathers to keep it from inhaling sawdust.[37]

The little beak is a big clue

Every kind of bird has its own kind of beak, and just looking at the beak, we can tell what the bird eats. An eagle has a hooked beak designed for ripping flesh. A duck has a flat wide beak designed for straining food from the mud at the bottom of a pond. A heron has a beak good for stabbing frogs and fish.

The songbirds in our backyards eat seeds or insects or both, so their beaks are designed for that. But each bird has a different specialty, so the shape of their beaks differs.

The world is full of delicious insects. Buzzing in the air, hiding in tree bark, burrowing in the grasses, lurking under dead leaves and crawling on plant stems. Different insects have different hiding places, and different beaks are designed to get them. Some beaks can probe deeply into tree bark, while other beaks can remove tiny insects from the underside of leaves, like a pair of teensy tweezers.

The shape of each songbird's beak is a trade off between

---

37   The texture of those protective face feathers – downy or hairy – give the Downy Woodpecker and Hairy Woodpecker their names.

seed-cracking and insect-probing. The broader and thicker the beak, the better for cracking seeds. And the worse for catching insects. The more slender and pointy the beak, the better for digging out insects, and the worse for cracking seeds.

Cardinals and grosbeaks have huge beaks and can crack seeds too big for most birds. But that kind of beak isn't much use for prying an insect out of tree bark. Wrens have long pointy beaks, good for getting insects from tiny spaces, but hopeless for cracking even the smallest seed.

A sparrow's beak is in between. A sparrow can crack some seeds and get some kinds of insects, but isn't a champion at either one.

A finch's beak is designed for cracking seeds, but smaller ones. So finch and cardinal don't compete. A starling jams its beak into the dirt and pries it open, exposing insects hiding in the soil. A crossbill has a unique beak designed to pry open pine and fir cones and get the seeds inside, a food no other bird can get.

A wren has a long pointy beak for catching insects. A grosbeak has a big beak for cracking big seeds. A crossbill has a unique beak for twisting seeds out of pine cones.

Aliens on the same planet

Birds' bodies seem so different from ours. If we were visiting another planet, the inhabitants might seem as different from us as birds do.

And yet, we have much in common with the birds. In some ways we have more in common with birds than with our fellow mammals. We'll talk about that in the next chapters.

CHAPTER ELEVEN

SEEING THE WORLD: BIRD SENSES

SO YOU'RE WALKING through the woods with your dog. "Hey, pup, look at this pretty flower!"

Dog goes, "Huh, a flower, who cares? Hey, smell this great raccoon poop!"

Poop is fascinating stuff – to a dog. Just by sniffing the poop, he knows that a raccoon made it. His nose tells him the raccoon was female, what she's been eating, how long ago she made the poop, and how healthy she is, and if she is pregnant or nursing babies. All this from a careful smelling of poop.

And pee is full of information, for a dog. When a dog marks a tree with his urine, he is telling every other dog who passes by, "I was here." That is why a dog will stop and sniff a place where other dogs have peed. The fire hydrant is, for the dog, like a neighborhood newsletter.

Many kinds of mammals use pee to outline the boundaries of their territories. Mice divide up a human house into territories and mark the territorial boundaries with pee. They put up signs that say "private property," but the signs can't be seen with the eyes – they are meant to be smelled with the nose.

The noses of most mammals are way more sensitive than ours. A dog knows if his master has petted another dog, and even who that dog is. A dog's nose can detect cancer earlier than medical tests. Dogs can tell by smell when a human is about to have an epileptic seizure.

A dog riding in a car likes to put her head out the window, not to watch the things the car is passing, but to smell all the fascinating smells carried by the wind. A dog's nose is thousands of times more sensitive than ours. And besides that, a dog's brain can process the information from the nose much better than our brains can.

To us, smells blend together into combination scents, so perfume makers blend different scents to make new perfumes, and chefs blend different spices to create new flavors. But when a dog smells a combination of smells, the dog perceives each smell separately. That's why it doesn't work to try to fool a drug-sniffing dog by by covering a smell with other smells. It's like if we were told to find a certain person in a group photo. It wouldn't matter if other people were in the photo.

On the other hand, show a dog a group photograph and tell him to pick out a person he knows. Easy for us, because when we look at a picture, we can see all the separate details. But for a dog, the picture is a single image, a complicated shape, like a combination smell seems like a single smell to us. It's hard for a dog to separate out the individual elements of a picture if none of them is moving. (But anyway, how can you identify someone if you can't smell them?)

Dogs and humans live in different worlds. Dogs live in a world of smells. We live in a world of sight.

When we talk about perceiving, we use language of sight. We say "I see what you mean" and talk about "seeing from someone else's point of view."

If dogs used words, they would probably say "I smell what you mean" and talk about "smelling from someone else's point of sniff."

Most animals would probably agree with the dogs that the world is made out of smells. But not all of them would say that. A bat, who navigates by bouncing sound waves off things, might say the world is made up of sound. A snail, with no eyes or ears at all, might say the world is made up of taste. A mosquito, searching for us by following trails of carbon dioxide we exhale, might say the world is made up of different gases in the air. A star-nosed mole, navigating by touch with the end of its nose, might say the world is made of the different textures of dirt. And what might a starfish say? Or an ant?

Only a few animals, other than birds, would agree with us that our eyes are the main thing that show us the world. Our fellow primates, the monkeys and apes, would vote with us that the world is made up of things we see. And butterflies and bees and some other insects. And the birds.

So why have we been talking about all these other animals, instead of birds?

Because we should realize how remarkable it is that the birds' senses are so much like ours. Birds live world of sight, like we do. When looking around at the world, we and the birds see more or less the same thing. And it's easier to communicate with someone who sees the world the way we do.

Actually, birds see better than we do, in every way. They see farther than we do. They see tinier things than we do. They see more details than we do. They see more colors than we do. They can see faster than we do.

In fact, birds see better than any creature on Earth.

Birds can see much farther than anyone else. Eagles and hawks can see the farthest of all. If you were an eagle, you could read the words on this page from fifty feet up in the air (if you were an eagle who could read). If you were an eagle, you could see a mouse moving in the grass from so high up that a human couldn't see you at all. Birds have the sharpest vision of any animal, and eagles the sharpest vision of all birds, giving them the best vision of any creature on Earth.

Birds see more detail than we can. Birds have a lot more light-catching cells in their eyes than we do, so much more light enters their eyes, making the world brighter and crisper and sharper to them. More light means clearer focus, both close up and far away, and it means that colors look more intense to the birds, and birds can perceive finer shades of colors than we can, especially green.

Birds can see much tinier things than we can. A sparrow can see seeds in the dirt that would be practically invisible to a human. A kinglet can see insects that a human would need a microscope to see. A robin searches for earthworms by looking for tiny movements in the dirt between the grass stems.

Birds see faster than we do. A movie in a theater would not look like continuous action to a bird; the bird would see a series of separate pictures. In fact, the movie projection speed (24 frames per second) is much slower than the wingbeat of a hummingbird (50 to 80 flaps per second) so it should be no surprise that hummingbird vision is the fastest of all.

Birds can see photographs as clearly as we can. And birds can recognize things and people they know in a photograph. But is that a surprise? Of course a bird can make sense out of pictures. Birds have to be able to resolve two-dimensional images. From up in the sky, the ground below looks like a flat picture. And a migratory bird can remember a landscape after flying over it once.

Birds have a wider range of vision than we do, since their eyes are on the sides of their heads. So they see all around them. And the direction of up/down is as important in a bird's brain as left/right and forward/back; a bird's world is three-dimensional in a way that ours is not. (But we do have one slight advantage over animals with eyes on the sides of their heads: we are better able to tell how far something is. A bird can judge the distance of an insect right in front of it, but looking at a tree yards away, we could make a better estimate of how far it is.)

And many birds can see more colors than we can. The next color on the rainbow after violet is called "ultraviolet," which means "beyond violet." To us, it is invisible, but to birds, bees, and butter-flies, ultraviolet is super eye-catching.

Many birds have ultraviolet markings in their plumage. In fact, among some birds, male and female look alike to us, but the males have ultraviolet markings that we can't see and the birds can.

Birds' plumages may have more brilliant and varied colors than we humans realize. To us, feathers colored ultraviolet look white. But not an ordinary white – rather, a bright white that glows in the sunlight. And, the way red and yellow can make orange, ultraviolet can mix with other colors to create new colors. To us, a color blended with ultraviolet looks fluorescent or day-glo. But to a creature who sees ultraviolet, the blend may make a whole new color. The red on a male Downy Woodpecker's head has a startling glow when the sun hits it right. To other Downies, that may be a color we can't imagine.

A lot of flowers "advertise" with ultraviolet colors, since hummingbirds, bees, and butterflies are attracted to ultraviolet. Urine looks yellow to us, but it's really yellow-ultraviolet. Birds of prey can track rodents by the ultraviolet glow from drops of urine they leave behind. A human friend (male) told me that he was peeing outdoors, and a hummingbird came up and tried to poke its beak where the pee was coming out. My friend tried to wave the hummingbird away, but the hummingbird dodged his hand and kept going after the stream of pee. (My friend assured me that it didn't get any.)

Even though we can't see the color ultraviolet and it just looks white to us, we can tell the difference between the ordinary white on the Bluejay's face and the ultraviolet on its wingtips and tailtips, because the ultraviolet markings glow in the sunlight.

A keeper of a goshawk mused:

The world she lives in is not mine. Life is faster for her; time runs slower. Her eyes can follow the wingbeats of a bee as easily as ours follow the wingbeats of a bird. What is she seeing? I wonder, and my brain does backflips trying to imagine it, because I can't... This hawk can see colours I can't, right into the ultraviolet spectrum. She can see polarized light too, watch thermals of warm air rise, roil, and spill into clouds, and trace, too, the magnetic lines of force that stretch across the earth. The light falling into her deep black pupils is registered with such frightening precision that she can see with fierce clarity things I can't possibly resolve from the generalized blur. The claws on the toes of the house martins overhead. The veins on the wings of the white butterfly... I'm standing there, my sorry human eyes overwhelmed by light and detail, while the hawk watches everything with the greedy intensity of a child filling in a colouring book.[38]

A creature with a super-powered sense needs to handle the data coming in through that sense. Dogs developed brain power to process the information coming in via the nose, and birds developed the brain power to handle the information coming through the eyes. Much of a bird's brain is devoted to interpreting what it sees. In a sense, birds think through their eyes.

Birds not only see better than we do, but (as we will talk about more) they are more observant than we are, and they remember what they see far better than we do. Even things they see only once. A migrating bird can remember its entire migration route after flying it once. A jay can remember a caching location that it visited only once, months before, and go right to the exact spot, not an inch off. And it remembers not just one caching spot, but thousands.

So it should be no surprise that birds can tell humans apart and can recognize and remember individual humans. That is why birds can have friendships with special humans they know.

---

38 From *H Is for Hawk*, by Helen MacDonald (p 48).

Sense of hearing

Second to sight, we live in a world of sound. And so do the birds. And communicate between us mainly happens through sound (even more so before the invention of writing). The same with birds (as we discussed in Chapter Three). So how does the birds' hearing compare to ours? There doesn't seem to be much scientific research on birds' sense of hearing. But, based on how far they can hear my voice and other birds, I think the acuity of birds' hearing (their ability to hear sounds that are quiet or far away) is about the same as ours.[39] Woodpeckers locate insects in dead trees by listening for them, and robins may use their sense of hearing in addition to sight to locate earthworms underground – but a human with undamaged hearing could do the same thing. (Most humans' hearing is damaged in this noisy modern world.)

The range of birds' hearing is more limited than ours, because birds' small eardrums can't hear pitches that are too low. How low is too low? That varies by the size of the bird, but small birds can't hear musical notes lower than around G above middle C. (They can hear low-pitched *sounds*, but I don't think they hear them as music.)

But in one way birds hear much better than humans: birds hear *faster* than we do. Birds can hear details that we can't. A birdsong lasting one second may sound to us like only a couple of notes. But if we record it and slow it down, we may discover features too fast and fine for our human ears and brains to catch – grace notes, overtones, microtone shadings, trills, and other ornaments. Female songbirds can hear those features and prefer males who sing more detailed and varied songs. (Though male birds do most of the singing, females can sing too; female birds don't sing as much because they don't have as much testosterone, which gives a bird the drive to sing.) Songbirds have special areas in their brains that not only enable them to create birdsong, but to hear and appreciate the song of other birds (even other species).

---

39 Other than owls, who hear so well they can catch a mouse in the dark by sound alone.

Sense of touch and body sense

When we think of the sense of touch, we think of our fingertips. Our fingertips can tell us a lot. Just by touching something, we can tell if it is metal or cloth, honey or ice, plastic or fur. We can tell a spoon from a pencil or shoe from a glove or a rock from a stick just by feeling it with our hands.

But birds don't have hands. A bird's main organ of touch is its beak.

How can that be? Beaks are hard. They are made from keratin, the same stuff as our fingernails, a horse's hoof or a cow's horn. Keratin can't feel… can it?

Yes. In fact, a bird's beak is much *more* sensitive than our fingertips. Though a bird's beak is hard and tough, it is full of nerves.

Birds who have to find food in muddy ponds – dabbling ducks – can't see their food at all. To find food they have to feel around, using the nerves along the edges of their beaks. When a duck sticks its head in the water and its butt in the air, it is combing the mud for food.

Feeling around in a drawer, we could identify paper clips, pens, erasers and other objects purely by touching them. But ducks can identify much tinier things. Their beaks are so sensitive that they can tell the difference between bits of food and the sand, grit, and dirt mixed with the food, by feeling with their beaks, and also their sensitive tongues.

Feathers are part of a bird's sense of touch as well. How? Feathers don't have feeling… do they? Well, if just one hair on our head is moved, we can feel it, because there are nerves around the base of each of our hairs. A stiff hair, like a cat's whisker, is even more sensitive, and feathers are stiff that way. A bird can feel the smallest shift in the breeze through its feathers.

When flying through the air, a bird needs to keep track of what the air is doing. A hawk can hover motionlessly above the ground atop a column of warm air. A weary seabird, blown about by a storm, can find a ship in the middle of the ocean and take refuge there, because even if the ship is invisible in the fog, it causes tiny changes in air pressure, which the bird can detect.

Birds are so light that for them, a current of air is a strong force. The air sacs in a bird's body may help it to monitor changes in air pressure, telling the bird something about coming weather changes.

A bird has to be aware of the direction the wind is coming from and how fast it is blowing. Not only when it is flying, but perched, because a gust from behind could ruffle the bird's feathers. If the bird loses the precious air pockets under its feathers that are keeping it warm, it could die. So a bird pays attention to what its feathers are telling it.

For a bird, air is *something*. For a bird, air connects everything together. I was swimming in a river one day, playing with the currents, feeling how they became stronger where the river narrowed and gentler where the river widened, letting the current carry me downstream, then swimming back upstream against the current, and I got it. The saying that a fish is unaware of the water is a good metaphor, but I don't think it is true. I think the fish are aware of water, just as the birds are surely constantly aware of the moods and movements of the air.

Taste and smell

Scientists argue about whether most birds can even smell at all. Vultures can smell decaying carcasses, and pigeons may use smells in the air to guide them over long distances. But for most birds, sense of smell may not be that important.

What about sense of taste? Birds don't have many taste buds. But hummingbirds taste the sweetness of nectar. Do fruit-eating birds taste the sweetness of fruit? Maybe, but some also eat tasteless berries like hawthorn, even awful-tasting (and toxic to humans) berries like holly. So it's hard to know.

On the other other hand (or the other wing?) birds must have some sense of taste, because there are some butterflies whose taste birds can't stand, and other butterflies who *look like* the bad-tasting butterflies, so the birds leave them alone.

But birds don't seem to taste mold or rancidity in bird seed, even though moldy food can make them sick. So if we feed them, we have to make sure food is fresh.

Magnetic sense

Birds have one sense that we don't have at all – a magnetic sense. This is an internal compass that tells them the directions. We don't know if all birds have this sense, but migratory birds depend on it, along with the sun and stars, to keep them going in the right direction.

Magnetic sense – what must that feel like? I imagine that it feels like an internal sense of orientation. Maybe like telling the direction a sound is coming from.

The birds don't tell us what it feels like, though. They just continue to orient their migrations the way they have done for millions of years.

Creatures of the light

We, like the birds, live in a world of sight. We, like the birds, are creatures of the day. For us, as for the birds, the world is made of light. The world is made of what we see.

In fact, when a bird can't see, its brain shuts down. So darkness calms a bird. If a bird is injured or panicking, putting it in the dark can help calm it down. A falconer puts a hood over a falcon's head to keep it calm. When I was a child, we had a trick with our pet chickens. We could carefully place a chicken's head under its wing, and if we did it right, so she didn't see any light, the chicken would fall into a sort of trance. We could lay the chicken down on its side, and she would just stay that way for minutes, looking like a headless ball of chicken fluff. For a bird, the world is made of seeing. So the world goes away when the bird can't see.

The world comes back when the light returns. The birds greet the return of light to the skies with the dawn chorus, filling the world with their music, because the return of light is the return of the world itself.

We can celebrate the dawn together.

CHAPTER TWELVE

ANCESTRAL MEMORY: BIRD INSTINCTS

A KILLDEER MOM is leading her fluffy little chicks along the banks of a pond, teaching them how to find food in the sand and mud.

Suddenly, she sees a dog sniffing the ground, coming in their direction.

She doesn't have to worry about herself. She can fly away if she has to. But her chicks can't.

So she gives a quick call that means; "Freeze! And don't follow me!" Instantly, the chicks become motionless, invisible among the rocks and pebbles. Then killdeer mom gives a loud cry and runs in front of the dog, dragging her wing like it's broken. The dog takes off after her. She runs away. Somehow she manages to keep just ahead of him. Farther and farther they chase. Suddenly, killdeer mom takes off into the air, leaving the dog panting. The killdeer flies in a wide circle and returns to her chicks.

Dogs fall for this like a ton of bricks. I've seen it. Is killdeer mom smart, or what?

She didn't figure out the trick herself. She was born knowing it. Just as her chicks were born knowing what to do when she made the "freeze" call.

Killdeer (named for their call) nest on the ground, and the ground is a dangerous place. Although killdeer can camouflage themselves well, a predator could find them by chance. Sometime, a long time ago, a killdeer hit on the idea of this trick. It worked, and as a result, that killdeer's chicks survived. And they inherited knowledge of the trick. Maybe they did it just a little bit at first, but more killdeer who knew the trick survived than killdeer who didn't know it. After generations and eons, killdeer moms were born knowing this trick.

Now the trick is killdeer ancestral knowledge, or "instinct."

Another shorebird, the plover, came up with a different idea to deceive predators. A shorebird can see danger approaching when it is still far away, so when the plover sees a predator, still far off, it will move to a fake nest site and pretending to be brooding eggs or chicks there. When the predator gets close, the bird runs off, and while the predator is sniffing around looking for the fake nest, the real plover and her chicks get away.

The killdeer, like the plover, doesn't have to figure out its trick; it remembers. Even if it never did such a trick before, even if no one taught it the trick, even if it never saw anyone else do the trick, the bird remembers how to do it.

A bird's memory doesn't stop with what it has personally learned in its life.

A bird is born with its ancestors' memory. Not every detail of every ancestor's life, but the things that have worked for that species over the years.

Every species – animal or plant – tries out different things, through different members. Some individuals try one thing and some try another. Some individuals are born with some characteristics and some with other characteristics. The species learns by trial and error, and when something works, it is passed on to future generations.

A bird depends on ancestral memory because it doesn't have time to learn everything it needs to know. It has to be ready to raise a family of its own when it is only a year old, and that's not nearly enough time to learn it all from scratch.

Remembering through ancestral eyes

A young kiskadee reacts with terror when shown a stick painted in bands of black, red, and yellow – the colors of the deadly coral snake. The kiskadee can't learn this from experience. If the kiskadee wasn't born with the memory of those colors, it might not live long enough to learn about it.

A parrot keeper describes how her bird reacted to his first sight of a pair of owls:

> … he became terribly distressed, squawking and crying, "Wanna go back… wanna go back!" I rushed to him and asked, "What's wrong, Alex? What's wrong?" I looked out the window and quickly realized what alarmed him. A pair of western screech owls were building a nest in the roof over the patio. They apparently struck terror into poor Alex, even though he had never seen an owl in his entire life. I tried to calm him, with little success. I pulled the drapes, so he could no longer see the owls. Still no use. "Wanna go back… wanna go back!"

...[E]ven though they were outside the house and he was safely inside, he was still terrified.... And I could not calm him.[40]

I have seen domesticated white doves – after thousands of years of breeding by humans – flinch and duck when a hawk briefly appears on a television screen. And the keeper of a pet starling described her bird's first sight of a Cooper's Hawk:

One day, Carmen was hanging out in her aviary on a branch by the window. All of a sudden, a Cooper's hawk perched briefly on the big camellia tree just outside.... [S]he let out a shriek I didn't know she was capable of and hurled herself across the room and onto my shoulder, where she spent the next fifteen minutes panting and... shivering.... Here was a feral intelligence ... evolved and wild knowing [that] runs through blood, heart, and imagination – in birds, in each of us.[41]

A scientist did an experiment with baby geese. He made a cutout of wood, and passed it over the heads of the young geese. When he flew it in one direction, it looked like a bird with a long neck and a short tail, and in the other direction, it looked like a bird with a short neck and a long tail. When the scientist flew it like a long-necked bird, young geese ignored it, but when he flew it like a long-tailed bird, the geese reacted with terror.[42]

Why? The long-necked, short-tailed shape resembled a flying goose, while the short-necked, long-tailed shape resembled a goshawk

---

40   From *Alex and Me*, by Irene Pepperberg, p. 155-6.

41   From *Mozart's Starling*, by Lyanda Lynn Haupt, p. 207.

42   Schleidt, Wolfgang; Shalter, Michael D.; Moura-Neto, Humberto (2011). "The hawk/goose story: The classical ethological experiments of Lorenz and Tinbergen, revisited." Journal of Comparative Psychology. 125 (2): 121–133.

(goose-hawk). For a young bird, instinctive terror at the shape of a predator can save its life.

Ancestral memory isn't only about scary things. Birds recognize the food their ancestors ate: pelicans recognize fish, parrots recognize fruit, swallows recognize flying insects. (In fact, swallows don't recognize insects as food when they are not flying.) The bee-eater of Africa not only recognizes bees and wasps as its food, but it knows how to hit and rub a bee on a branch to make it expel the venom in its sting.

The keeper of a goshawk (a bird of prey) saw her bird looking intently at a book that had been left open on the living room floor. The keeper looked to see what the hawk was looking at, and on the page was a pen-and-ink drawing of some partridges.

> Intrigued, I picked up the book and held it in front of her. She kept her eyes fixed on the picture, even when I moved the book about in the air. No way, I thought. The drawing was in ink; it was stylized and sparse; it caught the feel and form of partridges, but there was no color or detail to it, I flipped through the book, showing her other drawings: finches, seabirds, thrushes. She ignored them all. Then I showed her a drawing of a pheasant. Her black pupils dilated; she leaned forward and stared down her beak at it. I was amazed... Something deep in her brain saw these sparse inked curves as fitting the category gamebirds. [43]

Birds remember the environments their ancestors lived in. Some birds remember tree canopies, others remember meadows, others remember seashores or rocky cliffs. And they are attracted to environments that remind them of what they remember. A Brewer's Blackbird doesn't *believe* that parked cars actually *are* a herd of buffalo, but the parking lot resembles the ancestral picture. And as generations of

---

43   From *H Is For Hawk* by Helen MacDonald, p. 117.

Brewer's Blackbirds grow up in parking lots, their memories may start to include cars as well.

In one experiment, some scientists taught pigeons to peck at a picture of a tree. When pictures of other trees came up, the pigeons pecked at those too, showing that, even though they were born and raised in a lab and had never seen a real tree, they recognized "trees" as a category. And when a picture of a leaf came up, the pigeons chose that picture as well. The pigeons not only remembered trees, but remembered that leaves are part of trees.

Ancestral guidance

Birds inherit not only memories of things their ancestors saw. They also remember the techniques their ancestors developed for their way of life.

For example, every bird is born knowing what kind of nest to make. The robin knows how to make its cup nest of sticks and mud on a tree branch. The hummingbird knows how to weave a nest of lichens and spiderwebs. The bushtits know how to weave a nest suspended in the fir needles. The bluebird knows to look for a hole on the side of a dead tree with a cozy compartment inside, while the swift knows to look for a hollow tree with an open top, fly down into it and attach its nest to an inside wall. The Bank Swallow knows how to dig a hole in a riverbank, while in the nearby cattails, the Red-winged Blackbird knows how to weave a basket of grasses and mosses. And out in the desert, an Elf Owl knows how to make a nest inside a cactus.

If the normal place for its nest is not available, a bird will look for something that reminds it of the kind of place it remembers. If broken-top tree snags are in short supply, a Chimney Swift finds a chimney to be close enough.[44] If a Cliff Swallow can't find a rock outcropping to shield its mud nest from the rain, the eaves of a house

---

44   In fact, as I write this, I can hear a nest of baby Vaux's Swifts in my own chimney.

roof will do. If a bluebird can't find a vacant hole in a hollow tree, it can use a birdhouse provided by a human.

Every bird is born knowing how to make its own kind of nest. It doesn't need to see another bird demonstrate it. It doesn't shop around looking for ideas from other birds and wondering what might work. Scientists call such inborn ancestral knowledge "instinct," and First Nations peoples like the Haudenosaunee call this knowledge "the original instructions" given by the Creator.

But ancestral memory is only a starting point. Skills still have to be learned.

A bird has an instinct to build a nest, but building a nest, with no hands, only a beak as a tool, is not easy. The skill of nest-building develops over years of experience. First-time nesters may do clumsy jobs. Their nests may fall apart, or be too easy for predators to find.

A bird of prey has an instinct to hunt, but actually catching prey is not easy. It can take years to learn the skills and strategies of hunting, and many birds of prey starve to death before they can become good hunters.

A songbird is born with the instinct to learn songs, but not with the knowledge of the songs themselves – the same way as a human baby is born with the instinct to learn language, but not with the knowledge of the language itself. To talk when she grows up, a human baby has to hear people talking, and to sing when he grows up, a baby songbird has hear other birds of his kind singing.

A migratory bird knows by instinct *when* to leave, and the general direction to go. But she doesn't know exactly *where* to go, or the route to take. If the knowledge of the route and destination were inborn, then all birds of the same species would take the same route and head for the same place, and they would use up all the food in those places, while missing other places with food. So the birds have to spread out along different routes and go to different destinations, which means they have to learn where to go.

To Indigenous peoples of North America and elsewhere, a species is like a person. When an Indigenous hunter kills a deer, traditionally he apologizes to it and thanks it—not the individual deer, but the Deer Spirit, for offering one of its bodies to help feed the people. The salmon ceremonies honor not individual salmon but the Salmon Spirit for helping the people (and other animals, like bears) to survive. The species will remember if it was treated with respect or not.

Each species has its own intelligence. A species tries out different ideas, and finds out what works, and gathers experience through its many bodies, and develops its own strategies for survival, and negotiates its relationship with other species.

The more we know about the instincts of each kind of bird, the better we can understand birds who belong to that species, and the better we can communicate with them in ways that make sense to them.

Instinct and us

Some people think that instinctual creatures are dumb. A baby gull instinctively pecks at a red spot on its father's beak to make him regurgitate food, but it will peck at any red spot put in front of it, even a red spot painted on a stick! The baby gull never stops to think how dumb that is.

Sometimes a male bird may attack his reflection in a window. He is reacting instinctively to the sight of another male bird of his kind on his territory. He tries to drive out the rival, but instead of fleeing, the reflection attacks him back. The bird may get obsessed and fight with his reflection all day, day after day, never making his nest or having babies. How could a bird be so dumb?

A junco father feeding his cowbird baby on my doorstep.

And how about the junco pair dumb enough raise a big cowbird baby?[45] Shouldn't they have figured out something was wrong before following their instinct to give food to the biggest mouth and letting their own babies starve? How could they be so dumb?

Because of things like this, some people equate "instinct" with "stupidity." Some people even say that instinct is basically a computer program and that instinctual creatures are like robots, totally unconscious of what they are doing.

But we should be able to understand how birds feel when they are following instinct, because we humans have instincts too.

For example, we humans have an instinct for "cute."

When something is "cute," that means that it triggers our instinctive reaction to babies.

The more an animal resembles a baby, the cuter it seems to us. Koalas, with their round bodies and stubby arms and legs, are cuter than anteaters. Raccoons, with their wide flat faces, are cuter than alligators. Deer, with their big eyes, are cuter than rats.

---

45   See Chapter Seven.

Cartoon animals are designed to remind us of human babies.
Compare this cartoon bluebird to a real bluebird.

The cuteness instinct makes us pay attention to babies. It's a lot of work to take care of a baby, but, fortunately we have an instinct to take care of and protect a baby we see. It doesn't even have to be a human baby, it could be a puppy or a duckling. If we can be smitten by a kitten, we should understand the junco who reacts to a cowbird like its own baby.

We, like birds, are born with ancestral memory. As soon as we are born, we remember how to breathe and how to eat. As soon as our eyes start to focus, we remember what a face is. We understand the smile, the hugs, the loving tone of voice. We know how to cry, to communicate when we have a problem. As soon as we hear people talking, we try to imitate those sounds.

Instinct leads us to crawl, then to walk. If we trip and fall, we know by instinct to put out our arms to keep from landing on our face. If something heads for our eyes, we know by instinct to close them. We have an instinctual fear the birds don't have, the fear of falling. No one teaches us those things. Like all species, we inherit the experience of countless generations before us.

Our ancestral memories echo through our lives.

Once upon a time, we humans hunted animals for food. We chased them and aimed things at them – rocks, spears, arrows, bullets. We practiced the skills of chasing and aiming through games and sports. Today, almost every sport – basketball, golf, soccer, darts, ping-pong, bowling, tennis, baseball, and even video games – involves chasing and aiming. We have an instinct to chase for the same reason cats do. Practicing instincts is fun.

Once upon a time, we searched the fields and forests for edible plants and other wild goodies. Today, word search games and hidden pictures let us use our instinct to search. And so do shopping and looking for unexpected bargains or serendipitous finds.

Once upon a time, children searched for birds' nests hidden in the grass and stole their eggs for dinner. (Yes, we humans were nest predators too.) Today, that ancestral memory comes through Easter egg hunts.

But we don't all share one single ancestral memory. Different birds of the same kind living in different places – one group in a forest, one group in a grassland, one group in a marsh – will learn different things. We humans have lived all over the world, and within our species memory are many different currents, each with its own ancestral memories, traumas and joys. Our ancestors' experiences whisper in the background of our awareness.

Chasing and aiming are fun, but nowadays we could survive perfectly well without them. But our deeper instincts are much more powerful, because the survival of our species still depends on them.

One of our deepest instincts is to connect with other people. To bond with special individuals. To belong to a group – a family, a team, a gang, a tribe. We have an instinctual need to work with others in a common purpose. We have an instinctual need to feel accepted and loved. And, beyond that, to be valued, looked up to, and respected by our group. We have an instinct to show our loyalty to our group, in ways like wearing the same things, saying the same things, following the same customs, or hating the same enemies. We have an instinct to defend our group if we feel it is threatened. And if we are left out of the group, we feel pain. We may do almost anything to keep from being rejected or excluded by our group.

Our need to belong can sometimes make us do foolish things. So we should be able to empathize with the "dumb" junco whose instinct makes him put all the food in the big cowbird mouth while his own babies starve.

And, like the junco, our instincts can be manipulated too. Not by cowbirds, but by advertisers and politicians, maybe even our peers. They can try to use our instincts to make us desire something, or love someone or hate someone, or do other things they want us to do.

But that junco won't be fooled a second time. When necessary, he can override his instincts. And so can we, if we are aware.

Birds can help teach us about ourselves

"Instinct" means inborn knowledge inherited from ancestors.

A creature is born with its instincts, whether they are specific and detailed instructions or vague feelings. Instinct is guidance, feelings, desires and fears that are inborn and shared with all the other members of the species. Some instincts are activated the moment the creature is born, like a baby bird's instinct to open its mouth and face upward, or a baby mammal's instinct to nurse. Some instincts come out later, like a baby's instinct to play. Some instincts don't awaken until a creature is old enough to have babies of its own. The schedule for the instinct to come out is inborn, just like the instinct itself.[46]

If we did have to think about everything, it would slow us down a lot. At least, it would if we had to think about everything in words. Thinking in words is extremely slow compared to direct knowledge that doesn't use words. Imagine if we had to put into words the thought "This will fall if I drop it," not just once but every time we picked up something. Imagine if, in our heads, we had to say words like "The pavement will hold up my foot" every time we set foot on

---

46   No one knows how or where, or even whether, instincts are stored in the brain. Many insects and spiders, with tiny brains, have elaborate instincts. Plants have no brains at all, yet they have something like ancestral memory. (Perhaps ancestral memories are stored in the "cloud"?)

the pavement, or if we had to constantly speak words in our head like "The wet floor could be slippery" or "My foot could get stuck in the mud" as we walk.

Maybe some people do constantly put their thoughts into words as they go about in the world – but we really have many layers of thoughts, and we can only put one thought-current at a time into words. If we are saying to ourselves in mental words, "That math test was hard," we are not at the same time saying to ourselves in words, "The mud I am walking on is sticky." Yet we are aware of what we are walking on and how to walk on it. To put the thought about the mud into words in our head, we would have to set aside the thought about the math test. Though we can put only one thought at a time into words, we are actually thinking many things at once, These thoughts and memories all weave together to create our world as we move through it.

The thought that is put into words is what we would call a "conscious" thought, while all the rest of the thoughts at all different levels might be called "subconscious," or "below-conscious." Whenever we are talking to another person, the words in our heads may be about the conversation, but we are also perceiving many things about the person that we are *not* putting into words in our heads. All those "underlayers" are a kind of consciousness, which we can be aware of., if we can get our word-thoughts out of the way.

The different meanings of the word "consciousness" cause confusion. In fact, that word has even even more meanings. For example, we are conscious in our dreams, yet we are not aware of our physical surroundings. And even when we are asleep and *not* dreaming, we are conscious at a deeper level, without being aware of any *things* at all. And our bodies have a kind of awareness, and at yet deeper levels we are affected by the ancestral memories shared by all humans, and at deeper levels yet we are connected with the consciousness of all living beings. (The different meanings of "consciousness" is such a big subject I will save it for another book.)

But for those levels of consciousness deeper than words, there is a word we often use. We call it "instinct."

This meaning of "instinct" has nothing to do with ancestral memory. It means an inner knowing that can kick in when there is no time to put our thoughts into words or not enough information for logical thinking. A driver "instinctively" puts on the brakes without taking time to put into words the thought "There is something in the road." We may "instinctively" feel that someone is up to something bad without having any information that we can use to reason logically. That kind of instinct is sometimes known as "gut instinct." Sometimes we call it "sensing." Sensing that happens without any information at all to base it on, we may call "intuition." (But the word "intuition" also has other meanings, which can confuse the discussion even more.)

So there are two different meanings of the word "instinct." Yet they are not so far apart. In either meaning, it means an awareness that bypasses logic, ideas, and words. (We are born with an instinct to eat long before we ever find out about logical reasons why we should eat.) Instinct feels like a sense of knowing in the body rather than the head. It is an inner knowing without knowing how we know.

In the birds, we can see how these two kinds of instinct, the ancestral knowledge and the present awareness, flow as a single current that guides a life.

Thinking in words and concepts enables us to reason logically, which is a human superpower that other creatures hardly have at all. Some people think that logical thinking is the only kind of thinking that matters. Some people think that animals have no thoughts or awareness because they don't have this superpower. They think that animals cannot think because they don't put their thoughts into words. Even if a dog learns words like "ball" or "walk," he doesn't form the thoughts "I want to go for a walk" or "where did the ball go" with those words. He doesn't need words to think. But some people think that since animals don't use words to form their thoughts, they go through life without no awareness at all.

Some people think that if we can teach computers the kind of logical reasoning that humans use, the computer will become "conscious" like a human. According to these people, the deeper levels of consciousness that humans have, and other living beings have, don't matter. According to them, we should just concentrate on manipulating data, like computers. But if we forget those deeper levels, they can atrophy, till we lose the awareness of who we really are inside.

In the wild, we can start to remember. In the wild, we can feel our deep instincts again.

Alone in nature, we can be with our own secret thoughts and feelings. Of course, in nature we are not really alone, with birds and other creatures for company. But outside the human mindfield, there are no human judgments to influence us. We don't have to worry what other people think of us. We can figure out which thoughts have been planted by others and which thoughts are truly our own.

And wild birds, among all wild animals, bring the wild to us. They come to our homes and help us to remember our own deep instincts. That is why wild birds can be our teachers.

CHAPTER THIRTEEN

TOP SMARTS: BIRD INTELLIGENCE

A FISHERMAN STEPS away from his fishing lines. When he comes back, he sees a crow pulling at one of the lines. The crow can't pull up the line far enough to get the fish out of the water. But, as the fisherman watches in amazement, the crow pulls up part of the line, steps on it, pulls again, steps, pulls, steps, pulls. Finally the fish is up on the dock. Then the crow pecks the hook free from the fish's mouth and flies away with the fish.[47]

Two campers in Arizona are putting out food on a picnic table. A Mexican Jay lands on the table, grabs a pack of cookies, and flies off with it. The package was unopened. How did the jay know it was food? There was a picture of cookies on it, and the jay had learned not only what cookies were, it had learned that a picture on a wrapper told you what was inside.[48]

---

47   This comes from a report on social media. But similar string-pulling behavior has been reported in other birds: Great, Blue, and Coal Tits (European cousins of chickadees), European Goldfinches, redpolls, siskins, budgerigars, and macaws, among others. See *The Minds of Birds,* by Alexander Skutch, p 69-70.

48   Reported on social media.

Years ago I had a big walnut tree in my yard. Birds love walnuts, but they can't break walnut shells. They could eat one only if it dropped on the street and was crushed by a car. The crows didn't wait for that to happen by chance. I often saw a crow drop a walnut on the street and wait for a car to run over the nut and crush it.

But often the cars would miss the nut. So some crows in Japan came up with a better system. They bring walnuts to an intersection with a traffic light. When the cars stop for the red light, a crow hops in front of a car and places a walnut directly in front of its tire. When the light turns green, the nut gets smashed. When the light turns red and the cars stop again, the crows eat as much as they can before the light turns green again.[49]

House Sparrows in New Zealand learned to open the automatic doors to get into a cafeteria by hovering in front of the sensor. Then they would go inside and steal food from the buffet.[50] Hummingbirds have been reported to activate outdoor drinking fountains by flying in front of the sensors, then taking a brief shower when the water spurts up.[51]

Some birds can count. Fishermen in China train cormorants, large diving birds who catch fish underwater, to catch fish for them. The fisherman puts a ring around the bird's neck so it can't swallow the fish it catches. He takes the fish from its mouth. But every eighth fish, the fisherman loosens the neck ring so the bird can swallow the fish. The cormorant learns to expect every eighth fish for itself. If the fisherman doesn't let the cormorant swallow fish number eight, the cormorant refuses to catch any more. So the cormorants can count at least up to eight.[52]

Other birds can count, too. Scientists presented pigeons with sets

49   https://www.pbs.org/lifeofbirds/brain/

50   Brockie, R.E., and Barry O'Brien (2004)., "House sparrows (Passer domesticus) opening autodoors." https://notornis.osnz.org.nz/system/files/Notornis_51_1_52.pdf

51   Reported on social media.

52   Burton, Adrian (2018)., "Can Cormorants Count?" https://esajournals.onlinelibrary.wiley.com/doi/10.1002/fee.1927

containing different numbers of figures and taught them to peck the sets in ascending order: one, two three, etc. The pigeons learned to peck them in the right order, from one to nine.

A birdfriender in England taught a Great Tit (European chickadee) to count (sort of) and to recognize the names of small numbers. She started off, when the bird came for a peanut, by telling the bird "You must tap for it," and calling sharply, "Tap tap." The bird, named Star, tapped a piece of wood twice in the same rhythm. The next morning, the birdfriender called out three taps, and the bird imitated that. The number was increased day by day until the bird imitated eight taps, which seemed to be her limit. Then the birdfriender started speaking the numbers before tapping, like "three." Soon the bird would tap out between two and eight taps based on hearing the word only.[53]

And parrots can add. A parrot named Alex was shown two sets of objects one after the other – say, four objects, and then two. When asked "How many total." the parrot would reply with the correct answer, up to six.[54]

Dogs and cats are smart, but a lot of the smart things that birds can do are beyond them. The only mammals (other than humans) as smart as the smartest birds are monkeys and apes. Birds are among the smartest creatures on Earth. Their smarts enable them to live among us. If they weren't smart, they couldn't adapt to the constant changes we bring.

The limits of ancestral memory

Imagine you're a completely instinctual creature. You know exactly what to do, from the time you are born. No doubts, no questions. How perfect would that be?

---

53   From *Living With Birds,* by Len Howard, cited in *The Minds of Birds,* by Alexander Skutch, p 59-60.

54   Pepperberg, Irene (2006). "Grey Parrot (*Psittacus erithacus*) Numerical Abilities: Addition and Further Experiments on a Zero-Like Concept." *https://alexfoundation.org › wp-content uploads › 2015 › 03 › JCP-Alex-Add.pdf*

But one day, something new happens. Something your ancestors never faced.

Let's say you're a baby sea turtle. Your mother had crawled out of the ocean and laid her eggs in the dry sand of the beach. There, the sun kept the eggs warm till you were all ready to hatch. When you hatched, you knew what to do: head back into the sea.

How do you find the sea? Wait till night and follow the brightest light at ground level. That light is the reflection of the moon in the ocean. The path of moonlight guides you to the sea. Your mother timed laying your eggs so that you would hatch at full moon.

You are born knowing how to do this. Your ancestors have been doing things this way since forever.

But this year, things have changed.

This year a highway was built along the beach. And on the other side of the highway are bright streetlights and brightly lit buildings. So you head toward the lights. Which takes you away from the sea, and right across the highway.

All around you, your brothers and sisters are getting crushed. Somehow, you make it across the highway. But now you are lost on the land. There you will die, unless some kindly human finds you and carries you to the ocean.

If a change happens slowly over many generations, a species can figure out how to handle it. Members try out different ideas, and see what strategies work, and a new instinct grows over generations, through the experience of its members, like the body of a tree slowly grows through the sunlight gathered by its leaves.

But if things change too fast, there may not be generational time to develop new instincts.

Then a species that puts less of its intelligence in the collective memory and more of its intelligence in the individual members has the advantage. Individuals can learn and figure out new things. They can be more flexible.

But what each member figures out or discovers won't be known by the others, nor will it be inherited by future generations. Unless members of the species can learn from and teach each other.

We humans solved this problem by creating language, to share what we learn with others. And we developed writing, a better way to pass on what we learn to the future generations.

We humans are born with less instinctual guidance than any other species. So we have more ability than any other species to come up with new ideas, because we have to.

For example, we have an instinct to eat, but (after babyhood) we don't know what to eat. We don't know by instinct how to get food or prepare it. We have to figure that out. As a result, unlike a pelican or a woodpecker, we aren't limited to foods our ancestors ate. We eat a lot of different foods and prepare them in an infinite variety of ways.

We have an instinct that we need shelters to live in, but we don't inherit specific instructions for creating them. People came up with different ideas in different environments. As a result, we have been able to live almost anywhere – the desert, the rainforest, the Arctic, even outer space.

So when people talk about "intelligence" of a species, they don't mean its inherited intelligence. They mean the ability of individual members to learn and figure out things they didn't inherit.

So in this chapter we are using the word "intelligence" that way too.

Individual intelligence helps a creature survive in the human world. Humans are always bringing new things into the world. New things like cookies and fishing lines. And new dangers, like windows and cars.

And we bring out new abilities in other creatures. Cormorants likely never had any reason to count before they got involved with humans. Dogs never understood words until humans taught them. Animals like raccoons, coyotes, rats, and crows, who survive among us in the city, not only were smart already, but probably have become even smarter over the generations because only the smart ones survive, and have smarter and smarter babies.

Birds who live around humans learn and figure out new things all the time. Just the other day, I was throwing peanuts to the jays on the deck, and a towhee was watching. Peanuts are new to the birds, and the towhee had never seen them before. But. observing the jays, the towhee decided to try to get a peanut himself. He hopped over to one peanut, but he couldn't get his beak around it. So I broke a peanut in half and threw one broken half toward him. The towhee still couldn't get his beak around it. He studied it from different angles, and noticed the broken edge of shell. The perfect handle! He grabbed the broken edge and flew away with the peanut. A few minutes later he returned. I threw the other half of the peanut to him. Without hesitation he seized the broken edge of the shell and flew off. The towhee had not only figured out something new, but remembered it after one try.

The common, everyday birds we see around us are among the smartest, most adaptable and open-minded of all birds. They have to be, to live with us. And our familiar bird neighbors are not just among the smartest of birds—they are among the smartest animals on Earth, of any kind.

Curiosity and intelligence

A smarter bird is more likely to become our friend. This is because the smarter someone is, the more curious they tend to be. Curiosity, the instinctual *desire* to learn new things, goes along with intelligence, the *ability* to learn new things.

As a teacher, I know that the smartest kids are the most curious kids. (Schooling that suppresses kids' curiosity and creativity makes them dumber, no matter what their grades or test scores.) The curious kids are the most fun to teach, too.

Chickadees are openly curious, and don't mind us watching them while they watch us, while other curious birds may watch us without being seen. Juncos watch us from their hiding places in the grass, and Song Sparrows from the bushes.

Hummingbirds are curious not only about humans, but about other birds. They investigate what other birds are doing. When other birds are eating from the suet feeders and the sunflower seeds, the hummingbirds poke at those feeders too. They watch the squirrels. And they check out the humans. Often a hummingbird, especially a new visitor, will fly up in front of my face and hover there, closely studying my eyes, my nose, my mouth, my forehead. It's a little weird seeing that hummingbird beak pointing to my eye.

A lady in upstate New York found a Ruby-throated Hummingbird who had not flown south for the winter, and let him spend the winter in a flower-filled sunroom in her house. She named him Squeak. She wrote:

Hummingbirds are naturally inquisitive. Squeak... investigated everything, including my hair, my eyes, my cameras and tripods... He was soon brave enough that he would follow me anytime I had something in my hand, floating around right beside me inspecting whatever it was I was holding.... [He] would hover around my head just looking at me for no apparent reason. No matter what I may have been doing, Squeak would dart over to investigate. Every time I walked into his room he would hover around me chirping and chirping, looking for a treat... Once, when I walked into the room, he hovered around my face, chirping and getting closer and closer to my eyes, looking for his treat. He got so close to my eyes I had to close them. The next thing I knew, he had inserted his beak into my nostril.[55]

One day I read about hand-held hummingbird feeders – tiny feeders an inch across and an inch deep. So I got some, filled them with sugar water, and went out and offered one to my friend Raspberry, a male Anna's Hummingbird. Raspberry backed away suspiciously. He hovered at a distance. He flew around me, but wouldn't come near. Then he took off.

Later that day, when I went outside, Raspberry flew up to my face. Then he flew down to my hand. He flew around my hand, studying it from every angle. He flew up and down my fingers, examining each finger carefully. Then he flew around to my other hand and examined it just as thoroughly. And he left.

When I offered the hand-feeder to Raspberry again, he came to it without hesitation.

Another hummingbird friend, Cranberry, invented a game of his own. When I am hand-feeding peanuts to the chickadees and nuthatches, Cranberry pantomimes going for a peanut in my hand too. He seems to want to join the party.

Discovering bird brains

Instinct doesn't require brains. Even creatures with very small brains, like insects and spiders have ancestral memory. Even plants, with no brains at all, But for an individual to figure out and learn new things, it needs a brain. [56]

So it seems to make sense that the more brains a creature has, the smarter it is. And for a long time, people thought that only

---

55 From *Squeak: A Hummingbird in My House*, by Annette Heidcamp. The author wrote a later book called *Rosie: My Rufous Hummingbird*, in which she described another hummingbird with a very different personality.

56 Unless you're an octopus. An octopus has a brain in each arm.

mammals could be smart, because mammals have the biggest brains. Birds couldn't be smart, people said, because birds have small brains; after all, they can't fit much in such small heads.

But when it comes to brain size, what really matters is the size of the brain *in proportion to the body*. The brain runs the whole body, so a bigger body automatically needs a bigger brain. In order to be able to learn new things, a creature needs extra brains beyond what runs the body.

And it turns out that, *in proportion to their bodies*, bird brains equal or exceed mammal brains. Among mammals, other than humans, chimps (long considered the smartest animal) have the biggest proportional brains, but crow brain sizes compare to chimps, and the brain sizes of small songbirds compare to monkeys.

And bird brains are more densely packed with neurons than mammal brains, making the total number of neurons comparable. As some scientists said, "Avian brains thus have the potential to provide much higher 'cognitive power' per unit mass than do mammalian brains."[57] That is just one more way birds made themselves light enough to fly.

Another reason many people thought birds weren't smart is that birds have such strong and well-developed instincts, and people thought that you couldn't be *both* highly instinctual *and* highly intelligent. The more ancestral memory, the less ability to learn new things, and vice versa – or so people thought. But birds show that a species can have *both* instinct *and* the ability to learn new things.

So when scientists realized that birds might actually be smart, they started coming up with experiments to study their intelligence.

---

57   Olkowicz et al. (2016). "Birds have primate-like numbers of neurons in the forebrain."
https://www.pnas.org/content/113/26/7255
See also *https://www.deviantart.com/concavenator/art/Animal-brain-size-788091245*

Experimenting with bird smarts

The scientists began with pigeons, who are cooperative and easy to train. Like dogs, pigeons readily learn to do things for treats.

Starting in the 1930s, a famous scientist named B. F. Skinner taught pigeons complicated tricks. Pigeons learned to play ping-pong with each other, turn in circles whenever a "Turn" sign went on, send color-coded messages to other pigeons, guide missiles on a radar screen, and other fancy stunts.

But Skinner wasn't trying to show that pigeons were smart. In fact, the opposite. He thought that they were dumb, and he wanted to prove that it doesn't really take smarts to learn.

Skinner's method was this: A task is broken down into tiny steps. The pigeon gets a treat for mastering each step, and finally it has to perform the steps in the correct order to get the treat, and the steps add up to a complicated trick. The pigeon doesn't need to understand the trick, it only has to know how to perform the steps in the right order. Other scientists have used these methods to teach pigeons to spell words by pecking letters in order. The pigeon didn't have to understand what it was doing, only learn the steps.

Skinner thought that humans should be taught this way too. Children could then be taught by machines instead of by human teachers. Like a pigeon, a child wouldn't need to understand what she is doing – all she would need to know is that for each step she masters, she gets a reward. (For a human, the reward could be points, a smiley face, a gold star, etc.)

Today, many children are being taught by computers that use Skinner's methods. If you are ever taught by a computer this way, remember, the pigeons did it first!

Pigeons also turn out to be better than humans detecting subtle differences in pictures. Pigeons can detect breast cancer in medical images, which for humans requires considerable training and experience. [58]

---

58   Levenson RM, *et al.* (2015) "Pigeons (*Columba livia*) as Trainable Observers of Pathology and Radiology Breast Cancer Images." PLoS ONE 10(11):

Many other experiments have been done with pigeon smarts. Pigeons turn out to have prodigious memories. Many experiments involved memorizing pictures. Pictures were shown to pigeons and the pigeons were rewarded for pecking them. Later they were tested to see how well they remembered those pictures. They got treats for identifying pictures they had seen before. A typical pigeon could memorize over a thousand images. And remember them for years. [59]

Pigeons have even been taught to read... sort of. The pigeons learned to recognize words that would get them a reward. How many words could a human remember written in an alphabet they don't know, say πουλί or ᚻᚩᚱ or பறவை or طيور, each word seen only once? The pigeons could memorize a thousand words or more!

But of course pigeons would be good at remembering what they see. As migrating birds, they need that ability to help them find their way. And from up in the sky, the ground looks like a flat picture.

On the other hand, when chickens were tested on remembering images, they flunked. But of course they would. Chickens live their whole lives in one place. They don't need to remember the ground that passes beneath them.

But different birds have different smarts. In a different test, chickens beat the pigeons. This was a test called "object permanence," which means remembering things that move out of sight. With pigeons, if something they wanted (food) was moved out of sight, they just forgot about it. But if something the chickens wanted moved out of sight, the chickens kept looking for it.

But of course chickens would be better than pigeons at remembering things that move out of sight. Chickens hunt for bugs, which

---

e0141357. *https://doi.org/10.1371/journal.pone.0141357*

59   Vaughan, W., & Greene, S. L. (1984). "Pigeon visual memory capacity." *Journal of Experimental Psychology: Animal Behavior Processes, 10*(2), 256–271. https://doi.org/10.1037/0097-7403.10.2.256 and Fagot, Joel, and Robert G. Cook (2006) "Evidence for large long-term memory capacities in baboons and pigeons and its implications for learning and the evolution of cognition." https://www.pnas.org/content/103/46/17564

run into hiding places. Pigeons eat seeds, which don't move or try to hide. So if their food moves out of sight, the pigeons don't have much instinct to search for it. A hawk would surely do great on an "object permanence" test.

But it wasn't food the chickens were looking for. What they were searching for was something much more important – mom. They were baby chicks, and mom was a red ball. At least, they thought she was.

When a baby chick hatches, it thinks the first thing it sees is mom. And usually, that's right. But these chicks were hatched by a machine, and the first thing they saw when they came out of the eggs was the red ball. So, for these chicks, that ball was mom. And when "mom" rolled out of sight, the baby chickens were desperate to find "her." So they aced the "object permanence" test. [60]

Chickadees would also score high on the "object permanence" test. Sometimes a chickadee comes up to me to ask for a peanut, and I've forgotten the vial of peanuts I usually carry on me, and I have to go inside the house to get some. Some birds would forget the whole thing and leave as soon as I am out of sight, but the chickadee will wait outside patiently, ready to fly to my hand as soon as I emerge. If I have to walk a ways to the house, the chickadee will follow me – I can hear its wings fluttering behind me. And sometimes, when I come out, several chickadees are there, ready to grab peanuts, apparently having figured out why the first chickadee was perching at the door.

California Scrub Jays have been the subject of many experiments in bird intelligence. Some experiments test the Scrub Jays' strategies at fooling a thief who might steal food caches. If a potential thief is watching – whether another jay or a human known to be a food thief – a caching jay may make fake hiding places, pretending to hide the

---

60   Marino, Lori (2017). "Thinking chickens: a review of cognition, emotion, and behavior in the domestic chicken." *https://www.ncbi.nlm.nih.gov/pmc/articles/PMC5306232/* More in Garnham, Laura, and Harna Lovlie (2018) "Sophisticated Fowl: The Complex Behaviour and Cognitive Skills of Chickens and Red Junglefowl," *https://www.mdpi.com/2076-328X/8/1/13/htm*

same food in three different places. That way, the watcher would have to remember three times as many locations, most of which would be empty. Then, if the spy leaves, the caching jay digs up the food and reburies it somewhere else.[61]

However, if someone who is not a thief is watching, the Scrub Jays don't try to hide their caches. Jays who don't know me will fly out of sight to hide their caches, but those who know me don't conceal their caching places from me. Once Skippy flew up to me to show off an exceptionally large acorn he had found, fatter than the peanut I was offering him, then he flew down next to the deck, in plain sight, and pounded his prize into the ground emphatically, like a hammer pounding a nail.

Scrub Jays beat chimps in experiments about fooling food thieves, leading some people to proclaim Scrub Jays the smartest animal in the world.[62]

Chickadees too are careful to hide their caches out of sight of other chickadees, and also of nuthatches. But they ignore juncos, who don't steal caches. [63] This shows that chickadees recognize different bird species and know that different species behave differently.

Some people find it amazing that birds could realize that other points of view exists, but of course they would. When a bird hides its nest, it is considering the point of view of a predator. And when an accipiter sneaks up on a songbird, it is thinking about the point of view of its prey.

Other scientists did experiments to test the Scrub Jays' understanding of time. Scrub Jays were provided with peanuts and

---

61   These jays were in a lab, so they couldn't just fly off somewhere away from the thief.

62   No surprise that a book titled *The Genius of Birds* features a Scrub Jay on the cover, like Skippy adorns the top of this chapter on bird intelligence.

63   Pravosudov, VV (2007). "Mountain chickadees discriminate between potential cache pilferers and non-pilferers." https://europepmc.org/article/PMC/2562407

somethingeven more delicious – small worms. The jays cached the extra food when they got full. Later, when they were hungry again, the scientists brought them back to that room, and the jays dug up the caches first. But they soon learned something: worms rot in the ground, while peanuts don't. And, with experience, they learned how long it took for the worms to rot. So when only a few hours had passed, they would go for the worms first, but when a few days had gone by, the jays wouldn't dig up the worms at all, only the peanuts.[64]

When Eurasian Jays are courting, the male gives the female gifts of food. In an experiment with Eurasian Jays, a male jay was given two kinds of worms, and, after eating, he gave worms as gifts to the female, choosing the ones she would like best based on what he had seen her eating before. [65]

The puzzle champions

Crows and ravens, cousins of the jays, are legendary for their cleverness. For the Native peoples of the Northwest Coast, Raven is both a bringer of knowledge and a sly trickster. Scientists decided to test their smarts by giving them puzzles.

An Aesop's fable from ancient Greece tells of a thirsty crow who found a bottle of water, but he couldn't get his head inside the bottle to drink the water. He came up with a solution: he put a pebble in the bottle, and another pebble, and another, and kept on until the water level rose high enough that he could reach the water and drink. Moral: Little by little does the trick.

---

64   Clayton, N. and A. Dickenson (1999). "Scrub jays (Aphelocoma coerulescens) remember the relative time of caching as well as the location and content of their caches." Journal of Comparative Psychology. 1999 Dec;113(4):403-16. doi: 10.1037/0735-7036.113.4.403.

65   Ostojic, Ljerka, et al.,(2016). "Desire-state attribution: benefits of a novel paradigm using the food-sharing behaviour of Eurasian jays (Garrulus glandarius)." Communicative & Integrative Biology. http://dx.doi.org/10.1080/19420889.2015 .1134065

Most of Aesop's fables are fanciful and have nothing to do with what real animals do. But when scientists gave this problem to the New Caledonian Crow – a crow who lives in on a small island in the Pacific, the bird did just what the crow in the fable did.

The scientists gave another puzzle to a New Caledonian Crow. They put food in an empty plastic bottle. The crow dropped the bottle into its water dish and let the bottle partially fill with water, then it took the bottle and let the water run out until the food came out too.

Various birds, including nuthatches, flycatchers, finches, jays, and aracaris (a tropical bird related to the toucans) have been observed using fir needles, cactus spines, or other tools to get insects out of tiny spaces.[66] But the New Caledonian Crows don't just pick up handy needles or spines. They make and sharpen pointed sticks, keep the best ones, practice and perfect their skills, and teach each other.

Scientists have done many experiments with the New Caledonian Crow. They put a piece of food in a little bucket and hung it down where the crow couldn't reach it. They gave the crow a thin piece of wire with a hook. The crow hooked the bucket and pulled it up. The scientists hung the bucket again, but this time they gave the crow a straight piece of wire, no hook. Now what will you do, crow? The crow bent the wire into a hook and pulled up the bucket.[67]

Then the scientists set up puzzles with multiple steps – like using a small stick to get a longer stick, using the longer stick to turn a latch, and so on. The crow solved the puzzles. It didn't use trial and error. The bird studied the situation, planned out the steps, and then carried them out.

Some scientists define "intelligence" as having a mental model of the world. Migrating birds and caching birds have such models. Even a bird building a nest has a mental model. But a bird who can

66   See *The Minds of Birds,* by Alexander Skutch, pp 67-9.

67   For more on the New Caledonian Crow, with lots of pictures, see the book *Crow Smarts: Inside the Brain of the World's Brightest Bird* by Pamela S. Turner and Andy Comins, or see an episode of *NOVA* called "Animal Minds, Part 1: Bird Geniuses."

visualize and rearrange steps in its head to do something new, has a more complex model. So some scientists call the New Caledonian Crow the smartest bird in the world.

The nomadic communicators

If a species has individual intelligence, its members need to be able to teach each other and learn from each other. Otherwise, what each member learns can be lost. So intelligent species need the ability to communicate.

And communication takes a special kind of intelligence. It's different from the intelligence that figures out puzzles. You have to take into account what someone else knows, wants and feels, which might be different from what you know, want, and feel. Creatures who live in social groups, like wolves, elephants, parrots, and humans, have this kind of intelligence. Dogs are geniuses at communication. They can understand us humans and our feelings better than any bird probably ever will.

So birds who live in flocks tend to be extra smart. And birds who live in *nomadic* flocks even more, because they have to make decisions, and make them together. Most nomadic birds live in places like the tropics and the outback of Australia,[68] where there are no regular seasons, so they have no regular migration pattern. They stay in one place as long as it's good, then go somewhere else. Their lives are unpredictable, so they can't rely on ancestral memory. They have to use intelligence.

That is why parrots, who belong to nomadic flocks, are among the smartest birds in the world. There are hundreds of species of parrots, including budgerigars (parakeets), cockatiels, and their relatives the

---

68 North America has some nomadic birds, including Cedar Waxwings, Red Crossbills, and Pine Siskins. To my knowledge, no one has studied the intelligence of these birds. But Cedar Waxwings have been observed coordinating to hunt damselflies and other flying insects, with some birds flushing the insects and others catching them. That seems pretty smart.

cockatoos, all nomadic. Some kinds of parrots can live sixty years or more, and they have time to get to know each other, to learn things, and to share what they learn.

Parrot flocks are made up of extended families and networks of friends. Like other nomadic birds, parrots are not territorial. When a tree full of ripe fruit is discovered, the whole flock descends on the tree together, and they all share the tree at the same time. When the fruit is gone, the flock looks for another tree. So territories wouldn't make sense for them.

Not being territorial, they can nest close to each other and even help each other with their nests. The members talk to each other constantly. They quarrel and make up. They bond through humor. People who keep pet parrots describe how they like to make humans laugh with their jokes and pranks. For parrots raised with humans, those humans are the flock.

Crows too live in semi-nomadic flocks. But the crow way of life is different, so their smarts are a litte different. Crows are omnivores, like raccoons and bears; they eat almost anything edible. Omnivores tend to have flexible minds and to be good at coming up with new strategies to solve new problems. So the crow specialty is finding creative ways to get food out of hard-to-get places. Parrots, on the other hand, live mainly on fruit and nuts. Their food is not trying to hide. So parrot intelligence doesn't specialize in solving food-trap puzzles. Their great genius is communication.

But crows also teach each other and learn from each other. One wet day, I was throwing peanuts to the crows in the parking lot, and one peanut fell into a puddle. When a crow pulled that peanut out, it seemed to like the result. Maybe the peanut was softer. When I threw another peanut, the crow dropped it into the puddle on purpose. Seeing that, another crow dropped its peanut into the water too! The crows watch each other and learn.

Mirrors and memories

A falconer was being interviewed on a video. A falconer is a person who hunts in partnership with a bird of prey. It's not always a falcon, but sometimes a hawk or another raptor. But this falconer had a Peregrine Falcon on his fist.

"So tell me," the questioner asked. "How smart is your falcon?"

The falconer shook his head. "Raptors are the smartest creatures on Earth, and the dumbest. Their minds just don't work like ours. I will never understand how they think. The other day, I took my bird to a place where we hunted three years ago. Just the one time.

She remembered it in detail. She noticed everything that was different. A couple of trees were missing, she flew over and investigated. One outbuilding wasn't there before, she checked it out from all angles. I didn't remember those details myself, but I had video, which showed she was investigating everything that had changed from before. She certainly remembers places better than I do.

"Amazing memory, you say? And yet she can't remember a moment ago! When we are hunting and she brings me a quail, I take the quail, distract her with a piece of food, and put the quail in my bag. And she doesn't say, 'Hey, what happened to my quail?' Nope, it's out of sight, out of mind. It's only been a moment, but she's already forgotten the quail. She's ready to catch another one. How can she remember some missing trees she saw three years ago and not remember a quail from one minute ago?"

A bird's memory doesn't work the same way as ours. Our memories are made of stories. We remember things by putting them together into stories, by connecting what is happening now with what happened before, and before that, and so on. The most recent things are usually the clearest things we remember.

But a bird's memory is like a series of snapshots, filed *not* by the *order* they happened, but by how similar they are. A bird connects what it is seeing now *not* with the most *recent* things in its memory, but with the most *similar* things in its memory, whether its own personal memory or its ancestral memory.

After all, if you are a bird on migration, flying over a mountain range, what is more important to remember – the lake you flew over last week, or the mountain range you are crossing, which you last saw a year ago?

If you cache food for winter, what is more important to remember – the place where you dug up a cache yesterday, or the place you are now, where you hid a cache six months ago?

If you are building a nest, what is more important to remember – last month, before you started the nest, or last year, when you built a nest before? And the nest you built the year before that, and the year before that, and your ancestors' nests for time immemorial?

A bird lives a cyclical life. It follows the same basic pattern, over and over, as the life of the species passes through the generations.

So why doesn't the falcon remember the quail that was there half a minute ago?

The falcon has a mental snapshot of that scene with a dead quail. But the falcon also has a mental snapshot of that scene *without* a dead quail. In fact, way more snapshots with no quail. And when she sees the scene with no dead quail, it matches those memories.

Pet birds can recognize humans they know in photographs. In fact, they can recognize a human they know *only* through photographs. I once knew a teenaged girl who had a pet starling. The girl had a crush on some pop musician and had posters of him, alone or with his group, all over her walls. When her teen magazines came, her pet starling could recognize the photos of her crush in the magazine, *even though the bird had never seen him in person* and knew him only from the posters on the girl's wall.

Birds returning from migration often first check the exact spot where they found a feeder last year.

Someone reported on social media that she had accidentally cut down a hummingbird nest with two hatchlings in it. She fastened the nest about two feet from its original location, but the mother hummingbird couldn't find it. The mother kept going to the original spot. If the babies had been old enough to make noise, she would have found them, but unfortunately they weren't. The babies had to be taken to rehab.

Even if a scene changes. birds have an acute sense of exactly *where* something is in space. A caching bird can remember thousands of caching locations, even when they are covered with snow and look different. Birds live in a three-dimensional world where up-and-down is as important as left-and-right and forward-and-back, and there are no landmarks in the air.

Our memories works differently. Like birds, we connect what we see with what we have seen before. But even more, we connect our memories with events before and after, in a chain. We remember things by turning our memories into stories, and by creating stories of our lives.

But a bird lives the story of its species, so it doesn't have to create a personal story. We too live the story of our species. but within that ongoing story, each of us lives a different life, with different experiences. So each of us holds our lives together by creating a story of who we are and what we have experienced.

We think in stories. We live in our stories. Some people narrate their stories to themselves in words. We remember things that happen by telling ourselves stories about them. We walk around with heads full of memories, and thoughts about those memories, and feelings about those thoughts, and wishes that something had been different, and on and on.

Stories don't just hold our own lives together. Stories hold our world together. The days of the week are a story. A country is a story. Money is a story. Even a sentence is a tiny story. Our stories interweave to create our world.

When something "makes sense," that means it fits in with our stories. When we ask the question "why," we mean "how does this fit into my stories?" We might even hate people whose stories are different from ours, because they could cause our stories to break, and without stories, we might feel that life has "lost its meaning."

But a bird doesn't need to ask itself who it is. A bird doesn't seek to find itself. A bird doesn't try to figure out its identity. A bird doesn't live in stories.

Since animals don't create stories about their lives, some people question whether an animal even knows that it exists. Some people say an animal has "self-awareness" only if it can recognize itself in a mirror. They put a mark on a creature's head or chest and show it a mirror, and, if the creature checks for the mark on itself, that means it knows that it exists. Chimps[69], elephants, and dolphins pass this test, while dogs (who depend on smell more than sight and wouldn't care about marks anyway) flunk the test. Magpies and pigeons pass the test, but most birds treat a mirror reflection like another bird.

So if a creature doesn't understand how a mirror works, it doesn't even know that it exists? Obviously animals know they exist. They try to stay alive, and they aren't unconscious robots following a computer program with no awareness of what they are doing. But the reason people come up with ideas like the mirror test is because we sense that animals somehow experience their lives in a different way than we do.

And they do. While we live in stories, a wild animal lives in direct reality.

How can we know this?

Because if birds lived in stories, the way we do, that would be bad for their survival. To make stories out of what we experience, we have to filter out most of what is happening around us. We can't include every tree and person and car we pass. We pay attention only to things that fit into our story.

A bird can't afford to do that. A bird has to pay attention to *everything* around it. A bird can't ignore things that don't fit into a

---

69   Oddly, no one seems to find out if a chimp will check its *own* head when it sees *another* chimp with a mark on its head, even though chimps and other primates take cues from each other.

story. A bird can't be distracted by ruminating about what someone said yesterday or what could happen tomorrow. Otherwise, it would quickly be weeded out of the gene pool. A wild bird has to give full attention to the moment it is in *right now.*

So a baby gull, who pecks at a red spot on its parents' beak to signal them to regurgitate food, will also peck on a red spot painted on a stick – even if we just painted the stick, right in front of it. The gull doesn't tell itself a story about us painting the stick. It thinks of what the red spot reminds it of *right* now.

But if we offer the baby gull a painted stick again, after once or twice it will remember the painted stick, and remember that the stick didn't give it any food. It will have a new picture, closer to what it is seeing now.

Ancestral instinct blends seamlessly with the present moment to create a bird's awareness.

Some people say that animals aren't even aware of past and future. But a bird making a nest or caching food for the winter is anticipating the future. A bird bringing food to its nestlings is remembering laying and hatching those eggs in the past.

But we connect before and after, past and future in long chains, and we see the present moment as a link in the chain. So we have a different relationship to time than birds do. Birds don't think about the past and the future constantly, the way that we often do. We may think so much about the past or the future that we are hardly aware of the moment we are in right now.

We see a bird just sitting there, turning its head this way and that, just watching and listening. Doesn't it get bored? No phone, no television, no computer, not even a comic book?

But if we were totally in the moment of now, there could be no such thing as boredom. The world around us overflows with amazing things. And the birds can help us become aware of our amazing world. When we connect with them, they can bring us into the present moment and make us feel more alive.

So to communicate with birds, we need to remember how they think. When a bird sees something, it matches what it sees with the most similar pictures it has in its mind, whether from its own personal experience or the experience of generations of ancestors. The more often a bird sees the same thing, the stronger that memory becomes. We want to create a picture in a bird's memory of something good, and keep making that memory stronger by doing the same thing again and again.

Patterns, abstractions, and language

To measure intelligence of humans, often a test called an IQ test is used. An IQ test measures skill at spotting patterns and extrapolating patterns (figuring out what comes next).[70] (And this skill that can be improved with practice, so, contrary to popular belief, IQ scores can be changed.) Finding patterns and extrapolating patterns is a human superpower. This talent has let us create mathematics, which is the study of patterns, and that in turn has enabled scientists to discover the patterns in nature.

But we aren't the only ones who can find patterns. Other creatures can do that, too.

Pigeons, for example. Pigeons not only remember the specific

---

70   Finding patterns is an important part of human intelligence, but it isn't all there is to intelligence. An IQ test doesn't measure how good a person is at learning and figuring out new things -- after all, the answers to the test have been set in advance. Nor does an IQ test measure creativity, independence of thought, critical thinking, deep thinking, originality, problem-solving ability, ability to generate new ideas, ability to make connections among seemingly unrelated things, ability to see the big picture, ability to visualize, ability to understand people, ability to understand multiple points of view, ability to interpret ambiguity, ability to notice details, open-mindedness, curiosity, insight, inventiveness, resourcefulness, imagination, perceptiveness, musicality, empathy, wisdom, or other aspects of human intelligence. Since finding patterns can be quantified, an IQ test reduces the whole complexity of a human mind to a simple number, like height. Computers (AI) have none of those human abilities, but since AI is better at finding patterns than we are, some people think AI can become "smarter" than we are.

images they saw, they can recognize categories of images. Even categories that, born and raised in a lab, the pigeons have never seen in real life, sauch as "dogs." They can recognize more abstract patterns as well. Letters of the alphabet are only abstract designs to a bird, yet pigeons not only learned to recognize English words on a screen, they could tell the difference between words that *could* be English words, like "plashed" and "flinner" and words that couldn't possibly be English, like "ggfqykw" and "ucbzjdm." They recognized patterns of English spelling.[71] And pigeons taught to choose paintings by a particular artist could recognize other works of the same artist. They could tell which images followed the same patterns.[72]

This means that pigeons can spot general qualities separate from any specific thing. That is called abstraction. If we talk about the color "blue" without talking about any specific blue thing, then we are talking about "blue" as an abstraction. Same if we say "honesty is good" without talking about a specific honest person or action," or the number "three" without saying "three what?"

Abstraction has long been considered a unique human ability. After all, what use for abstractions would a wild animal have? It doesn't need to think about "blue" as an abstraction, separate from any blue thing.

But a famous African Grey Parrot named Alex showed that he could use abstractions. Earlier we described how he could apply number labels like "three" to different groups of three objects, showing that he understood "three" as an abstraction.

And not just numbers. He understood colors and shapes as abstractions too. If presented with two objects, say a red metal square and a red wooden circle, and asked, "What same?" Alex would say

71   Scarf, et al, (2016). "Orthographic processing in pigeons (*Columba livia*)." *https://www.pnas.org/content/113/40/11272*

72   Watanabe, S. (2001). "Van Gogh, Chagall and Pigeons: Picture Discrimination in Pigeons and Humans." *Animal Cognition*, vol. 4, nos. 3-4, pp. 147–151.

"color." If there was a red metal square and a green wooden square, he could answer "shape." If there was a red metal square and a green metal triangle, he could answer "material." He could answer "how many red?" or "how many wood?" if presented with a tray of objects of various shapes and colors.[73]

Human language is based on abstraction. Any word we use is an abstraction. So if a parrot can use human words, with meaning, could it have conversations in human language?

Not quite. Besides words, human languages have syntax – the patterns of putting words together in sentences. We humans have an instinct to learn syntax. Alex learned very simple word order – like "want nut" or "want grape." But he didn't seem to learn syntax further than that.

On the other hand, songbirds have an instinct for syntax. Many songbirds have something like syntax in their songs – patterns of putting notes and phrases together, in patterns like how we put words together. In fact, scientists are studying how songbirds learn birdsong to gain more insights about the human brain and how we learn language.[74]

So, between parrots and songbirds, birds have both sides of human language. If only they could put the two halves together.

But we have one superpower that may be ours alone: imagination.

It's a safe bet that birds can visualize pictures in their minds. Not only do birds compare what they see to mental pictures, but birds probably can recall pictures to their mind. They use that ability to search for things, and smart birds like the New Caledonian Crow can figure out multi-step puzzles by rearranging their mental pictures in new ways.

But we humans can do more than that with mental pictures. We can picture things we have never seen. We can even picture *things that don't even exist*, and that is a superpower unique to humans.

---

73   See the book *The Alex Studies: Cognitive and Communicative Abilities of Gray Parrots*, by Irene Pepperberg.

74   Berwick, Robert C. et al. (2011). "Songs to syntax: the linguistics of birdsong." https://pubmed.ncbi.nlm.nih.gov/21296608/

How can we be so sure that birds don't have imagination? Because imagination would be worse than useless to a bird. If a bird pictured things that it has never seen, things that have nothing to do with what is around it, that would distract it from the here and now, and a distracted bird wouldn't survive very long. A bird who wasted its attention on imagining imaginary things would quickly be weeded out of the gene pool. The birds who have survived to have children have been those who *don't* have imagination. What has been passed down, stronger and stronger in each generation, is the ability to be completely present and aware of real life, the here and now.

If we want to tune in to how an animal thinks, we need to clear the imagination from our thoughts and see what is actually present in front of us in the real world in the real moment. Yet our power of imagination can help us to understand our wild birdfriends. We can imagine what life is like for someone else. We can imagine being a hawk soaring in the sky or a wild horse running on the plains – whereas a hawk surely never imagines itself as a horse, nor vice versa. And neither of them ever imagines what it is like to be a human. But *we* can use the power of imagination to enter the life of another creature, or another person. Even if we can imagine someone else's life only a little bit, that can be the beginning of communication and connection.

So bird intelligence is not just a lesser form of human intelligence. Bird intelligence is like ours in some ways, and different from ours in some ways. And we can learn from them. They can help us be more aware of the world around us and more fully present in the now. Learning from the birds doesn't mean giving up our human form of awareness; it means expanding it.

For a lot of people, birds are just cute and pretty to look at. For a birdfriender, birds are more than that. For a birdfriender, as for Indigenous people, the birds can be our teachers.

CHAPTER FOURTEEN

DO BIRDS SING BECAUSE THEY ARE HAPPY?
BIRD EMOTIONS

DO BIRDS SING because they are happy?

That is the first question many people ask when the subject of bird emotions comes up. After all, birdsong makes *us* happy. Birds *sound* so happy when they are singing. It's spring! The world is coming back to life! Sun is shining! Flowers are blooming! The woods are full of warbles!

But, other people say, singing has nothing to do with happiness. Birds sing to establish territories and attract mates. It's business. Therefore, those people tell us, birds feel no emotions when they sing.

In fact, some people say, birds and other animals don't even have feelings.

Only humans have emotions, some people say. If we talk about animals' feelings, those people say, we are *anthropomorphizing* them. To "anthropomorphize" literally means "to give a human shape."

Animals have instincts *instead of* feelings, those people say. And instincts, they say, are like computer programs. Just as a computer feels nothing while executing a program, an animal feels nothing when executing its instinctual software. Not even pain. It doesn't matter if the animal cries. After all, we could make a robot that could sound like it is crying, but that doesn't mean the robot feels pain or sadness.

But why would an animal act like it has emotions it doesn't feel? What purpose would that serve? And how is it that when humans do the same things – crying, playing, showing affection – those empty actions become filled with feelings?

Emotions create the desire to follow an instinct. Instinct is felt as emotion. So emotions help survival. Someone fleeing a predator will have more power to escape if they feel the emotion of fear. Someone trying to attract a mate will try harder if they feel the emotion of desire. Someone taking care of a baby will care for the baby better if they feel the emotion of love.

There are some basic emotions that may be common to all living things. One is desire. Any creature has an instinctual desire for the things it needs to survive. The emotion of desire makes us try harder to get those things. Desire takes various forms, including hunger, the desire to mate, curiosity, attraction, and wanting things needed for survival and reproduction, like a good place to nest and nesting materials.

Another basic emotion is the sense that "something is wrong." This emotion can take many forms, including fear, which is shared by practically all animals. But fear wouldn't do a plant any good, since a plant can't run away from danger. Plants also don't have brain chemicals associated with fear, since they don't have brains. But a plant may feel that something needs to be fixed.

Frustration is another emotion probably shared by all living things. Frustration makes us try harder to overcome obstacles.

And another basic emotion may be the sense of rightness – of satisfaction, contentment, happiness.

Instinct is felt as emotion. Fulfilling our instincts *feels* good. When we do things that help us survive and continue our species, we are rewarded with a feeling of happiness. A bird may feel pride and satisfaction when it does a good job of building a nest. Happiness and contentment is a signal that all is well.

Every creature has the emotions it needs, so different creatures have different emotions. A mother bear will do anything to protect her cubs, but a mother salmon has no idea what mother-love feels like. Baby salmon aren't cared for by their mothers, so salmon don't need the emotion of mother love. Salmon probably can't even imagine that emotion. And we may be unable to imagine some of the emotions of other creatures.

If we figure that birds have *all* of the same emotions we do, that would be making a mistake. We really would be anthropomorphizing.

So how can we know what emotions birds have?

There are three questions that can help us figure that out.

The first question is: Do birds *appear* to have that emotion? Can we see evidence that they have that emotion in front of our eyes?

The second question is: Would that emotion help a bird to survive and pass on its genes?

If the answer to *either one* of these questions is yes, then we can assume that birds have that emotion, or something like it. If the answer to *both* of the questions is yes, then we can be pretty sure they do.

The third question is whether they have the same brain chemicals associated with that emotion in humans. Scientists have found such brain chemicals. But we birdfrienders can't observe that directly, so we have to stick to the first two questions.

Our physical senses are closer to bird senses than to the senses of most of our fellow mammals. And some of our emotions ae closer to birds than to most mammals. Our shared senses and our shared emotions give us a common ground to understand birds and communicate with them.

But which emotions do we share with birds? Let's look at some emotions and see which ones birds may experience as well.

Love

Love is commitment to someone else's well-being. If we love someone, their welfare matters to us. Love is also an emotion, a sense of connection with someone or something.

Birds, like all creatures who care for their young, are committed to the well-being of their babies, and the welfare of the babies matters to them. But birds also experience another kind of love, unknown to most other creatures: romantic love. Few other creatures have any idea what it means to fall in love. But humans can understand.

Why do birds fall in love? Why do humans? And why doesn't every creature?

Among most creatures, including some birds, the mother can care for the babies without any help. So there is no need for the father to be involved. Most baby animals don't need care from their fathers. A mother cat doesn't need help from the father cat to raise her kittens. A mother chimp takes care of her baby until it is old enough to start learning from the other adult chimps, but it doesn't matter which male is her baby's father. Most mammals, after they mate, go their separate ways and forget each other.

But songbird children, like human children, need two parents to care for them. Most baby birds hatch blind and naked and helpless. In order to survive, they need two parents. So a family begins with two partners who fall in love. The survival of the whole species depends on the romantic partnership between female and male.[75]

For about eighty percent of bird species on Earth – including just about all the birds in our backyards – life is all about finding someone to love.

A squirrel or a deer just wouldn't get it – the strange bird obsession with romance. But we humans can get it. This is one more way we are more like birds than like most of our fellow mammals.

Bird mates are devoted to each other. They kiss and groom and nibble each other. They whisper sweet nothings into each other's ears. Some birds bring their mates gifts. Some mates pretend to be baby birds and feed each other. Some perform a ritual in which they pass a berry back and forth. The devotion between bird mates is intense and powerful.

When a bird is in trouble, its mate may stay with it. A bird may even take care of an injured mate, bringing it food.

Someone once found a male robin with a broken wing in a

---

75 Do birds ever form same-sex couples? Among some species, sometimes. Among some gulls and some geese, females sometimes partner to raise chicks together, making brief liaisons with males to get their eggs fertilized. And if two birds of the same sex are in captivity together with no member of the opposite sex available, they may bond as mates.

snowbank. She picked up the robin to take him to the vet, and his mate, who was with him, let herself be picked up too. The vet said that the wing had been broken for a long time, but the robin was healthy and well fed. The injured bird's mate had been feeding him and taking good care of him.[76]

Birds may even risk their lives for their mates. A tracker was watching a pair of cardinals foraging, in separate spots. As pairs often do, they kept in touch by chipping back and forth. Then the female cardinal fell silent, and the male cardinal became agitated in his chipping. And the tracker saw:

... the female in sudden flight, and behind her was a sharp-shinned hawk closing fast.... Just as the hawk was about to reach the female, the male burst onto the stage at a dead, bright-red sprint and flung himself right between his lady love and the hawk. Distracted, the sharpie faltered and swerved to pursue the male... but the male escaped... I was stunned. This was one of the most powerful scenes involving birds I had ever witnessed. Was it an incredible act of courage, as we would define it?[77]

A man once shot at a female shrike in flight (before killing native birds was made illegal) and hit her wing. As the injured bird tumbled to the ground, her mate flew under her wing and supported her wing with his own body so they could fly away together. The man could have shot both of them at that moment, but he was too awed – both at the way the male risked his life to save his mate, and at the amazing way that he did it.[78]

76   Related in *Eye of the Sandpiper: Stories From the Living World*, by Brandon Keim, p. 65.

77   *What the Robin Knows: How Bird Reveal the Secrets of the Natural World*, by Jon Young, p. 33.

78   *Child, JS, "Intelligence of the Shrike," The Auk*, Volume 17, Issue 1, 1 January 1900, p. 68.

People who band birds sometimes find themselves being harassed by the mate of a bird they are banding. As far as the mate knows, it could be risking its life by confronting the bird-trapping human. And when the trapped bird is released, its mate would fly right over to it to make sure it was all right.

Some birds mate for life. Some birds stay together for years and then may split up. But some birds break up after raising the kinds and find a new mate next season.

So we might ask those birds – if you two were so much in love, why did you get divorced before a year was out? And then, come spring, you find different mates? And you do this every year? Who should believe you when you say you are looking for true love?

Human instinct tells us that a true love should last forever. That is because it takes a long time to raise human children. But most bird children are on their own in less than a year. There is no purpose to the couple staying together after that.

But they may choose to. I have seen Song Sparrow couples stay together through the winter. Others remarry the same mate in the spring, which may testify to their happy relationship.

Bird couples don't have equally happy marriages, though. Some mates are always together, paying attention to each other, while others seem like impersonal co-workers. Some couples seem affectionate and cooperative, while others are downright quarrelsome. I have a devoted Red-breasted Nuthatch pair who are together all the time and even visit my hand together to snag peanuts.

Whether the flame of romance is short or long, it burns brightly. Birds course with the same kinds of hormones that make teenagers fall in love so passionately. They don't break each other's hearts when they break up, so they have no hesitation to give their hearts again, next year and every year.

And birds don't let the romance get stale, even those who mate for life. Every spring, courtship happens all over again, as though for the first time, and the lovers renew their vows.

And yet... oh dear, it turns out that lovers can cheat on each other sometimes. When supposedly out gathering food, one mate or the other may sneak over for a little tryst with a neighbor. Scientists figured this out by testing the DNA of baby birds. Turned out some babies had the wrong father.

But still, for romantic love, we can give a definite "yes" answer to the two questions about bird emotions: we can see evidence that birds feel romantic love, and romantic love helps their species to survive. So does love for their babies.

Yet, can a wild bird feel love for a human being?

A pet bird who doesn't have another member of its species around to mate with will often take its human keeper as its mate. Few humans are prepared for the intensity and obsession of bird love. A bird will kiss and groom and nibble its human mate. It may bring its human mate gifts – and expect them to eat the gifts. It wants to be with its human mate constantly. The stereotyped pirate with a parrot clinging to his shoulder has a feathered mate who never wants to leave him.

But what about a wild bird? It doesn't need a human as a mate. Can it feel love for a human friend?

Birds can have friendships with other birds, though we can't know how much a bird loves its friend. But we know that birds show their love for mates and children by giving them food. And birds show love for mates by giving them pleasure, including through music. So when we give a bird food or music, we may be activating its feelings of love the same way we do to a dog or cat by petting it, which activates its feelings of love by reminding it of when it was a baby being licked by its mom.

And I believe that birds understand our kind intentions toward them. So it is quite possible that a wild bird may love us.

Caring and Empathy

Birds can care about other birds besides their mates and children. A birdkeeper discovered that one of two baby Gouldian Finches was blind. Once she was out of the nest and supposed to be feeding herself, she couldn't, so her parents kept feeding her. That's not so surprising, but her brother fed her, too. Somehow he knew she needed help.[79]

There are reports from the wild of handicapped birds being taken care of by other birds. A birder in Costa Rica observed a Fiery-billed Aracari and a Chestnut-mandibled Toucan whose deformed bills made it impossible to hold food, who stayed healthy apparently because their flockmates helped feed them. He heard reports from other birders of a disabled Black-faced Wood Swallow and Black-headed Grosbeak who were fed by their companions.[80]

A hummingbird rehabber described one of her hummingbirds who helped others:

> Iris put her strong nurturing instincts to work... modeling how to eat from new feeders, catch fruit flies, hide in the ficus tree at night, and stand up to bullies. She was especially solicitous of the smallest and most frightened underdogs in each group. Whenever she noticed a fearful bird hanging back, she alighted on the perch beside him, tapped his chest lightly with her bill, then encouraged him to join the fray by dropping down and snapping up a fruit fly.[81]

Birds can even help birds of other species. One afternoon, I witnessed something astonishing. I was throwing peanuts to the Steller's Jays, and a Spotted Towhee was watching. The towhee flew down to the deck, but didn't go for a peanut because he was afraid to get close

---

79 From *The Birds of Pandemonium,* by Michelle Raffin, p. 192-3.

80 From *The Minds of Birds,* by Alexander Skutch, p. 117-18.

81 From *Fastest Things on Wings,* by Terry Masear, p. 171-2.

to the much larger jays. I threw a smallish peanut to the towhee, which landed near the towhee's feet, and threw a very large peanut in another direction, for a Steller. Since jays like the biggest peanuts they can get, I figured the Steller would go for the big peanut and leave the towhee's peanut alone.

As I'd hoped, the Steller flew over and grabbed the larger peanut. She prepared to fly off with it and peck it open on a tree branch. Meantime, on the deck, the towhee tried to peck his peanut open, but he wasn't having much success, because he couldn't hold the peanut in place with his small feet. The Steller dropped her peanut and headed for the towhee's peanut instead. But she didn't fly off with it. She held it with her feet and started pecking it open right on the deck. And she didn't eat the peanut halves as she extracted them. She just dropped them. When all four peanut halves were lying on the deck, she hopped back to her own peanut, grabbed it, and flew away. The towhee came back and ate the pieces on the deck.

I was flabbergasted.

Did I just see the Steller open the peanut *for* the towhee? On purpose? Was that possible?

Could it be that an atmosphere of cross-species generosity at my feeders influences some of the birds?

Since then, I have heard of other reports of birds feeding birds of other species (not cowbirds or cuckoos!) On the internet I saw a video of a Black-and-white Warbler feeding Red-breasted Nuthatch nestlings. A bird scientist reports:

A Gray Catbird fed and mothered an orphaned brood of Northern Cardinals. A House-Wren gave food to both Black-headed Grosbeak parents, who ate some and passed the remainder on to their nestlings. After the young grosbeaks fledged, the wren fed them directly. A few days later, this wren brought food to a family of House Sparrows. A Swainson's Thrush assisted in feeding nestling American Robins. A Black-and-white Warbler repeatedly fed nestling Worm-eating Warblers, against the opposition of their parents. A House Sparrow brought food to three fledgling Eastern Kingbirds. A Scarlet Tanager fed young Chipping Sparows. A male Red-legged Honeycreeper reportedly fed a fledgling Scarlet-rumped Tanager twice his size. These are only a few randomly chosen cases of interspecific helping.[82]

In one of those cases (the wren feeding the grosbeaks) a bird fed other adult birds. So the Steller who helped the towhee wasn't totally unique.

Birds may empathize with other birds even when they can't help them.

One day I heard a loud screech next to the deck, and a Steller's Jay popped up from the ground. She shot straight up to a small cherry tree and continued screeching and screeching. And Stellers from all around flew over and perched around her, screeching with her. They aimed their screeches toward an opening under the deck. Evidently a feral cat hiding under the deck had tried to ambush the Steller on the ground.

The first Steller took off and flew from tree to tree, still loudly screeching, and the other Stellers followed her. Though they soon fell silent, she kept screeching in outrage. They followed her and surrounded her until she finally calmed down. They seemed to be offering sympathetic support, "You're not alone, we're here for you."

Another day, I went out, and the sliding door didn't close completely. It was left open just a couple of inches. But that was enough space for a Steller's Jay to get inside. And he couldn't find the way out and went into a panic. By the time I got back, he was a wreck, frantically bouncing off one window after another, hitting the walls, panting with stress.

---

82 From *The Minds of Birds*, by Alexander Skutch, p 132-33, citing his own book, *Helpers at Birds' Nests: A Worldwide Survey of Cooperative Breeding and Related Behavior.*

I opened the door wide and talked to him in a soothing voice, trying to coax him out, but he was way beyond any calming down. I had no choice but to try to catch him. That, of course, made things worse. Now, on top of being trapped, he was being pursued. What a nightmare for both of us.

While this was happening, Skippy the Scrub Jay landed on the deck. He hopped to the open doorway. Skippy is one of the birds who freely comes in and out. But he just stood in the doorway and watched us. Oh no, what must he think? Seeing me chasing a terrified Steller's Jay all around the room? Am I going to lose the two years I spent getting Skippy to trust me?

Skippy didn't fly away, though, so he wasn't frightened by what he was witnessing. I looked at him, and to my astonishment, he was panting, just like the Steller was! Skippy was, apparently, empathizing with the stress of the Steller!

Skippy kept panting until I finally caught the Steller and let it go. Then he stopped panting and relaxed.

The Steller, for his part, didn't seem to hold the incident against me. He flew to a tree limb near the deck and sat there, panting, for a long time. I went out by the tree and talked to him till he stopped panting.

But Skippy amazed me. First, because he seemed to have grasped the situation – that I was trying to rescue the Steller, I had not suddenly turned into a predator. But even more because he showed me that apparently a bird can empathize with another bird in trouble, even a bird of another species.

Can we witness caring and empathy in birds? Sometimes, apparently. And would these emotions help birds to survive? Yes, caring for mate and children helps a species to survive, and mutual help among birds can help birds survive too. So we can probably say that birds have emotions something like caring and empathy. And since birds can show kindness to other birds, they may be able to understand our kind intentions toward them.

Grief

One sunny June day, I heard a robin singing.

I looked up and saw him on a Douglas fir branch. He was showing off some of his best singing, even though he already had a territory and a mate. As the presiding robin in my yard, he was the leader of the dawn chorus. His was the first voice to sound in the early morning, and the last voice to sound in the dusk.

A few hours later, I passed the tree again. And there on the ground were the wing feathers of an adult male robin.

A cat had done it. If there had been a bunch of fluffy breast feathers on the ground, that would have indicated a Cooper's Hawk, who tears out the breast feathers first to eat the internal organs. But a cat tears off – or chews off – the long feathers to make it easier to drag the body through the brush.

I was shocked. A short time before, I had been watching that very bird – the robin owner of my yard, my robin singer, the leader of the dawn chorus.

What about his family? Where was his mate? I didn't hear any bird alarms going off, so the cat had managed to hunt unseen. Did his mate even know what had happened?

That evening I listened for the evening chorus, to see if it would sound different without his voice. I didn't hear any robin song. But from around the same fir tree where he had perched, I heard a robin call "*Kuk... kuk... kuk....*"

The robin alarm call. A slow, mild alarm. "*Kuk....*" The female, looking for him in his favorite spot. As she flew from tree to tree, her *kuks* became faster, louder, more urgent, until they were rattling at machine gun speed.

And then her "*kukukukukukuk*" went up in pitch, higher and higher till it seemed to end in a scream. Like the wailing "*NOOOOOO!*" of a human suddenly confronted by unthinkable tragedy. It shocked my heart to hear it.

Then, faintly from a distance, I heard an echo of that wailing cry. A robin in a neighboring territory was answering. And then another echo from another robin in a different direction.

Maybe they were sympathizing with her. Maybe the robins were spreading the news that someone had fallen, and everyone needs to watch out.

Maybe it was an affirmation that life goes on.

The very next day I saw her gathering nesting material. Maybe she had found a new mate already. It was still early enough in the season to start another nest. And news may have spread quickly that a prime territory was available. But who was her new mate?

The day after that, I heard a new male robin singing, from a nearby fir tree.

I looked for him among the branches. When I spotted him, he immediately flew away. He wasn't used to me. But that evening, I heard a prominent robin voice in the chorus, and then again in the dawn chorus the next morning.

Everything seemed normal in the bird world again. If I had not stopped to watch the first robin, if the cat had not left his wing feathers next to the path, if I had not been listening for the robin voice that evening, I wouldn't have suspected anything. I might never have realized the male robin in my yard had been replaced.

How many times have such things happened around me without me ever noticing?

So do birds feel the emotion of grief? We can ask the two questions. First, do they show evidence of grief? Second, would the emotion of grief help them to survive?

The answer to the first question is yes. Birds often do appear to show grief for their dead mates. Birds who mate for life may show the strongest grief. Hunters who shoot wild geese have witnessed a dead goose's mate coming to mourn over the dead body, even at the risk of its own life.

But what about the second question? How would the emotion of grief help a bird to survive?

It probably doesn't. In fact, grief can distract from survival. A bereaved bird may even risk its own life when mourning for its mate. So why would birds have that emotion?

Grief may be the price paid for love.

But birds get over it. Once a bird has a new mate, it probably stops thinking about the mate who was lost. The cycle of life begins again. For the sake of survival, grief needs to be short.

What if a baby bird gets eaten by a predator? Do the parents grieve?

Probably they do, but it must pass even more quickly. So many babies are lost that birds cannot afford to spend time grieving for them. The grief may be intense, but it seems to be brief.

To survive, a bird must let the past be the past, and carry on.

Anger, rage, hatred and vengeance

Birds can show anger when rivals invade their territories or when someone threatens their babies. But can birds feel hatred?

We should distinguish *hatred* from *hate*. "Hate" can mean aversion ("I hate this show," "I hate lima beans"). "Hatred" means wanting something bad to happen to someone, as in "I hate your guts and I want you to suffer and die!" Birds *hate* lots of things and stay away from them, but I used to think that *hatred* was only a human emotion.

Until one morning. Going out to get the mail, I saw a squirrel on a power line high over a street, being divebombed by two crows.

That's not unusual – squirrels can raid bird nests, and crows divebomb squirrels to drive them away. But these crows weren't trying to drive the squirrel away. In fact, they were keeping the squirrel from getting away. Each time the squirrel tried to run one way, one of the crows would divebomb from that direction and prevent its escape.

The two crows divebombed from opposite directions, coordinating so that the squirrel had to dodge them both at the same time.

Over and over again the squirrel nearly fell. A fall from so high would have killed the squirrel.

The squirrel must have wiped out these crows' brood. But animals eat other animals every day. I was shocked and amazed to see animals bent on revenge. Hatred radiated from the crows like a physical force, like waves of heat from a bonfire. It was so strong it made me shudder.

I watched for about half an hour. I saw close call after close call, but the squirrel didn't fall. During that time, several people walked down the street, oblivious to the drama happening above their heads. I had work to do, so finally I went inside.

Two hours later, I came back out. To my astonishment, it was still going on!

My dog Mitzi ran out with me. She started barking, which distracted the crows for a second, just long enough for the squirrel to take a flying leap into the walnut tree.

Mitzi ran over to the walnut tree and started barking at the squirrel. And the crows drove the squirrel down down down the tree trunk, till it was about two feet above Mitzi's head. Mitzi was thrilled. Never before had she gotten this close to a squirrel. She barked insanely and jumped on the tree trunk as though her legs were springs.

Finally, I called Mitzi, and she reluctantly came to me. The squirrel disappeared, and the two crows slowly flapped away.

I never thought that hatred and vengeance existed in the animal world. Now I know.

Fun

Birds can fly! Surely flying must be the greatest fun in the world? Gulls surf the ocean breezes. Hawks soar high in the sky. Swallows swoop to snap up mosquitoes. Ravens do acrobatics with air currents, even flying upside down. Those birds undoubtedly have fun flying.

For most of our backyard birdfriends, though, flying costs too much precious energy to do it frivolously.

Still, the songbirds don't miss out on *all* the fun of flying. On windy days, songbirds may spread their wings and let the wind carry them like leaves. Or a songbird may grab hold of a twig and swing in the wind, up and down, back and forth. It can't fall off because its feet lock on the perch. For a bird as light as a leaf, the bouncing bushes and waving trees are like a vast amusement park full of rides.

A Song Sparrow bounces up and down on the yard ornament.

And a bird may not even wait for the wind. Ravens slide down snowy roofs and icy windshields of parked cars. Song Sparrows and chickadees land on my yard ornament and let the blade bounce them up and down.

The emotion of fun is a survival emotion. It makes us practice real-life skills. In fact, our instincts tell us that the things that help us survive are exactly the things that are most fun to practice. A cat practices hunting skills when it chases a string. Bunnies practice escaping predators when they play tag. A human practices thinking skills by working out puzzles or paying chess. A hawk practices hunting skills when it surfs the breezes.

I once had a pet starling. She was a fledgling when I rescued her, so, unlike pet starlings adopted as nestlings, she never talked. But her hunting instincts had kicked in by that age, and she taught me about insect-hunting birds. Though her prey was tiny, she was like a tiny raptor. She taught me that insectivorous birds are predators and hunters.

Her style of play was completely different from that of a seed-eating bird. Her games reenacted hunting for insects. She was ferociously curious about hidden spaces, holes, nooks and crannies, where insects might be hiding. She would climb on me, poking her sharp bill into every fold of my clothing, into my ears, into my nostrils – anyplace that could be a hiding place for insects. (Except my mouth – she seemed to have an instinct to stay away from that.)

Sitting on my hand, she would wedge her beak between my fingers and pry my fingers apart – just in case I had any delicious insects hiding between my fingers, you know. Starlings hunt this way in grassy fields – they jab their beaks into the ground and then pry their beaks open, to get insects out of the ground.

Her favorite toy was mealworms. She didn't eat them. But she liked me to wave a mealworm around her so she could chase it, like a cat chasing a string.

She would peel holes in stacks of newspaper, as though searching for insects. Then she would drop a mealworm onto the newspapers and wait for it to crawl into a hole and hide. She would slowly peel the newspaper, page by page, looking for the mealworm. When she found it, she would wave it around triumphantly. Then she would toss it into the air, let it fall onto the newspapers, and wait for it to hide again. When the mealworm finally died, she would lose interest in it. I'd give her a new, live one and she would play the game again.

Do birds have fun? Let's ask the two questions. First, they certainly *appear* to have fun. Second, the emotion of fun can help them survive. So we can say birds have fun. This one is easy.

Pride and competitiveness

Do birds feel pride and competitiveness?

Well, let's ask the two questions. Male birds *appear* to feel pride and competitiveness when showing off their songs or plumage. And those emotions help a bird pass on its genes. Anyone who is proud of what he is doing will do a better job than someone just mechanically going through the motions. And a male who is fiercely trying to outdo the other males will win female hearts better than one who doesn't really care.

Hummingbirds show off not just for their mates, but for humans, too. When a hummer hovers in front of my face with his head feathers spread to catch the sunlight, it's on purpose. Hummingbirds are natural showoffs.

Male hummingbirds are natural showoffs. They can control the angle of their iridescent display feathers to shine their colors exactly where they want, when they want, and they do that to impress female hummingbirds – and humans. Sometimes I'm working in the yard, and suddenly I'm shocked by a flash of blazing red flame in front of my face. Raspberry likes to make dramatic appearances.

A hummingbird rehabilitator reports that when fledglings beginning to fly hear her applauding their success, "they seem motivated to repeat the miracle. Some fly back and forth over and over, deliberately completing one rotation after another until I stop encouraging them."[83] They are proud of themselves.

Something like the emotion of admiration must also exist in the bird world, since the male birds try to evoke it in the females. Do we see evidence of that emotion? Yes. Would it help birds to survive? Yes. These emotions drive birds to excel, so they help the species survive and continue.

---

83   From *Fastest Things on Wings: Rescuing Hummingbirds in Hollywood*, by Terry Masear, p. 139.

Gratitude

One morning I come out to find a Steller tail feather lying across my doorstep. A long tail feather, deep blue with penciled bars across it.

In Bird Fall, when birds shed their feathers and grow new ones, it's not a surprise to find a feather.[84] A few days later, another Steller tail feather is lying across my doorway.

Then a few days later, lying across my doorway is another tail feather – not from a Steller, but a flicker. The longest feather from the middle of the tail, brilliant orange-red with a sharp black tip.

Maybe those feathers didn't land there by accident?

Many birds give gifts to their mates while courting. Crows may give gifts to friends as well as mates. Some crows even gift human friends who feed them, leaving coins and bottle caps and plastic toys and the like.

But birds don't give each other feathers. Still, the Stellers may have observed me picking up a feather and admiring it. Did the Stellers figure that a feather could be the perfect gift for me? And a long tail feather a special prize? And did the flicker see what the Stellers were doing and get the idea to leave a feather of its own? Or did a Steller spot the flicker feather on the ground, pick it up and bring it? I don't know.

Asking the two questions leaves us inconclusive about the emotion of gratitude. It's not certain that we can observe evidence of gratitude in birds. And it's not clear how this emotion would help birds to survive. But I believe that birds understand our kind intentions toward them, and I feel that they can feel something like gratitude.

Depression

Animals in the wild can suffer pain and grief and hardship and frustration. Yet one thing that wild animals don't suffer is depression.

How can we know that? Because depression is an *anti*-survival

---

84   It is against the law to keep feathers from native birds, so of course I can't keep them.

emotion. If someone is depressed, they don't feel like putting much effort into life. A wild animal who got depressed wouldn't survive very long.

That doesn't mean that animals can't feel depression. We can find depressed animals in zoos, factory farms, in laboratory cages, in dog pounds – any place where animals can't fulfill their instincts and live as their ancestors tell them they are meant to live. We can feel depressed around depressed animals. We know how they feel. When we can't fulfill *our* instinctual needs – our need for love, for connection, for belonging, for beauty, for purpose, for freedom. for a sense that we have a place in the world, and other needs we have as humans – we can suffer depression too.

But wild animals living in freedom don't get depressed. They are able to fulfill their instincts. They have freedom to be who they truly are. They have connections to their ancestors and to their descendants. They belong fully to the living world around them. They have a purpose: to stay alive and to give life to the future generations. When we are with wild animals, we can share their sense of belonging and connection, their sense of guidance, their sense of freedom. So being out in nature, or simply watching the birds in our own yard, can help *us* with depression, too.

Story emotions

There is a type of emotion that, I believe, only humans have. I call them "story emotions," because these emotions depend on stories.

Many story emotions are painful. For example, self-pity. Sometimes an injured or handicapped creature shows up at my feeders – a bird with a broken wing, a squirrel who has lost an eye. But it doesn't seem to be thinking, "Why me? Why can everyone else fly and I can't? Why is life so unfair?" Wild animals don't expect the universe to be fair, so they don't feel betrayed when it isn't. They just deal with life as it comes.

Another story emotion is resentment. A crow can hold a grudge, but it surely doesn't think about the target of its grudge when they are not around, the way we do when we are resentful. Out of sight, out of mind.

Animals don't seem to have regret about the past. A rescued dog doesn't ruminate about its wasted years. If it's happy *now*, it's happy. Nor does an animal worry about the future. Wild animals prepare for the future, but they don't ask, "What if this doesn't work? What if something happens that never happened before? What if a disaster ruins everything?"

Blame – blaming someone else or blaming oneself – is a story emotion. A bird may be upset to be caught by a predator, but it doesn't blame. Whatever happens, happens. A bird doesn't create a story about it.

Story emotions like self-pity, resentment, regret, guilt, worry, humiliation, envy, despair, and blame can become traps for us. They can pull us into a vortex. They can suffocate us. They can haunt us with past sorrows.

Fortunately, our wild friends can help us step back from our stories. They can help us reset ourselves. Birds and other wild creatures live in the here and now, and they invite us to join them.

Sense of beauty

I save this for last because it seems to have nothing at all to do with survival. Yet it may be the deepest emotion we have in common with birds: the sense of beauty.

Although we can see abundant evidence that birds love beauty, there is no logical or practical reason for it. The love of beauty doesn't seem to help survival – not for the birds, or for us, either.

We can value something without feeling that it is beautiful. We can be attracted to something without feeling that it is beautiful. Most creatures are attracted to mates by smell, not by looks. And something we find beautiful doesn't necessarily attract us. A tiger or a glowing lava river may be beautiful, but we might not want to get too close to it.

Why do flowers look beautiful to us? Why does beautiful music affect us? The colors of a flower are only different wavelengths of light, and music is only patterns of sound waves in the air. Why is *anything* beautiful to us?

And *how* is anything beautiful? Beauty does not exist except in the *feeling* that something is beautiful. If we did not have a sense of beauty, then nothing could *be* beautiful. Why should we love beauty, and be inspired by beauty?

Beauty reminds us that life is about more than survival.

In older human times, beauty has been a guiding principle of life. Among Indigenous peoples, even mundane implements should be beautiful – a pot should hold water in beauty, a cradleboard should carry a baby in beauty. As a Nimipu grandmother told me, "The reason we are here on this Earth is to add to the beauty of the world. We repay the Earth and the Creator for giving us life by making life on Earth more beautiful."

And I once heard a Tsalagi pastor say, "God gave us a sense of beauty so He could communicate to our hearts directly. Beauty is God's language."

Perhaps that is why we imagine angels, God's messengers, with wings. Feathered wings, like birds.

The Dine healers chant, "Beauty before me, beauty behind me, beauty above me, beauty below me, beauty all around me, I walk in

Beauty…" To them, restoring the sense of beauty is vital to restoring a sick person's health.

If a creature cannot fulfill its instinctual needs, it cannot be truly healthy. A human who lives without beauty doesn't feel fully alive.

People love birds mainly because they are beautiful, and because they add beauty to the world.

Love of beauty is part of what makes us human.

And love of beauty is part of what makes birds birds.

Do birds sing because they are happy?

So, back to the question at the beginning. Does a bird sing because it is happy?

No. The bird isn't singing because he is happy. The bird is happy because he is singing!

Does a dog chase a ball because he is happy? No, the dog is happy because he is chasing a ball. Does a cat nurse her kittens because she is happy? No, the cat is happy because she is nursing her kittens. Do we hang with our friends because we are happy? No, we are happy because we are hanging with our friends.

Every creature is happy when it can fulfill its instincts.

And a bird may sing for practical reasons, but the happier a bird feels when he is singing, the better he will sing.

And maybe sometimes a bird *does* sing when it is happy. When a female bird sings, when a bird sings in Bird Fall with breeding season over, when an Anna's Hummingbird perches and sings for hours any time of year, the bird may be singing for happiness.

We and the birds have things in common that can help us understand each other. We both live in a world of sight and color. We both love music. We both experience romantic love. We both seem to understand caring. But among all the things we share, love of beauty may be the most important bond of connection between us and the birds. Beauty is a language we share.

Part Four

THE BIRDS AND US

CHAPTER FIFTEEN

OTHER WAYS TO BE FRIENDS OF BIRDS

LITTLE OVER A hundred years ago, in North America, a lot of people used to shoot birds for the fun of it. Not for food, nor for any other reason except fun. It didn't matter if a bird was beautiful, or rare, or important to farmers – shoot it! There was even a custom on Christmas Day to go out in teams that would compete to kill the most birds!

A bird defender named Frank Chapman wanted to stop this. He figured out that the best way to get people to stop doing something isn't to tell them they are bad, but to offer them a better alternative.

So he came up with a different way to have fun looking for birds on Christmas Day. Instead of killing the birds, people could count them.

The first Christmas Bird Count was in 1900. Only 27 people participated that first time. But the next year more people joined, and each year more people.

Mr. Chapman was a member of an organization of bird defenders called the Audubon Society, which had been started only a few years before by a man named George Bird Grinnell. The Audubon Society adopted Mr. Chapman's idea of having bird count days, and today they happen not just around Christmas but also at certain other times of year, and tens of thousands of people all over the United States and Canada help count birds.

Also members of the Audubon Society were two women who lived in Massachusetts, named Harriet Hemenway and Minna B. Hall. They were especially concerned about a bird called the Great Egret and its cousin the Snowy Egret.

The Great Egret is a magnificent pure white heron about a meter tall, and its cousin the Snowy Egret looks the same but smaller. During breeding season, these egrets have long, flowing display feathers on their back, and a fashion had developed to use these snowy plumes to decorate women's hats. So people slaughtered the tall, elegant white birds to collect those feathers. And the time of year when the egrets wear those feathers is nesting season, when they are raising babies, so every pair of egrets killed (both sexes have the display feathers) meant three to five babies were left to die.

One ounce of egret plumes was worth the equivalent of two thousand dollars —twice as much as gold. Six egrets were killed for each ounce of feathers, not to mention the babies who died. The Great Egret and Snowy Egret appeared headed for extinction, but the rarer they became, the more valuable their plumes.

And many other kinds of birds were being killed for their plumes as well. Flamingos and Roseate Spoonbills, for their rosy-pink feathers.

Small birds were used as decorations as well – they were stuffed and set on hats as though perched up there.

Ms. Hemenway and Ms. Hall got pledges from hundreds of women not to buy hats with plumes or dead birds on them. They worked hard to get laws passed to protect the egrets and other birds. But even after laws were passed, it was not easy to stop the bird slaughter. Plume hunters ignored the law. In fact, several bird defenders who tried to stop the plume hunters from killing egrets. were murdered. These brave heroes include bird wardens Guy Morrell Bradley and Columbus G. McLeod, and Audubon Society employee Pressly Reeves.[85] But the murder of Mr. Bradley was highly publicized, which helped to make the public aware of what was happening to the birds and led more people to stop buying hats decorated with plumes.

Soon after the beginning of bird count days, a man named Ernest Harold Baynes came up with another way to get people to stop shooting birds. In 1910, Mr. Baynes organized a bird club in his town of Meriden, New Hampshire. Other "bird clubs" existed, but they were for shooting birds. This was the first bird club ever devoted to birdfriending.

Mr. Baynes got practically the whole town to join his bird club. The students at the local school birdscaped an area to create one of the country's first bird sanctuaries. Soon, the town of Meriden became known as the Bird Village.[86] The birds there became so tame that anyone could stand out anywhere and hold up a hand full of food, and birds would land on their hand in numbers. Chickadees would

---

85   For more about the two women who started the movement to save the egrets, see "How Two Women Ended the Deadly Feather Trade" *https://www.smithsonianmag.com/science-nature/how-two-women-ended-the-deadly-feather-trade-23187277/* For more about the story of the first murdered bird warden, see "The Most Dangerous Job In America," *https://getpocket.com/explore/item/the-most-dangerous-job-the-murder-of-america-s-first-bird-warden*

86   See *Wild Bird Guests: How to Entertain Them,* by Ernest Harold Baynes, published in 1915.

tap on windows to tell people inside they were hungry. Pine Gros-beaks would feed in people's laps and land on the heads of children.

Then Mr. Baynes invited people from other towns over to visit. He would tell someone to hold out their hand, with food in it, and then watch their amazement as the birds flew down to eat out of their hand. Then he would ask them, "Do you realize that people in your town kill these birds, just for the fun of it?"

Of course, the people couldn't stand the idea of those cute and lovely birds being wantonly killed. More and more people started calling for laws against killing birds. First laws were passed in local communities, and finally, in 1932, due to the hard work of many bird defenders, a national law was passed to protect birds throughout the United States.

The law not only made it illegal to kill native birds,[87] but also to collect eggs and nests and feathers, and to keep native birds as pets. It is even illegal to keep feathers found on the ground. People don't get in trouble just for keeping a feather they found on the ground, but it's still against the law to have it, because that law ensures that someone killing birds for their feathers can't try to use the excuse "I just found them."

For some birds, these laws came too late. But other birds were saved. The Great Egret and Snowy Egret, which people died to save, made a big comeback. Today, I can see them at a wildlife refuge near my home. And the symbol of the Audubon Society, the biggest organization of bird defenders in North America, is the Great Egret.

---

87 With certain exceptions. Game birds like quail and ducks can be hunted at certain times of year. Crows can be killed by farmers who say they are damaging crops. Non-native birds like pigeons, House Sparrows, and starlings are not protected at all. Such non-native birds can legally and ethically be kept as pets.

A Great Egret wearing the breeding-season plumage that almost made them extinct, and a pair of Great Egrets at my local wildlife refuge.

The heroic bird defenders of the past saved a lot of birds so that we can see them today. And any of us can be a bird defender too, even a kid. We can do things like protecting birds from cats,[88] making sure birds don't crashing into windows, or asking people who want to trim trees or bushes (and throw pieces into the chipper to be ground up) to please do it in the fall when the trees and bushes are not full of bird nests. Birds give all of us the chance to be heroes.

Wildlife rehabilitators

A wildlife rehabilitator can work very hard to save just one injured bird, even though saving one bird out of billions won't affect the population of the species. To a wildlife rehabilitator, every bird is precious. Wildlife rehabilitators are people who take in injured or orphaned wild animals and help them get better so they can return to the wild.

It isn't easy to be a wildlife rehabilitator. It's a lot of work and takes a lot of knowledge. To become a wildlife rehabilitator, someone starts by volunteering to help at a wildlife rehabilitation center. cleaning up

---

88   Even one outdoor cat can have a huge impact on wildlife. See "A Single Male Cat's Reign of Terror" *https://www.theatlantic.com/science/archive/2019/07/cat-birdsaustralia/595048/* and "It's 10 PM, Do you Know Where Your Cat Is?" *https://hakaimagazine.com/features/its-10-pm-do-you-know-where-your-cat-is/*

and doing chores and learning how to care for the animals. Finally they can get a permit or license to be a wildlife rehabilitator themselves, which makes it legal for them to care for native wild animals. Then people who find an injured or orphaned wild animal have someone to take it to for help (after making positive sure it's really orphaned and the parents aren't just hiding).

Wildlife rehabilitators don't try to make friends with birds they rescue. In fact, they try to be careful *not* to make friends with them. When feeding an orphaned baby bird, they may hide behind a screen or use a bird-shaped puppet so the baby won't realize it is being fed by humans. Otherwise, it may even think that the humans were its parents and that humans are its own kind. And after the bird is finally released, when it gets hungry it might go up to any strange human and beg for food, and that can be dangerous for the bird. People are not allowed to visit wildlife rehabilitation centers, because the animals will be safer if they are not used to seeing humans get close to them.

(A birdfriender doesn't have to worry about their birdfriends getting too tame for their own safety, because the birdfriends are already grown up, and they know they are birds and not humans, and they know the difference between their human friends and strange humans, and they know how to keep a safe distance from strangers.)

Though a wildlife rehabilitator can't make friends with a bird they are saving, they feel connected with that bird when it is back out in the wild, and that is as rewarding to them as conversing with a birdfriend is to a birdfriender.

They do their work because they care. Caring is one of the things that makes us human. Caring makes us different from computers. The more we care, the more human we are. Wildlife rehabilitators save animals, but in a way perhaps they also help save the humans.

Habitat protectors

A hundred years ago or so the world was much more full of birds, but most of us are too young to remember that. But, from the information gathered on the Bird Count Days, we know that the bird population is going down a lot. In only fifty years, the world bird population has gone down by almost a third. At this rate, in another century we may have hardly any birds left, except for pigeons, crows, starlings, and House Sparrows. The world could be left without the Snowy Owl and the Merlin Falcon, the Scarlet Tanager and the Painting Bunting, the Blue-headed Sapphire Hummingbird and the Blue-footed Booby.

Why? Not because people are shooting them, nowadays, or killing them for their feathers. The main reason the birds are disappearing is because their habitats are disappearing. Forest birds are losing their forests, marsh birds are losing their marshes, meadow birds are losing their meadows.

Many of us feed birds, which can make life a lot easier for those particular birds, but the birds could survive without us feeding them. To survive, what birds really need is habitat. Habitat means a place that has all the things a particular species needs to survive. When a patch of woods is turned into a parking lot or a tallgrass meadow is paved over, or a habitat goes away because of climate change, the birds who lived there lose the places to find food and build their nests. With no places to raise babies, the birds can disappear from an area.

Today, for bird defender groups like the Audubon Society and the American Bird Conservancy, protecting habitat is the biggest priority. By supporting such organizations, people can protect habitat around the world. But people can also create habitat in their own yards.

There are easy ways to create a bit more habitat. For example, instead of removing fallen leaves, leaving them for the birds – dead leaves attract insects for thrushes and other birds to eat. Piles of cut branches make insect-hunting ground for wrens. A hollow tree provides a place for flickers, owls, and bluebirds to raise their babies.[89] Grass grown without chemicals lets robins hunt worms and bugs without being poisoned, and "weeds" on the lawn can feed birds with their seeds. Grass left unmown can provide food and nest sites for ground-feeding and ground-nesting birds,

Some people put a little more work into creating bird habitat. They put in plants that help the birds. Berry bushes for the waxwings. Flowers for the hummingbirds. Native plants that attract insects. Bushes that provide protected sites for nests. This is called *birdscaping*.

Cities are full of spaces that can be turned into habitats for animals.

But oh dear, the habitat yard is not a neat and manicured lawn. It looks a bit like a wild natural area. The neighbors might complain – until they see how full of life it is. Then maybe they would join together to make their neighborhood even richer with life. A mix of habitats close together will be the richest, so each neighbor could create the kind of habitat they like best – a pond, a little woodland, a meadow (that's the easiest – just stop putting chemicals on the lawn, stop removing the "weeds" and wildflowers that feed birds and other wildlife, stop picking up leaves, and let some grass grow tall). Habitats could also be created in public parks, on school grounds, in office parks, and in the strips next to highways. Even a few acres could support birds as diverse as woodpeckers, ducks, quail, and owls, along

---

89   Dead trees are very important habitat for many bird species. For more information, see *https://cavityconservation.com/*

with other creatures like snails and salamanders and frogs, maybe chipmunks and rabbits and deer.

And butterflies and bees, who are also going way down in numbers. If small habitats are connected with wildlife corridors, animals who travel on foot, like rabbits and foxes and deer, may show up too.

Small wildlife forests planted around the city help cool the city in the hot summer and dampen city noise. They serve not only as sanctuaries for wildlife, but as human sanctuaries too – "sanctuaries for human sanity," someone has said.

And wildlife forests, being more densely planted than timber forests, absorb carbon dioxide from the air much faster than timber forests, thus helping with climate change, and they support more different kinds of plants and animals.

Wildlife sanctuaries make the planet healthier. They make the world more beautiful. And they help us feel that we belong here.

We can help save bird habitat in faraway countries as well. Birders who travel to other countries to see the birds show those countries that saving the birds' habitats brings in money, so those birders are helping to defend the birds' habitats.

Of the whole planet, the tropics have the most birds by far. Besides the birds who live there all the time like parrots and hummingbirds, many migratory birds we see during the summer fly south to spend the winter in the tropics. They wouldn't survive without those tropical habitats. If the tropical habitats disappear, many of our warblers and other colorful migratory birds would disappear too.

There are many ways we can help defend tropical bird habitats. For example, we can buy shade-grown coffee (also known as bird-friendly coffee). Most coffee farms cut down the forest and monocrop the coffee. Monocropping means allowing only one kind of plant to grow and removing all other plants. The monocropped plantation is cultivated with big machines, and chemicals are used to kill the insects, taking away the birds' main food and sometimes even poisoning the birds.

A forest has been cleared for a coffee plantation. Very few birds can live there.
But the birds still have the forest habitat seen in the background.

But forests don't have to be removed in order to grow coffee. Coffee can be grown in the shade of the forest. In fact, shade-grown coffee is more delicious. And many small coffee farmers don't want to cut down the forest, which they don't have to if people buy their shade-grown coffee. In an Asháninka village I visited in the Peruvian Amazon, every family had one or two coffee trees growing in their jungle gardens, which was enough to bring each family the money for things they needed to buy. They didn't need to buy many things, since they grew their own food and made their own houses and clothes. And as the families worked in the gardens together, they were surrounded by birds and butterflies that brought them joy.

No matter where in the world we may live, a good life for birds and a good life for humans go together.

Birdwatchers, birders, and birdquesters

Bird defenders and bird habitat protectors don't care if the birds know they are helping them, and wildlife rehabilitators try to purposely keep the birds from knowing that. Birdfrienders, on the other hand, want the birds to pay attention to us, because how else can we make friends with them?

But other people want the birds *not* to pay attention to them. They want the birds to ignore them and act as though they were invisible, so they can watch the birds live their own lives in their own way. These people are *birdwatchers*, *birders*, and *birdquesters*.

A *birdwatcher* is anyone who watches birds, anywhere. A robin stalking earthworms on the lawn, the pigeons in the park, the crows in the trees.

Some people turn up their noses at such ordinary birds, because they think that the only birds worth paying attention to are those that are colorful or rare. But for a birdwatcher, the bird to watch is the one who is here right now. People who don't bother looking at "common" and "ordinary" things miss treasures hidden right in front of our eyes. The clouds reflected in a mud puddle. The veins of a leaf. A birdwatcher sees the magic in the most common bird.

Anybody can be a birdwatcher. Anyone can start watching birds any time. It isn't necessary to know anything about them. We can discover them ourselves.

When we are watching the birds, no one tells us what to look at. No one writes a script for what we see. No one edits it to control what we are supposed to look at. There are no special camera angles or dramatic music. What we are seeing is not made up or faked or simulated. It is actually happening in the real world. We witness the birds with our own eyes and feel them with our own feelings.

While a birdwatcher watches any bird who happens to come along, a *birder* looks for birds on purpose. Birders go to wild natural areas to see the birds living their lives in their own world in their own way.

We can be both birdfrienders and birders. It helps us understand our birdfriends better if we go out birding sometimes, the way we can understand a friend better by visiting them at home and seeing how they live.

Birders listen to birds as well as watching them. Some birders can locate an elusive bird hiding in a tree by sound and can identify a bird by its sounds alone. In fact, there are birders who are totally blind!

Many birders keep a "life list" of all the bird species they ever have seen (or heard). A birder is always looking for a "lifer," a bird they've never seen before, to add to their life list. Some birders even travel to different countries to see new birds they can add to their life list. This encourages those countries to conserve bird habitat, because they see people coming and spending money there because of the birds.

Backyard birders are birders who watch birds in their own yards. And just as a birder can keep a life list of all the birds they have ever seen anywhere, a backyard birder may keep a "yard list" of all the bird species who have ever visited their yard.[90] A backyard birder may attract birds by putting out birdfeeders, birdbaths, or birdhouses. Or, best of all, by birdscaping – creating bird habitat in their yards.

Most birdfrienders start out as backyard birders, because in the yard we can see the same birds every day, and they see us every day too, and we can get to know each other.

Some birders are *birdquesters.* (I made up that word, but such people exist.) Birdquesters search for treasures, but real treasures in the real world, not imaginary treasures on a screen. The treasure is a rare bird sighting or a prize bird photo. The birdquester's real feet fall on real ground, and they feel real sunshine and real wind. A birdquester can have the fun of hunting without hurting anything. They sharpen the skills of silent stalking and keen observation. They gain the power to discover hidden secrets that are invisible to most people.

---

90   I don't have a life list (I lived for years in South America, the greatest bird continent, and saw way too many birds I could never identify) but my yard list has over sixty species, of which about twenty species are regular visitors at least part of the year. That's about average for an urban or suburban yard in an area with lots of trees.

Their senses awaken and they start to see the movements under the shadows of the leaves, hear the wild sounds floating through the air, feel the bumps of the path touching their feet.

A birdquester can share pictures with birdquesters in other parts of the world who have different birds. A prize photo or rare bird sighting doesn't create envy or FOMO, because a beautiful photo can give joy to everyone, and anyone else might be the one who gets the treasure tomorrow.

Many birders or birdquesters go out in groups. They can stay together in a group, or they can socially distance, spreading out like a flock of birds searching for food. The more eyes looking, the more birds may be spotted. Someone who can find birds by their sounds and point them out to everyone else can be everyone's hero.

Birding can be a gentle way to get exercise – or a challenging way. Birding can bring together people of every race, nationality, age, sex, gender, religion, and political opinion. Families can go birding together, since birding is something that people of all ages, from babies too young to walk to people with canes, can do together, and some wildlife sanctuaries are even wheelchair-accessible. Young people can go birding together with friends in real life, making real friendships with real people – not just "friend" lists on social media. People who love birds have open hearts, so they can become true friends. Neighbors can get to know each other as they get to know the local birds. Church groups can celebrate God's creation together as they admire the wonder of the birds. The birds help open our eyes to the miracles around us. Birding helps us to cultivate a grateful heart.

Birds invite us to look up from the screen and look at real life. A screen is not as exciting as real life. If something in a movie or role-playing game ever happened in real life, that would be a huge deal! But when the biggest explosion happens in a movie, a minute later we barely remember it.

Someone posted, "The other day I ran into a flock of flamingos in VR. They were very pretty, that was okay. Then I went outside and a hummingbird flew in front of my face! A real hummingbird! That was more exciting than a thousand fake flamingos!"

On a screen, we are bombarded with so much noise and fast images that we have to shut most of it out. We can't possibly fully look at all that comes to our eyes. We have to turn down the volume on our senses. Then, when we go out in nature, where things are quiet and subtle, we may miss everything—at first.

Nature is the opposite of screens. Nature doesn't try to make us pay attention to it. In fact, much of nature is hidden. It reveals itself only when we are paying close attention.

Nature unfolds at its own speed, and we have to slow down our minds to see it. But when our senses start to reawaken, we see more and more. We see things that others would miss.

Some birders prefer to go birding alone. A lone birder may hike to a high place and look down from the heights like a bird. Or may sit by the water, watching not only the birds but the endlessly changing patterns of light on the water movements. In nature, outside the human mindfield, we can discover who we are.

Watching the birds can help us with stress and anxiety. The birds don't ruminate about the past, nor are they tense about the future. Birds don't care what someone said. They don't worry about someone judging them. They don't compare themselves with each other. They don't care about getting "likes." They don't worry about grades. They don't fret about deadlines. They are not in a hurry. They don't get angry when things don't go their way. They prepare for the future, but they don't worry about the future. They don't ask, "What if what I'm doing doesn't work? What if something happens that never happened before? What if a disaster ruins everything?" If something unexpected happens, they just deal with it.

Danger is always lurking in the birds' world. Yet they are not tense or stressed-out. They are alert, but relaxed. They know what they need to do, and how to do it, and when to do it. They live in graceful trust.

Watching birds can help us with depression. Social media can leave us feeling empty, lonely, and depressed. And school can kill our curiosity and creativity and wonder. School, once modeled on factory assembly lines, now is modeled more and more on computer programming. Human qualities that can't be computerized, like imagination, dreams, caring, love, humor, curiosity, are not valued or encouraged. No wonder so many people feel hollow and depressed.

You know who doesn't get depressed? A computer. Because a computer doesn't feel anything at all.

You know who else doesn't get depressed? A wild animal living free. An animal living in a cage, unable to fulfill its instincts and truly be itself, can get depressed. Just like we can if we never experience freedom and never have the chance to find out who we really are. But an animal in the wild, though it may experience pain and hardship, never gets depressed. Any wild animal who gets depression and quits caring about life would be quickly weeded out of the gene pool. When things get tough, a wild animal tries all the harder to survive.

A teenaged birder posted, "I used to be obsessed with what my friends thought of me. I felt like I didn't belong. Sometimes I was depressed and thought of giving up, other times I was angry. One day I was all by myself watching the birds and I saw how hard their lives were, yet they were never angry about it. I saw how much they wanted to live, and I discovered that I wanted them to live too! And then I thought, why do I want *them* to live if I don't want *myself* to live? And then I got it."

And when we can't go to the wild, birds bring the wild to us. The birds help us remember that we are not just machines. We are living creatures in a living world. Birds can help us remember that we are alive. And that we belong here.

Bird scientists

Bird scientists are very important for the survival of birds. All around the world, bird populations are going down. To save them, we need to learn as much as we can about how the birds live and what they need.

And any of us can be a bird scientist. Even a kid!

What? Wait a minute, don't scientists need years of training and laboratories and special equipment?

Well, in most branches of science, yes – but bird science is different. All of us can study birds and make new discoveries. All we need to do is step outside! And if we share our discoveries and add to humanity's store of knowledge about the world, we are scientists!

Of course, a *professional* bird scientist (called an *ornithologist*) does need years of training. But ornithologists are luckier than other scientists – they have *community scientists* to help them.

Who are community scientists? Us!

Thousands of eyes and ears around the world gather information about the birds around them.[91] Me, for example. In Chapter 5 of this book, I talk about the two kinds of jays who share my region, whose behavior I find fascinating. Other people who live with one of both of those two jay species can observe them to see how they act the same and differently from my jays. The same with other birds. By comparing observations of the same kind of bird living in different places, and seeing what behaviors are always the same and what behaviors are different, we can figure out how much of what they do is inborn (ancestral memory) and how much of what they do is learned or cultural.

You may see birds doing the same things as other people have seen, or different things – but, either way, your observations can help all of us to understand the birds better. Just like, in order to understand people better, we need to figure out both the ways we are all the same and the ways we are all different. By comparing our various

---

91   Contact the Cornell Lab of Ornithology to join their army of community scientists.

observations about the birds and things they do, we learn more about what the birds need to survive.

And birds are everywhere, just waiting for us to discover new things about them. I made new discoveries right in my living room. In the summertime, Vaux's Swifts nest in my fireplace chimney (not used for fires in the summer). I can't see them, but I hear periodic explosions of peeps when the parents arrive with food. One day, I heard loud shrieks of alarm down in the fireplace. I discovered that a nestling had fallen down into the fireplace. I took it out and tried to help it, but it died overnight. After that, the chimney was silent. No more bursts of cheeping that meant the parents had come in with food. What happened to the other babies? Had the entire brood disappeared?

But, weeks later, the young swifts flew out the chimney, well-fed and healthy. So the babies had still been there all along, and were still being fed. They had just stopped making noise.

I reported this to a scientist who studies Vaux's Swifts. My observations contained three pieces of information that were new to him and, as far as he knew, new to science: one, that Vaux's Swifts can make a loud shriek; two, that the nestlings can shut up, permanently, if they think there is a threat around; and three, the parents don't need to hear all that cheeping from the babies to keep feeding them.

Unfortunately, ornithologists, like other scientists, want to gather data on specific questions they are studying, and usually they can't use one-off stories (called anecdotes) people have about birds. So my discoveries about the Vaux's Swifts have never been published (till now).

Thousands – no, millions! – of observations of birds by millions of people are going to waste!

Descriptions of bird behavior are scattered all around social media, but quickly vanish in the ether. When writing this book, I studied reports and videos on social media, to compare my own experiences with observations of bird behavior by other people. That way, I could figure out what was common and what was unusual. For example, my hummingbirds share the feeders peacefully – I have even seen hummingbirds sitting next to each other taking turns at the same feeding port. Turns out that is unusual; lots of people report that their hummingbirds fight and try to drive each other away.

If only there were a place where people's experiences of bird behavior and could be gathered together in one place. We could compare our observations and share our experiences and learn so much together. We could get better at communicating with them. We could help the world to realize how smart birds are and how individual their personalities are.

So birdfriender.net will have forums to provide a place to share and compare bird stories. The forums are not just for birdfrienders, but for all different kinds of friends of birds – birdwatchers, birders, bird defenders, birdscapers, and bird scientists. And for wildlife rehabilitators, and bird-inspired artists and musicians, and people who dream about birds.

Why do birds matter?

If we say, "Because they are beautiful," then we are saying that beauty matters.

If we say, "Because they are living creatures," then we are saying that life matters.

If we say, "Because they are part of the balance of nature," then we are saying that the balance of nature matters.

If we say, "Because they help our mental health," then we are saying that mental health matters.

If we say, "Because I love them," then we are saying that love matters.

Birds can help us to remember that we are part of the family of life.

CONCLUSION

"BUT TO ME, THEY WILL ALWAYS BE GLORIOUS BIRDS"[92]

THE MOST FAMOUS birdfriender in history was a man named Francesco, who lived about 800 years ago. In English, his name is Francis, and he came from the town of Assisi, in what is now Italy, so we know him as St. Francis of Assisi.

Francesco was a monk. In fact, he was the leader of a group of monks, who tried to live like Jesus and his disciples. They owned

---

92 A concentration camp survivor, watching the seagulls at sunset, in the film *Harold and Maude*.

nothing and walked from town to town doing good and helping people.

Francesco loved all of God's creation. He always reminded people
that "God saw that it was good."

He had a gift for communicating with animals, especially birds. Birds
would eat out of his hands and even land on his shoulder. Statues of him
show him cradling a bird in his hand, and paintings of him depict him
surrounded by birds, and sometimes by other animals as well.

One day, in the year 1210, Francesco and his monks were walking to a town. As they passed a field, Francesco noticed that the trees
were full of birds. And these birds were acting unusual. They seemed
to be watching the group, as though expecting something.

Francesco walked over to the birds, and he started to preach to
them. To the amazement of the other monks, the birds seemed to
listen intently. As he spoke, they opened their beaks, stretched out
their necks, bowed their heads reverently, and spread their wings.
When Francesco was done speaking, they all began to sing in chorus.
The birds kept singing until he blessed them, and then they flew off
in the four directions.

The other monks wrote down what Francesco said to the birds.

My sweet little sisters, birds of the sky, you are indebted to
heaven, to God, your Creator. In every beat of your wings
and every note of your songs, praise him. He has given you
the greatest of gifts, the freedom of the air. You neither sow
nor reap, yet God provides the most delicious food for you;
rivers and lakes to quench your thirst; mountains and valleys
for your home; tall trees to build your nests; and the most
beautiful clothing, a change of feathers with every season.
Clearly, our Creator loves you dearly, since he gives you gifts
so abundantly. So my little sisters, please beware the sin of
ingratitude, and always sing praises to God.

Because of how the birds appeared to understand and listen to what Francesco said, this event is known as the miracle of the birds.

St. Francis with a bird in his hands, on his shoulder, and on his head.

Maybe we can't expect the birds to understand a sermon. But birds can understand a lot of things.

A bird can understand that a human is a fellow creature, like itself, even though we look so different. A bird can understand that it is possible to try to communicate with humans. A bird can understand when we want to help it. A bird can even like us.

Not all birds all the time. But some birds sometimes. That is a miracle. Birdfriending is a kind of miracle.

But there is a sad part of birdfriending that I didn't want to talk about. Still, it has to be spoken.

Before we start making friends with the birds, we don't pay attention to individual birds (and the birds have the same attitude toward us). When we start to make friends with individual birds, we recognize them. We even name them. And that is how we know when a bird disappears. Sometimes a birdfriend or squirrelfriend I love doesn't show up again. Ever.

So I'm always afraid for my birds. I give thanks every time I see one of my friends alive.

Most songbirds have the potential to live for ten to fifteen years or more, but a wild songbird who survives more than two years is a tough or lucky bird. Most wild birds don't make it to their first spring.

So when I see the same birdfriend next year, I am grateful. If I see the same birdfriend for three or four years, I rejoice. And I know I have helped that bird buck the odds. Feeding the birds may not have much effect on the overall bird population, but if I can help my own friends to survive, that gives me joy.

And no matter where we are in the world, the birds are there, to remind us of beauty. Some people say that is a job God gave them. The birds help us to remember that we are not mere machines. Machines cannot feel beauty. Birds help us remember that we are alive. They help us remember that we are living creatures in a world of living creatures.

Like the birds, we are looking for our way in this changing world.

And we get by with a little help from our friends.

BIRDS PICTURED IN THE BOOK

Front cover: Chestnut-backed Chickadee

Introduction: Red-breasted Nuthatch, Song Sparrow, Northern Flicker, American Robin

Chapter 1: Brewer's Blackbird, Rock Pigeon, American Crows, Gull, American Robin, Bewick's Wren, Mourning Dove

Chapter 2: Chestnut-backed Chickadee, Red-breasted Nuthatch, White-breasted Nuthatch, Steller's Jay, California Scrub Jay, Pine Siskin, Downy Woodpecker, Anna's Hummingbird, Green-Tailed Towhee, Tufted Titmouse, California Scrub Jay

Chapter 3: Red-breasted Nuthatches, Song Sparrow, Black-capped Chickadee, Steller's Jay, Cooper's Hawk, Red-Tailed Hawk, American Robin

Chapter 4: Dark-eyed Junco, Dark-eyed Junco (juvenile), Anna's Hummingbird, Black-capped Chickadee, House Finch (juvenile), Northern Flicker, Anna's Hummingbird, Scrub Jay, Steller's Jay, Song Sparrow, Song Sparrow, Steller's Jay, Mourning Dove, Spotted Towhee, Steller's Jay, American Robin, Mourning Dove, Steller's Jay. Mourning Dove, Turtledove, Song Sparrow, Mourning Dove & Northern Flicker, White-crowned Sparrow (2), Mourning Dove, Northern Flicker, American Crow, Dark-eyed Junco

Chapter 5: Steller's Jay, California Scrub Jay, Bluejay, Steller's Jay (6), California Scrub Jay, California Scrub Jay (2), California Scrub Jay

Chapter 6: Anna's Hummingbird, Golden-crowned Sparrow, Fox Sparrow, American Bushtits, Chestnut-backed Chickadee

Chapter 7: White-Crowned Sparrow, Brown-headed Cowbird, Gray Catbird, American Bushtit nest, Mourning Dove, American Robins

Chapter 8: Black-headed Grosbeaks, Red-breasted Nuthatches, American Robin, Downy Woodpecker, Downy Woodpeckers & Black-capped Chickadee, Dark-eyed Juncos, Brown-headed Cowbird, Brown-headed Cowbird & Song Sparrow, Northern Flickers, Mourning Doves (2), Dark-eyed Junco (juvenile)

Chapter 9: Song Sparrow, Steller's Jays, Song Sparrow, Steller's Jay

Chapter 10: Bewick's Wren, Trumpeter Swan, Canada Geese, European Starlings, Black-headed Grosbeak, Bewick's Wren, Red Crossbill
Chapter 11: American Bushtit, Bluejay, Golden Eagle
Chapter 12: Killdeer, Dark-eyed Junco & Brown-headed Cowbird, Mountain Bluebird
Chapter 13: California Scrub Jay, Dark-eyed Junco (juvenile), Steller's Jays
Chapter 14: Mourning Dove, Song Sparrow
Chapter 15: Anna's Hummingbird, Great Egret (2)
Conclusion: Gulls, Song Sparrow, American Bushtit
Back cover: Song Sparrow

Photo credits

All photos by author, except:
p. 21, Gull: Paul Forrester, freeimages.com; p, 41, Green-tailed Towhee: Roger Shaw, with permission; p. 45, Tufted Titmouse: pixabay.com; p. 47, California Scrub Jay: John Paulus, with permission; p. 51, Song Sparrow: Keith, Wikimedia Commons; p. 89, Bluejay: Darren Swim, Wikimedia Commons; p. 105, White-crowned Sparrow: National Park Service; p. 120, Brown-headed Cowbird: freeimages.com; p. 120, Gray Catbird: pixabay.com; p. 130, American Robin nestlings: Laslovarga, Wikimedia Commons; p. 164, flying machine: wikiwand.com; p. 169, swan: Barry Skeates, Wikimedia Commons; p. 170, boat wake: Edmont, Wikimedia Commons; p. 171, starling murmuration: Airwolfhound, Wikimedia Commons; p. 173, bird syrinx: wikiwand.com; p. 173, panpipe: George Grove, Wikimedia Commons; p. 176, Red Crossbill: www. naturespicsonline, Wikimedia Commons; p 180, Golden Eagle: adamantios, Wikimedia Commons; p. 182, Bluejay: kikoACT01, Wikimedia Commons; p. 189, Killdeer: Andrew C. Wikimedia Commons; p. 197, Mountain Bluebird: VJ Anderson, Wikimedia Commons; p. 227, Turtledove: Andy Morffew, pxhere; p. 261, Great Egret in breeding plumage: Chuck Homler, Wikimedia Commons; p. 264, Miyawake forest: freeimages.com; p. 265, coffee plantation: Ineed Coffee, Wikimedia Commons

Acknowledgments
Thanks to John Paulus, Linda Neale, Livia Horowitz, Nathan Horowitz, Rev. Jay Nichols, Jenny Kirwan, Todd Andrews, Konatsu Ono, and the late David Marshall.

BIBLIOGRAPHY

Ackerman, Jennifer (2017). *The Genius of Birds*. Penguin.

Baynes, Ernest (2018, originally published 1915). *Wild Bird Guests: How to Entertain Them*. Hardpress.

Caughey, Melissa (2017). *How to Speak Chicken*. Storey.

Grandin, Temple (2006). *Animals In Translation*. Houghton Mifflin Harcourt.

Haupt, Lynda (2017). *Mozart's Starling*. Little, Brown Spark.

Heidcamp, Arnette (1991). *A Hummingbird in My House*. Crown.

Heim, Brandon (2017). *Eye of the Sandpiper: Stories of the Living World*. Comstock.

Heinrich, Berndt (2016). *One Wild Bird at a Time*. Houghton Mifflin Harcourt.

Hoose, Phillip (2012). *Moonbird*. Farrar, Straus, & Giroux.

Howard, Len (1956). *Living With Birds*. Collins.

Kirpluk, Barb (2005). *Caw of the Wild: Observations from the Secret World of Crows*. Iuniverse.

Kroodsma, Donald (2015). *The Singing Life of Birds*. Houghton Mifflin.

Lederer, Roger (2016). *Beaks, Bones, and Birdsong*. Timber Press.

MacDonald, Helen (2016). *H Is For Hawk*. Grove Press.

Marzluff, John, and Tony Angell (2013). *Gifts of the Crow*. Atria.

Masear, Terry (2015). *Fastest Things on Wings: Rescuing Hummingbirds In Hollywood*. Houghton Mifflin Harcourt.

Montgomery, Sy (2010) *Birdology: Adventures with a Pack of Hens, a Peck of Pigeons, Cantankerous Crows, Fierce Falcons, Hip Hop Parrots, Baby Hummingbirds, and One Murderously Big Living Dinosaur*. Free Press.

Pepperberg, Irene (2002). *The Alex Studies: Cognitive and Communicative Abilities of Gray Parrots*. Harvard.

Pepperberg, Irene (2009). *Alex and Me*. Harper Perennial.

Raffin, Michelle (2014). *The Birds of Pandemonium: Life Among the Exotic and Endangered*. Algonquin Books.

Robbins, Jim (2018). *The Wonder of Birds: What They Tell Us About Ourselves, the World, and a Better Future*. Random House.

Rothenberg, David (2006). *Why Birds Song: A Journey Into the Mystery of Birdsong*. Basic Books.

Skutch, Alexander (1996) *The Minds of Birds*. Texas A&M.

Smith, Susan M. (1991) *The Black-capped Chickadee: Natural History and Behavioral Ecology*. Comstock.

Stiteler, Sharon (2008). *City Birds, Country Birds: How Anyone Can Attract Birds to Their Feeder*. Adventure Publications.

Stokes, Donald and Lillian (1979). *A Guide to Bird Behavior, Vols 1-3*. Little, Brown.

Turner, Pamela S and Andy Comins (2020). *Crow Smarts: Inside the Brain of the World's Brightest Bird*. Clarion.

Young, Jon (2012). *What the Robin Knows: How Birds Reveal Secrets of the Natural World*. Houghton Mifflin Harcourt.

Zickefoose, Julie (2012). *The Bluebird Effect: Uncommon Bonds With Common Birds*. Houghton Mifflin Harcourt.

INDEX

Italicized page numbers indicate illustrations